THE SECONDARY BANKING CRISIS, 1973–75

THE SECONDARY BANKING CRISIS, 1973–75

Its Causes and Course

Margaret Reid

First edition 1982
Reprinted 1982, 1983

Published by
THE MACMILLAN PRESS LTD
London and Basingstoke
Companies and representatives
throughout the world

ISBN 0 333 28376 7 (hardcover)
ISBN 0 333 36325 6 (paperback)

Printed in Hong Kong

Contents

Preface

Although many people have probably heard of the crisis which hit the so-called secondary sector of Britain's banking system in 1973–5 and led to the launching of the big banks' rescue 'Lifeboat', detailed knowledge of this major occurrence – almost certainly the biggest emergency in British banking this century – is not widespread. It has therefore seemed to me desirable that, before this important episode in financial history is further obscured by time, its causes and course should be more comprehensively studied. It is beyond the ambit of a single book to recount the story fully, but my work is an attempt to give a rounded sketch of the whole affair in its historical context, with a certain amount of detail.

I would be the first to admit that the result leaves plentiful scope for further contributions to the subject, and I hope that it will encourage healthy discussion – and discourage any playing down – of this significant and instructive chapter in Britain's business experience. I should like to think that my work may provide, for existing bankers, the occasion for discussion of the events themselves and the issues they raise; for aspiring bankers, a warning of certain rocks to avoid; and, should history unkindly repeat itself, for later generations of bankers, a 'war book' for fighting a future emergency.

Between December 1973 and September 1978, it fell to me as a journalist on the *Financial Times* to report many developments in the prolonged secondary bank affair. Inevitably, the pressures of daily journalism precluded full-time concentration over many months on research into the background of such a financial saga as this, let alone the writing of a book. I was, however, fortunate in having the opportunity for such research and writing when I was elected to a Journalist Research Fellowship at Nuffield College, Oxford, for the academic year 1978/9.

I should like first to express my gratitude to the Warden, Mr Michael Brock, and Fellows of Nuffield College for their hospitality during the year I spent at the College, and to the *Financial Times*, which granted me leave of absence and other assistance. I am also grateful to Mr Kevin

Leigh, Mr Tony Northeast and their colleagues in the *Financial Times* Library for much help. I was able to discuss my proposed work from its inception with the Rt. Hon. Douglas Jay, MP, and Professor David Henderson, of University College, London; both have encouraged me throughout, for which I warmly thank them.

In view of the limited published information about my subject, I have had to rely a great deal on discussion with many of the people who had knowledge of it from various viewpoints. Most of those whom I approached felt that it was in the general interest that this major part of Britain's recent financial history should be understood and were ready to assist my knowledge and interpretation of events, within, of course, the limits they thought appropriate and without breaking the normal rules of banking confidentiality. From a multitude of sources I have pieced together the story as I see it and I must emphasise that responsibility for what I say is mine alone.

Grateful as I am to all who have helped me, I feel most particularly in debt of those who have generously devoted time to reading my manuscript in whole or in part. I should like to express special gratitude to Sir Eric Faulkner, formerly chairman of Lloyds Bank and of the Committee of London Clearing Bankers, who read almost the entire first full draft and gave me comments of great value. I am also most grateful to Mr Martin Reid, my brother, for invaluable comments and criticisms. In addition I should like to thank Miss Margaret Stephens, my aunt, and Sir Charles Ball, for most kindly reading and commenting on an early draft. A particular word of thanks is also due to Sir John Prideaux, formerly chairman of the National Westminster Bank and of the Committee of London Clearing Bankers, for his comments on a particular episode in the extraordinary economic climate of late-1974 and for illuminating discussion of various points.

Very many people have spared time to see me and to all I am grateful. I should like particularly to record my gratitude to the late Lord Armstrong and to express my thanks to Mr Ronald Artus; Mr Karol Ashken; Mr George Blunden; Mr Hilton Clarke; Mr Simon Coorsh; Sir Kenneth Cork; Mr Michael Craker; Lord Croham; Mr Jack Dellal; Mr John Fforde; Sir Archibald Forbes; Mr Peter Graham; Mr Keith Hughesdon; Mr Hugh Jenkins; Mr Richard Langdon; Mr David Lewis; Mr Leonard Mather; Mr Pat Matthews; Lord O'Brien; Mr John Quinton; Mr Brendon Sewill; Mr William Stern; Sir John Thomson; Mr Gerry Weiss; Mr Malcolm Wilcox; Mr Derek Wilde; and Mr Arthur Winspear.

I also wish to thank Mrs Kathleen Rogers, of Oxford, for her admirable and patient typing of my manuscript through various drafts.

In a work of this kind, where much of the material is drawn from sources other than published ones, it is not possible to give references for all statements. I have included a considerable number of references to publicly available material, and have, on occasion, referred to interviews given to me. Where no reference is given, it must be assumed that the source is information to which I have had access but which I do not wish to attribute to a particular source.

London, April 1981   Margaret Reid

Part I THE OUTBREAK OF THE CRISIS AND THE LAUNCHING OF THE LIFEBOAT

1 Action Stations at the Bank of England

> In wild periods of alarm, one failure makes many, and the best way to
> prevent the derivative failures is to arrest the primary failure which
> causes them.
>
> Walter Bagehot, *Lombard Street*, 1873

Midwintertide of 1973 brought one of the year's longest nights in more
senses than one to the City of London's financial centre and its citadel,
the Bank of England. From 9 a.m. on Wednesday, 19 December, until 3
a.m. on the following day, a sequence of secret meetings took place at the
Bank. Prominent among those involved were Mr Gordon Richardson,
the new Governor, previously a merchant banker and barrister; Sir (then
Mr) Jasper Hollom, the youthful-looking Deputy Governor; Sir (then
Mr) Kenneth Cork, the head of the accountancy firm W. H. Cork Gully
who was best known as a company doctor and 'undertaker' and later as
Lord Mayor of London; and a number of key figures from large
investing institutions and banks.

The length of this top-level gathering was a record. But its occasion
also had no exact precedent. The subject was the plight of Cedar
Holdings, one of the many secondary or fringe banks which had grown
up rapidly alongside the older-established banks and whose failure, it
was feared, could have dangerous repercussions throughout the banking system.

Cedar, which specialised in the then controversial business of second
mortgage lending to individuals and which also held property interests,
had expanded very rapidly; its pre-tax profits had climbed from £87,000
in 1967–8 to £1.9 m in 1972–3. But now this company, which had relied
heavily on funds borrowed as short-term deposits from the money
markets, was on the edge of collapse. It had experienced such a swift
outflow of deposits that – unable quickly to reclaim cash against its
loans to some 70,000 borrowers – it would be able to survive only if it
received immediate major cash backing. The adverse swing in the

fortunes of this very rapidly expanded but previously prospering business had followed a recent tightening in the Government's economic policies, involving a jump in the Bank of England's key Minimum Lending Rate to a record 13 per cent, and, only two days earlier, a tough Mini Budget from the Conservative Chancellor of the Exchequer, Lord (then Mr Anthony) Barber. Cedar's business had also been hit by the repercussions of a crisis – and a quick Bank of England-sponsored rescue operation – three weeks earlier at another secondary bank, London and County Securities Group, whose directors included Mr Jeremy Thorpe, at that time Leader of the Liberal Party. In its emergency, however, Cedar had a significant strength in the presence among its large shareholders of four major investing institutions, Phoenix Assurance and the pension funds of the Unilever industrial group and of the nationalised electricity supply industry and the National Coal Board. The four institutions held 23 per cent of Cedar's shares but were entitled to raise this to 35 per cent through the conversion of loan stock.

Cedar was typical of a large crop of new banking concerns which had grown up in the previous fifteen years. This work will later examine the causes of their development, including the emergence of the new money markets which supplied much of their finance and the expansionary policies of Mr Edward Heath's Conservative Government which led, in 1971–3, to a strong upsurge in the money supply. A further encouraging factor had been the benign attitude of the Bank of England towards the extension of London's banking fraternity at a time when its own surveillance capacity was not growing in step with that community's rapidly increasing size. In any case, the Bank's bias had been against close control of the banks, as was made clear in 1972 by the previous Governor, Lord O'Brien, in these words: 'Our tradition in Britain is of a less formal system of supervision than is customary in some other developed countries; and my long experience has not weakened my faith in this tradition.'[1]

The crisis which was now requisitioning such high-level attention was not merely the emergency at Cedar, but a rapidly escalating wider problem. It was certainly by no means unprecedented for the Bank of England to concern itself with the problems of a tottering bank. But on this occasion a further important cause for alarm was the danger that Cedar's troubles, if not solved, would be transmitted, through a domino effect, to the many other secondary banks which, with much vulnerable short-term borrowing and many assets tied up in the increasingly troubled property industry, were themselves showing signs of being at risk in the harsher new economic environment. With such a considerable part of the financial sector potentially in jeopardy, who could say what dangers a highly publicised failure might not present for the whole banking system?

All this accounted for the urgent action by the Bank of England, which was aiming to stop the rot by getting a rescue operation mounted for Cedar. This would require the co-operation of the four institutional investors and of Barclays Bank, Cedar's main clearing bank, through whose Barclays Bank Trust Cedar's shares had been brought to the stock market – not without some heart-searchings in the Barclays group – in 1971. The leading personalities concerned in these organisations had accordingly been called together.

To underline the gravity of the occasion and the strength of the central bank 'suasion' to be brought to bear, an impressive staging had been arranged for what was to prove the marathon series of meetings. For those cast in the role of rescue party – the representatives of the institutions and Barclays Bank, their advisers, and the Bank of England officials concerned, some forty people in all – a suite of three rooms on the Bank's first floor was provided. These were the spacious Court Room, where the Bank's Governors and directors meet and which contains a weathervane, at that time registering 'deep depression'; the Octagon Room opening into it; and an anteroom. A separate committee room downstairs had been allotted to Cedar's chairman, 72-year-old Mr Jack Morrison, and its other executive directors, including two managing directors, Mr Michael Morrison, the chairman's son, and Mr David Fischer.

Early in the day, Mr Richardson, who was then facing his most severe test since he had become Governor the previous July, addressed the assembled representatives accompanied by Sir Jasper Hollom and senior Bank staff. On the other side of the table, receiving the Governor's appeal – or rather demand – for a support package were top men speaking for the four institutions which had for some years backed the hitherto very profitable Cedar with millions of pounds of share and loan capital. The party included senior officers of the institutions, such as Mr Bill Broadfield of the Union (Unilever) pension fund, who was a non-executive director of Cedar, and Mr Hugh Jenkins, investment manager of the National Coal Board pension funds, who was shortly to join the Cedar board. But on this unusually important occasion the institutions were also represented at a higher level, Phoenix by its chairman, Viscount De L'Isle, who also chaired the large secondary bank First National Finance Corporation and who was perhaps better known as a former Air Minister and Governor General of Australia. Present too was one of industry's top financial personalities, Mr Cob Stenham, financial director of Unilever and chairman of the Unilever pension fund. Mr Burton Johnson, financial adviser to the Electricity Council, represented the management committee of the electricity supply industry pension fund, of which he was chairman. Mr David Clement, the Coal Board's finance director who also chaired its pension funds' joint investment sub-committee, joined the gathering a little later in the day, as did Mr Tim Bevan, chairman of Barclays Bank UK management company and afterwards chairman of the Barclays Bank group, and Mr Deryk Vander Weyer, Barclay's senior general manager, who later chaired Barclays Bank UK. City advisers on hand included Mr John Gillum, a director of Samuel Montagu, Cedar's merchant bankers, and Mr Ray Wheeler, a director of Hambros Bank, which was acting for the institutions.

The Governor urged the representatives of the institutions to consider what rescue could be mounted and pressed them to make their response in the light of the more general dangers to be anticipated, were Cedar to be allowed to fail. He 'gave us a good talking to', one of those present remembers. This session was relatively calm compared with some which were to follow within hours. But it was made clear that the Bank did not mean to receive a negative answer – and the pressure it could mount was powerful.

The institutions had not hitherto faced up to the possibility of having to replace virtually all Cedar's existing borrowings (other than its longer-term loan stocks, much of which they had themselves subscribed for) if these should be withdrawn. But this was what was now at issue. The Bank of England was asking them to devise a method of refinancing, as necessary, the whole of Cedar's £72 m money book of borrowings, much the greater part of which had been raised from the wholesale money markets, although some £10 m came from about 10,000 smaller depositors. Because of the troubled company's difficulties, the quotation of its shares was due to be suspended on the Stock Exchange the following morning, a move which had the potential of touching off general alarm. The Governor and Deputy Governor were insisting – 'decreeing' in the words of one of those present – that before the opening of the Exchange in the morning cover must be provided for all the deposits which might be withdrawn. Nothing less could, in the Bank's view, guard against the blow to public confidence which would be produced by panic-stricken small depositors hammering vainly on closed doors for the repayment of their savings or the unpredictable consequences of big lenders through the money markets being unable to get back deposits they had placed with Cedar. In short, the assembled party had got to stay in the Bank until the right sort of package was wrapped up; it was going to be a hard day's night.

'We went into the Bank of England one day at 9 a.m. and came out the following day at 3 a. m.' Mr Jenkins recalls. 'It became very apparent on the night of the rescue that we were concerned with something more than Cedar Holdings. One had to look at it in the context of the knock-on consequences, were Cedar to go.'[2]

From the length of the succeeding discussions it is obvious that agreement on the rescue operation was not easily reached. The intense haste being imposed made for confusion, since there was uncertainty about the nature of the available alternative choices, and doubts about the implications of the collapse which would threaten Cedar in the event of no rescue being mounted. The institutions, as custodians of very large funds on behalf of present and future pensioners or insurance policyholders, had to consider whether it would be justifiable to hazard fresh large resources in the defence of this troubled and by no means top-flight concern. Would they be throwing good money after bad? The occasion also meant crucial decisions for Barclays Bank which, as a debenture holder, would have been in a position to call in a receiver to Cedar, failing a support operation.

For all concerned, the hours were anxious. The four institutional investors were not entirely of a mind, partly because the diverse scale and composition of their holdings in Cedar made for some variation in their viewpoints which did not encourage the easy adoption of a common front. Also, there were some differences among the attitudes of the four institutions. Observers recall that Phoenix, led by Lord De L'Isle, and the electricity pension fund, appeared most willing to respond promptly to the Bank of England's urging. A more critical response came from the Coal Board representatives and, perhaps most of all, from the Unilever pension fund chairman. Searching and critical questioning of new propositions was all part of a normal day's work for Mr Stenham, as financial director of Unilever, one of the largest of industrial enterprises, and he was for hours not satisfied about the case for the proposed large rescue venture in which it was proposed that Unilever's pension fund should take part. The Bank of England was indeed asking a very great deal when it sought commitments, at the shortest notice, about the production of many millions of pounds of support money.

As the day went on, the Bank piled on the pressure and it was doubtless aware that people would not lightly cross it. As the series of discussions took place among the potential rescuers, their advisers and Bank of England officials, some sharp exchanges occurred in the increasingly tense atmosphere. Somebody who attended the meetings recalls that one of the blunter conversations was between Mr Stenham and Sir Jasper Hollom. Mr Stenham is quoted as having said 'This is immensely complicated – we all need time to think', to which, it is recalled, Sir Jasper replied 'You have got half an hour'. This was far from well received by Mr Stenham, and he is said to have suggested that the remark would more appropriately have been addressed to one of Sir Jasper's clerks. Another exchange between the two men which became decidedly pointed was when Sir Jasper suggested that he might telephone Unilever's chairman, Sir Ernest Woodroofe. Mr Stenham riposted that that was unlikely to be well received by Sir Ernest and that he, Mr Stenham, had come as chairman of the pension fund with full powers to deal with the matter. Another person present recalls somebody urging the need for agreement to a rescue package on one of the Coal Board pension fund chiefs, who replied to the exhortation 'You'll have to do this, you know', by saying 'I've got my miners to think of'.

Eventually, however, the representatives of the four big institutions all came round to accepting the need for a rescue package and agreed, after any necessary consultation with their own organisations, to make available the required large sums. Such was the hard lesson which the Bank of England drove home, and was soon to impress on many other institutions which had gone into the recently fashionable secondary banking and property fields, about the burdens which must be shouldered in these now troubled sectors.

All concerned then grappled through further long hours with the problems of assembling the formidable rescue package and determining its size, shape and character. The outlines began to emerge: the four institutions would provide £50 m between them, and Barclays Bank would make £22 m available, with the right, broadly, to be repaid ahead of the institutions. It was an essential element in the solution that the institutions, which were to assume voting control as part of the deal to keep Cedar afloat, would in due course take over the bulk of the company's multi-million pound property portfolio. This would take Cedar out of a business not related to finance and generate cash towards the repayment of the rescue advances.

Of course, there would have to be strict conditions, a tight curb virtually halting new lending and a close monitoring of the continuing business. Moreover, since effective control would be moving over to the rescuers, some eventual changes in the top management were to be envisaged. But now it suddenly became apparent that there were serious hesitations about accepting the proposed rescue package among Cedar's top executive directors, who owned large shareholdings: the Morrisons and Mr Fischer had the bulk of the 35 per cent held by members of the board. As it turned out, an important role in resolving these and other difficulties was to be played by Sir Kenneth Cork.

Just before six p. m. that evening, Sir Kenneth was engaged in a meeting about another company at Barclays Bank Lombard Street headquarters when he received an urgent summons to go over to the Bank of England to join Mr Bevan and Mr Vander Weyer of Barclays over a yet more pressing problem. 'I went up at six o'clock to the Governor's boardroom', he recalls. 'There was this gathering about Cedar Holdings, a company I had never even heard of before. Everyone was arguing about what to do, though most of the plan had been hammered out before I got there.'[3]

Sir Kenneth was now asked for his advice on how the plan should work and he did something to assuage remaining doubts of the institutional interests about the responsibility they were assuming, stressing, after a preliminary review of the facts, that Cedar's wide range of borrowers should give a much safer spread of security than could have been offered by some other kinds of business. Several of those present remember the helpful, calming influence he exerted as a fresh arrival at this stage. Sir Kenneth was also invited to participate in drafting a document with heads of agreement for the rescue package. 'We went into another room and knocked out heads of agreement and brought it back. They knew I was used to banging out heads of agreement; lawyers might be too tough', he says.

The draft was then taken down to the separate gathering of Cedar's chairman, managing and executive directors, who were asked to sign it. They were reluctant. Deadlock threatened, and the time was approaching midnight, only nine-and-a-half hours before the Stock Exchange was due to open for business – and to receive the news of Cedar's suspension, which might set off a wider explosion.

Sir Kenneth's persuasive powers were then called upon and at 11.30 p.m. he went down to Mr Jack Morrison, Cedar's chairman, and the other executive directors and found them he remembers, ' . . . very unhappy. Here was their company, till then very prosperous, suddenly faced with a situation where they felt they had lost their interest'. He returned upstairs an hour later, having obtained their consent through a board resolution to sign the heads of agreement for the planned rescue deal, after stressing that the basis of the price offered for the property was more favourable than could be expected from disposal of a collapsed concern's assets.

The package of loans and credit to cover Cedar was thus duly wrapped up by the four institutions and Barclays Bank. The Bank of England, in its first, then unannounced, financial commitment towards solving the mounting crisis, added a little comfort in the shape of an undertaking to contribute up to £2 m towards any loss the rescuers might ultimately sustain.

Recollections of the 17-hour marathon series of meetings are still vivid. 'We first saw the Governor. Jasper Hollom was very much in evidence. Both acted magnificently. They knew the nature of the problem and their *sang froid* was remarkable. They were cool but very firm. Kenneth Cork was a very central adviser', recalls Mr Jenkins, the investment manager of the coal board pension funds. 'I can remember that huge room full of people – and the other conference room that runs off it. We went from one room to another, moving about in small groups. We really got down to brass tacks at about seven in the evening. There were consultations and reconsiderations. The dialogue was going on between the institutions in a position to rescue Cedar, and Barclays Bank, plus merchant banks, lawyers and Kenneth Cork. By the evening the board of Cedar had been brought in.'[4]

As usual at such extended gatherings, refreshments were produced at intervals. From the evening onwards, whisky and snacks were served upstairs to the rescuers. Refreshments were also sent to the beleaguered Cedar board which remained below; one memory is that ham sandwiches were provided – not the happiest choice for a board with several Jewish members. Another recollection is that the emergency atmosphere within was accentuated by a pervasive physical chill, due to the fuel crisis. Many of the negotiators wore their overcoats.

One of those present at a subsequent board meeting of the Unilever pension fund, recalls that Mr Stenham, when reporting, as chairman, what had happened at the Bank of England, said 'we did the best we could in unbelievably difficult circumstances and it was amazing that the result was so satisfactory. But what a way to carry on'.

The position over Cedar itself had been held in check, though a long process of retrenchment and tough negotiation over some of the rescue terms still lay ahead. But meanwhile in the City the general crisis was worsening rapidly.

2 The Lifeboat Launched

We lent [money]' said Mr Harman on behalf of the Bank of England 'by every possible means and in modes we had never adopted before . . . to an immense amount . . . and we were not on some occasions over nice [over-choosy]. Seeing the dreadful state in which the public were, we rendered every assistance in our power. After a day or two of this treatment, the entire panic subsided and the "City" was quite calm.

> Walter Bagehot, *Lombard Street*, 1873,
> on the 1825 crisis

Having eventually, in their midnight marathon, cobbled together the £72 m support package for Cedar Holdings, the embattled bankers snatched a few hours' sleep. But hopes that the developing wider crisis would be damped down by the Cedar rescue quickly proved unjustified. Cedar's share quotation was duly suspended at the start of stock market dealings on the morning of Thursday 20 December, and the news of the rescue package was announced at about the same time. But the public revelation of the crisis at such a sizeable group sent new shock waves through the City, as the extent of the flight of deposits which had been taking place was realised. Rumours of problems at other fringe banks swept through the financial community and, within two-and-a-half hours of the Stock Exchange's opening, share of many secondary banks dropped by about a third, wiping millions of pounds off their value.

The Cedar crisis, dramatic as it was, had not come as an unexpected shock to City of London insiders who knew that, in the previous three weeks of disturbed conditions, many hard-pressed secondary banking companies had lost short-term funds through depositors switching cash to the safe haven of the large banks in what Mr Richardson, the Bank of England's Governor, later called 'a fit of collective prudence'.[1] These other banking businesses, often also in acute anxiety about how they would present their accounts for the end of the year, had urgently made known their troubles to their clearing banks, which had provided some

11

first-aid through stand-by borrowing facilities. Many had also hastened to the Bank of England, whose Discount Office was operating a system of early warning of impending trouble, under which information was swapped among the big banks more readily than in normal conditions.

As a result of these worrying developments, the Governor had already been discreetly in touch with the chairmen of the large High Street clearing banks and had even held a secret meeting with them the previous afternoon while the Cedar marathon was under way elsewhere in the Bank. At this gathering, the possibility of a joint rescue operation, involving up to £1000 m of support loans for the secondary banking sector, should the atmosphere of crisis not abate, had been mentioned.

The fact that news of Cedar's rescue, so far from calming the atmosphere, provoked mounting fear in the City about the situation of many other secondary banks opened the way for a crucial decision. Up to this stage, the Bank of England had retained some hope that the gathering crisis could be tackled piecemeal, by wrestling with the problems of individual banking companies. But now, in the view of those at the head of the Bank of England, events pointed unmistakeably to the need for a more generalised attack on the emergency. This is how a top person at the Bank of England recalled that organisation's thinking about the handling of the mounting crisis in what must stand as a classic of British understatement: 'We did have this marathon on Cedar Holdings and that came out all right. It was immediately following that that we concluded that 'ad hoc' was all right as far as it went, but that it was probably time to assemble a team.'

Action was now swift. The chairmen of the Big Four clearing banks which, despite competition from the now troubled newcomer fringe concerns, still made up the great bulk of the banking industry, were called secretly to a meeting with the Governor on the afternoon of the following day, Friday 21 December, at the Bank of England.

Fringe banks were not the only worry for the clearing bank chairmen who attended this crucial session. The world was in economic turmoil at the end of 1973. A State of Emergency was in force in Britain because of an impending industrial confrontation with the miners, threatening a fuel shortage in addition to the emerging prospect of steep rises in world oil prices. The clearers, already heavily lent after the 1971–3 boom, and with new 'corset' curbs just imposed on them, as will be explained later, in the Mini Budget, were concerned how they were to meet all calls upon them. Would their industrial customers, carrying a high level of stocks, but with production cut back by a three-day working week, need larger overdrafts to continue to pay wages? Were foreign debts to British exporters, and large clearing bank financing of these exporters, safe in the light of certain signs of trouble at one or two banks abroad? Then, still more pressing, there was worry lest the panic which was affecting the secondary banking community should reach even the big clearers and the long-established merchant banks. Could these leading banks themselves be caught up in the avalanche which was threatening to bring down a crop of smaller banks? 'This would have been worse than the Wall Street crash of 1929, which British banking had survived so well', one senior clearer afterwards reflected. All these considerations inclined the clearers' chiefs to give a responsive hearing to the central bank's plans.

At the crucial summit meeting presided over by Mr Richardson, the Bank's Governor, on Friday 21 December, business was completed with much more despatch than in the crowded mid-week marathon about Cedar, though the decision arrived at was vastly more far-reaching. The secret gathering lasted just ninety minutes. The chairmen present with Mr Richardson and the Deputy Governor, Sir Jasper Hollom, were Sir (then Mr) Eric Faulkner, chairman of the Committee of London Clearing Bankers (CLCB) and of Lloyds Bank, Sir Archibald Forbes, the Scottish industrialist and chartered accountant who chaired the Midland Bank, Sir (then Mr) John Prideaux, the National Westminster Bank chairman, and Sir (then Mr) Anthony Tuke, who had become chairman of Barclays Bank in succession to Sir John Thomson less than two months earlier. The clearers' chairmen were accompanied by chief or senior general managers from their banks, while the Governor and Deputy Governor were supported by senior Bank of England colleagues.

Mr Richardson formally proposed that the Bank should organise an operation whereby the clearing banks would jointly provide support loans to hard-pressed secondary banks to fill some or all of the gap left by the flight of funds from them. He pointed to the risk to the banking system of a further spread of alarm and stressed the need for a team effort to fend off the current dangers. It was an appeal both to common interest and the national interest.

Depositors of money with appropriate secondary and fringe banks were generally all to be protected, since it would be impossible, or at least undesirable, to limit this help to small personal depositors only. It was important that the rescue operation should also guarantee the position of big depositors, since any failure by a fringe bank to pay back large money market deposits would have damaging repercussions on the creditor which had lent the money. The idea was that shareholders, as distinct from depositors, in the troubled secondary banks were not entitled to direct protection of their interests, although, of course, they would often be indirectly helped by the proposed support plan.

Essentially, the proposition was for a 're-cycling' arrangement. Since depositors had been withdrawing their deposits from the secondary banks and confiding them to the safe keeping of the large clearing banks, the idea was that the clearers should, on conditions, jointly lend money back to the secondary concerns. The fear that these fringe banks' assets might prove too deficient to finance full repayment of this aid, or might shrink so that they became so, was not uppermost in the banking chiefs' minds at the time. However, it was a feature of the scheme unfolded by the Governor that the combined support pool should be used to give hard-pressed secondary banks time for recovery and not to postpone the insolvency of non-viable fringe concerns.

The clearing bank chairmen readily enough accepted the Governor's plan, but a good deal of discussion took place, in which it was noted that the scale of the problem could still not be fully gauged. The clearers had not all been equally close, as bankers, to the new secondary sector. The bigger two clearers, the National Westminster and Barclays, naturally had more secondary banks among their own customers. Of the other two, the Midland, at this stage, still saw some advantage in the concept of individual rescues, *à la* Cedar, rather than a general operation. The argument along these lines was trenchantly voiced by the Midland's chairman, Sir Archibald Forbes, although, in the prevailing emergency, he agreed to go along with the idea of a joint approach.

With the crisis at the pitch it had reached, there was an obvious consensus that this was not the time to linger over apportioning responsibility. Some clearing bankers did consider that the Bank of England, through its beneficent attitude towards the growth of new banking businesses with their competitive challenge to the big boys of the industry, had played its part in the build-up towards the emergency. Certain clearing banks thought that they had themselves given less encouragement to the fringe banks in the recent boom than had some fellow-clearers and were not ecstatic about sharing rescue bills on a common basis. The Bank of England, for its part, doubtless felt that, had the Government taken its advice, which will be referred to later, to slow the boom down sooner through higher interest rates, the trouble would not have arisen. But so far from mutual recrimination, the theme by the time of the Governor's meeting was one of co-operation to fend off a crisis whose dangers were by then unmistakeable, but whose potential was still incalculable.

Some concern was voiced by the bank chairmen at the impetus which had been given to the mushrooming of the fringe bank sector by the Department of Trade and Industry's very liberal issue of documents, under section 123 of the Companies Act 1967, certifying that companies were carrying on a banking business. The Governor showed sympathy with this, promising to take the matter up with the Department.

But the most important question raised by the clearers was whether the Bank of England, or indeed the Government, planned to participate in the joint operation to the extent of agreeing to provide any money towards the loans, or indeed to share in any losses. Not so, it seemed. But the chairmen pressed that the central bank should have a stake. After all, the Bank was very closely involved as proposer and prospective leader of the support operation. Moreover, the Bank had shouldered a small proportion of the risk in a combined and ultimately very costly participation by the clearers earlier in 1973 in a rescue, which will be referred to later, of the Scottish Co-operative's bank. This vital issue of the central bank's possible participation in the financing and risks of the joint operation was left over for a few days. One point also made was that some back-up help might come from large institutional shareholders, such as insurance companies, with investments in secondary banks.

Before this historic meeting broke up, the bankers approved the draft of a carefully worded Press notice to be issued by the Bank later in the afternoon of 21 December. The decision to launch the 'Lifeboat'[2] – as the combined support operation was to become familiarly known – had been taken.

It should be noted here that at least some of the top general managers of the clearing banks were far from convinced, at this stage, of the case for a general rescue operation and, rightly of course, expressed their hesitations to their chiefs. 'It was a proper difference of role', one recalls. 'The chairmen took a broader view.'

The Bank of England's Press statement was pitched in the low-key style of central bank pronouncements at times of crisis and read as follows: 'In recent weeks a number of so-called "fringe banks" have experienced a withdrawal of deposits obtained through the money markets. The resultant pressure on their liquidity has been severe and normal stand-by facilities have had to be used. In some cases these facilities have proved inadequate to meet the pressure experienced, and further support has therefore been sought from banks and other institutions. In response to these developments the Bank of England have established in conjunction with the clearing banks machinery whereby such cases can be promptly considered, and the situation as a whole kept under continuous review. This machinery, which is working well, is being further strengthened, and in cases where additional support is shown to be necessary and justified, arrangements for reinforcing the liquidity of the deposit-taking companies concerned have been and will be made in order to protect depositors.'

The announcement did not refer to the pooling agreement as such, since the heads of agreement for it were not settled and signed until the following week and were never published. Knowledge that there was a joint funding arrangement emerged more gradually, and was not formally disclosed until much later. Nor did the statement stress the unprecedented character and anticipated possible £1000 m scale of the operation the big banks were embarking on. Nonetheless, the message of reassurance quickly reduced tension – in fact before knowledge of the emergency had made much impact beyond the City of London itself. The calming process was helped by the Christmas holiday; the next working day was Monday 24 December, Christmas Eve, traditionally a time when little business is done in the City.

When stock markets reopened after the holiday, share prices stabilised, the *Financial Times* 30 share index rebounding 17.8, after recent weakness, to 336.0 on 27 December. On the same day, when Mr Richardson presided over another meeting with the chairmen, of the Big Four and other clearers' representatives, the subject of a Bank of England contribution to the Lifeboat operation was taken up. The bank chiefs, led by Sir Eric Faulkner, argued strongly that the central bank, as the leader of the rescue or 'support' group, should have a significant financial stake in it. The Governor and the Deputy Governor had done some more thinking about this over the holiday and now made it clear that the Bank desired to play an appropriate part in this way, if the chairmen wished it. After discussion in which other possibilities were talked about, the Governors agreed that the Bank should take a stake of 10 per cent, the figure the chairmen regarded as 'significant', in the financing and risks of the operation. It was also decided to invite participation from the Scottish clearing banks, Bank of Scotland, Clydesdale Bank and Royal Bank of Scotland with the related Williams & Glyn's Bank, all of which agreed to come in.

Heads of agreement for the support operation were then settled. For all rescue operations undertaken to protect depositors in banks, fringe banks and other financial companies dependent on money markets or private depositors, the group agreed to act together in the closest co-operation on lines which were specified, and to consider bringing in other suitable financial institutions, whether inside or outside the banking sector, to help in the operation. A 'control committee' to run the Lifeboat support operation was set up with Sir Jasper Hollom as chairman. From this position he played a crucial role throughout the course of the rescue strategy over a number of years. The other members of the committee were senior representatives of the participating clearing banks. The Bank of England provided the secretariat.

The clearing banks' 90 per cent share was divided up in the ratio of their eligible liabilities, broadly their deposits. Provision, which will be enlarged upon later, was also included for sorting out recipient fringe banks into different categories (a few were to be supported at the sole risk of a single clearer); for attaching conditions to the support loans; for certain investigation into assisted companies; for the appointment of a 'related bank' from among the clearers to act as the main channel for communication with each recipient of aid; and for the setting up of machinery to collect and advance the large sums involved.

No upper limit was specified for contributions by the participants in the Lifeboat support group; the arrangements were however subject to review. The heads of agreement were then signed; they were formalised later in a substantive agreement dated 28 June 1974. The Lifeboat committee first met on 28 December 1973 in the Octagon Room at the Bank of England, where it was to continue working intensively to deal with the prospective 'casualties' and to decide which should be helped and on what terms. The prompt action meant that all hard-pressed concerns which were to be supported received necessary assistance before the year's end; the Lifeboat also took over the financing of certain loans already advanced to fringe banks by individual clearers in the previous few weeks.

A major feature of the British banking system's giant new survival kit, and one provided for under the heads of agreement, was the establish-ment of a 'money desk' at the Bank of England. As the Lifeboat committee decided each day on the amount required to be advanced in the following twenty-four hours, the money desk would call on each participating clearing bank by telephone for its contribution. These contributions were produced immediately and without question. If the borrower needed more support during the day this would be provided by the 'related bank' and shared out appropriately the next morning.

It is one of the most remarkable events in banking history that the big banks unhesitatingly put up the vast sums required for the Lifeboat, often to protect concerns which had lately been competing wildly with them for business, for the greater good of safeguarding the whole financial system.

According to what was sometimes said at the time, it could only have happened in Britain. The Americans, so the reasoning ran, would never have managed such a quick answer to this kind of emergency: it would have taken three months for the Federal Reserve to have consulted all the interests concerned. In France, the Finance Ministry would have stepped in and taken full control at once. As for the West Germany, the banks there were perhaps hardly close enough at the time to each other – or to the central bank – to have committed themselves to an operation on the scale of the Lifeboat.

Looking back on the crisis in the calm conditions more than four years later, Mr Richardson, the Governor of the Bank of England, highlighted the motives behind the Bank's action in assembling the Lifeboat team when he gave evidence to the House of Commons Select Committee on Nationalised Industries in January 1978: 'We had as our purpose protecting depositors, and the purpose of protecting depositors was simply to avoid a widening circle of collapse through the contagion of fear. . . . The danger was real and, of course, we had seen it in the past. We saw it, for example, rage through the American banking system in the early 1930s, when hundreds of banks were closed and finally a total closedown of the banking system was involved.'[3]

Assessing the gains from the unprecedented venture, Sir Eric Faulkner, the leader on the big commercial banks' side as chairman of the Committee of London Clearing Bankers when the Lifeboat was launched, afterwards remarked: 'The British banking system's slide into possible chaos had been halted on the very brink; the threatening avalanche of deposit withdrawals from the clearing banks had been avoided, for none of them suffered any identifiable withdrawals; international confidence in the British banks continued uninterrupted; international trade was unaffected.'[4] The worldwide benefits to confidence in Britain were to be underlined by the stability of sterling throughout 1974, despite the multiplied oil price.

One of the most striking aspects was that many people were unaware that there was a crisis at all. This applies also to at least parts of the Government. The Treasury was kept informed by the Bank of England, but the dramatic events and the issues involved seem to have made little sharp impact at the highest levels, so much was the burden handled at the east end of the axis of the British State's financial power known as 'the authorities' (the Treasury and the Bank of England). It is a long-standing joke, not quite unconnected with a genuine rivalry, that the Treasury sees the Bank of England as its 'East End branch', while it is itself, of course, regarded by the Bank as *its* 'West End branch'. There is no doubt that, in the response to the fringe banking crisis, the decision-making rested overwhelmingly at the east end of the axis.

Mr Brendon Sewill, a special assistant and political adviser to the Chancellor of the Exchequer, Lord Barber, recalls: 'Although each day I looked through the Chancellor's "In tray" in order to identify any particularly politically sensitive subjects, I recall no alarm bells ringing over the secondary banking crisis. All the concern at that time was concentrated on oil prices, coal miners and the incomes policy.' He remembers hearing about the Scottish Co-operative and London and County Securities crises, but of both being seen rather as the results of management misjudgments. The subject of the secondary banking crisis is not mentioned by Mr Douglas Hurd MP, Political Secretary at 10 Downing Street to Mr Edward Heath as Prime Minister from 1970 to 1974, in his book *An End to Promises*[5], which deals with many of the events of the period, particularly the winter of 1973/74.

The Bank of England was, in short, left to get on with combatting the emergency very much on its own, with little questioning or close watching from the Treasury or the Government. The Bank's intervention was so firm, prompt, and discreet that it effectively muffled the threatened crisis.

Before the future course of the Lifeboat operation is considered, it is now appropriate to go back a number of years and review the earlier causes of the crisis, including the monetary boom of 1971–3 which nourished the rapid growth of the secondary bank sector.

Part II BACKGROUND AND CAUSES OF THE CRISIS

3 Developments in the Financial System, 1958–73

> The Empire may have disintegrated and the UK may now be a third rate power, but the City of London has staged a comeback which would be the envy of any child movie star reaching maturity.[1]

> Professor Ira Scott

In retrospect, the crisis in December 1973 can be seen as the culmination of a fifteen-year period of rapid change in the City of London's banking and financial mechanisms. In 1958 new influences, partly political and partly economic, began to make for an environment which was more hospitable than before to new money enterprises.

After nearly twenty years of wartime and post-war restriction the Conservative Government sought to return the economy to something like peacetime normality by sweeping away certain curbs on financial activity. Stock markets had already perked up after long stagnation and the standard of living showed some rise. It was the era of the celebrated remark by Mr Harold Macmillan, the Prime Minister: 'You've never had it so good'.

Credit controls were gradually eased and, in October 1958, hire purchase controls were dropped. Shortly afterwards the regulation of borrowing through the long-standing Capital Issues Committee was ended. There was accordingly no longer any official control over the raising of money, other than the Bank of England's supervision of the timing of some public issues of securities. Those who wanted to borrow cash were from then on no longer required to satisfy a Government-appointed body that their project was desirable in the national interest. This cleared the way, at a time of gradually rising living standards, for hire purchase, banking, property and other financial ventures, whose creation depended essentially only on their prospects of profitability. Expansion of hire purchase firms had already been encouraged by a spell

23

of lending curbs on the big banks from 1955 to 1958. Now, more generally, the stage was set for a range of new money-making activities, partly to feed the appetite of the British population for increased consumption – on credit.

Many of the new financial concerns which were to figure in the banking crisis of the mid-1970s began business in the late-1950s and early 1960s. But not all the newer creations were successful, even in the short run. Tough competition and lack of experience drove many smaller hire purchase firms out of business within a few years and left larger operators with bad debts. There were some well-publicised failures of smaller financial concerns, notably Pinnock Finance (Great Britain), and Davies Investments, whose creator afterwards took his own life. The fact that some ill-fated enterprises had relied heavily on advertising for the public's savings – often at attractive interest rates – caused concern when collapses occurred. In 1963 the Protection of Depositors Act was passed to limit the freedom of companies to advertise without making available certain stipulated information about themselves, though banks were exempt from the requirement. The new law was a small step towards more official regulation on behalf of savers and depositors. It represented some departure from the hitherto prevalent belief that it was up to investors to safeguard their own interests. 'A fool and his money are soon parted' was a maxim which, at least until then, had been frequently quoted as the prevailing City philosophy.

A development in the structure of the City of London's markets which was to have far-reaching significance for new financial ventures, because it opened up an important source of funds for them, can be traced back to 1955. From that year, the Treasury required the local authorities to raise part of their finance in the open market instead of relying wholly on Government loans. This led to a quest for sources of shorter-term borrowing, in which the hire purchase companies also participated. It was not long before large industrial groups and others with surplus cash were alerted to the opportunities for deploying substantial sums of their money in lending to these new borrowers on terms more advantageous than those available through the traditional outlet of deposits with the big High Street clearing banks. Broking firms, eager to scout around for deposits and bring borrowers and lenders together, soon sprang up.

In short, a novel phenomenon gradually emerged on the financial scene – a market performing a new intermediary function by drawing in deposits at more attractive interest rates than could be obtained on ordinary deposit accounts at the clearing banks and making them available for use by a wide variety of borrowers who could afford to pay interest rates above those charged by the clearers, whose own lending was often restricted. Soon many banks of various kinds outside the ranks of the clearers were supplying surplus funds to the new money markets and borrowing from them, creating a sizeable new 'inter-bank' market. In due course, a further refinement appeared with the creation of a market dealing in certificates of deposit, 'IOUs' for deposits.

At first the emerging money markets were often described as 'parallel', since they grew up alongside the old-established discount market, through which the big banks traditionally place out their surplus cash with the discount houses, against security. But in time, the new markets were more broadly known as 'wholesale' markets, since they trade in funds of sizeable amounts, as distinct from the generally smaller sums collected by big 'retail' High Street clearing banks from numerous depositors. These wholesale money markets, which continued to expand, proved a key factor in the development of the new secondary banks, to be further surveyed in the next chapter, as well as becoming important sources of finance for local councils and other long-established bodies.

A useful summary of the new sterling wholesale markets was given by the Bank of England in its evidence to the Wilson Committee on financial institutions: 'Since the early 1960s a second sterling market [in addition to the traditional discount market] has developed, mainly in inter-bank unsecured deposits . . . but also, to a significant extent latterly, in Certificates of Deposit [CDs] . . . Participants are not restricted to banks and include local authorities, building societies and other financial institutions and many other commercial and industrial companies. This market is sometimes thought of as a series of discrete markets . . . but [it] is essentially a unitary unsecured sterling money market.'[2]

An important characteristic of the wholesale money markets which thus developed is that deposits placed through them are unsecured. In this they differ from call money placed by the clearing banks with the traditional discount houses, which do provide security and can always obtain money to finance repayments by discounting their assets for cash at the Bank of England. There is no such lender of last resort to the unsecured wholesale markets – although in essence what the Lifeboat operation meant was that the authorities did arrange for the top level of the banking system to perform just that role, on an emergency basis, in the secondary banking crisis.

Another major development which began in the late-1950s, but which lies outside the main theme of this book, was the creation in London of a new wholesale market in foreign currency deposits, known as the Euro-dollar or Euro-currency market. Curbs on United States domestic interest rates, and some relaxations in world exchange controls, created the conditions for an 'offshore' market in dollar and other internation-ally mobile funds. London seized the opportunity and provided the mechanism for such a market, which grew much larger than the sterling wholesale market operating alongside it and attracted many American and other foreign banks to London. By the end of 1973, $91,000 m (£39,000 m) was outstanding in London's Euro-currency market, compared with nearly £14,000 m in the sterling inter-bank and CD markets.

The growth of these markets was a major structural change much welcomed by the Bank of England, which was conscious of the diminishing world role of sterling and saw the fresh activity as opening a worthy new chapter for London as a financial centre. The Committee of London Clearing Bankers later remarked that '. . . the growth of the new [Euro-currency] markets was helped by the positive attitude of the Bank of England, especially its "open-door" policy towards all reputable banks from overseas who wished to set up in London'.[3] This welcome to foreign banks was part of the Bank's favourable attitude towards the growth of the banking community which extended also to the encouragement of new British banking ventures.

The growth of the wholesale money markets which attracted funds from industrial and commercial companies and various financial institutions was accompanied, from the late-1950s and early 1960s, by the develop-ment of wholesale banking, not only by new British secondary and fringe banks but by long-established merchant banks and international banking groups as well. Wholesale banking consists, broadly, of the provision of bank loans in sizeable amounts and the financing of this activity with appropriate money market borrowings. This is as distinct from retail banking, where there is no close relationship between the multitude of deposits collected by the big High Street banks, through their branches, and the loans, investments and other assets in which these resources are deployed. While the safe management of a retail bank, and the security of its depositors, depend to a large extent on adequate holdings of cash and near-cash assets as a cushion against withdrawals, rather different precautionary principles are appropriate for wholesale banking.

Matching is a concept vital to the prudent management of a wholesale banking operation. The idea is that liabilities should, to a reasonable extent, be balanced by assets corresponding to them in amount, period and currency. This ensures that adequate funds will be available in the shape of a maturing asset to repay a deposit when it falls due. Exact matching is more than safety requires since cash assets, standby borrowing facilities and reserves afford a cushion, and a bank's own skills and reputation should enable it safely to lend for periods longer than those of its borrowings, within controlled limits. A considerable degree of 'mismatching' or 'maturity transformation' – borrowing short and lending longer – is thus within the bounds of acceptability, and the art of conducting a safe and profitable wholesale bank lies in the correct judgment of the degree of proper departure from precise matching. A very closely matched operation of borrowing and lending may bring little profit; on the other hand, a high degree of mismatch is obviously very risky.

Although principles of matching – and other prudential ratios for wholesale banking – are familiar topics, and still subjects of debate in the early 1980s, they were less recognised and certainly not codified in the 1960s. A rare contemporary academic commentary on the matter was given in 1968 by Professor Jack Revell in his paper 'Changes in British Banking: The Growth of the Secondary Banking System'.[4] In this Professor Revell used the term 'secondary banks' in the wider sense of the full range of those active in wholesale banking, including top British merchant banks and UK offshoots of foreign banks, rather than of the narrower category of second-line and fringe British banks to which the description was later generally applied.

After noting the much slower growth between 1958 and 1966, of the 'deposit' (clearing) banks than of the 'secondary' (wholesale) banks, he remarked: 'Just as liquidity is the basic principle of deposit banking, so is matching the basic principle of secondary banking. The principle is . . . of considerable importance, and it needs spelling out because its application is quite new in British banking.' Underlining the mutual dependence of the new sterling money markets and of the wholesale ('secondary') banking sector, he noted: 'The growth of the new parallel money markets and the spectacular growth of the deposits of secondary banks are inextricably intertwined . . . Secondary banking could not exist without an active inter-bank market'. In a prophetic reference to the dangers which arose later when fringe banks tapped the unsecured money markets excessively, he added: 'The bank which is placing a deposit with another bank . . . has lost control of the ultimate use of that deposit. . . . It would seem that a failure anywhere could ripple through the system. . . . There is no doubt that any widespread financial crisis would spread all the more quickly because of the existence of this network of inter-bank deposits'.

Many banks newly engaging in wholesale banking in the 1960s and early 1970s undoubtedly managed their liabilities with enough regard for matching to be proof against subsequent troubles. But by no means all did so. Certainly the philosophy of matching was hardly a common subject for debate at the lunch tables, or indeed in the boardrooms, of the new enterprises which became known as secondary or fringe banks. One leading personality in that field appeared puzzled at the term in subsequent discussion with the author and quickly dismissed it as 'rubbish'.

The years in which the wholesale money markets were growing up, and nourishing the expansion of the secondary banks as well as of wholesale banks generally, were not altogether happy ones for the big High Street clearing banks. The tranquil economic climate of the late-1950s gave way from the early 1960s to less easy times, when recurrent sterling crises necessitated restrictive Government policies involving the reimposition of controls and later of direct 'ceiling' curbs on the lending of the larger banks. Many of the smaller, newer, banking concerns, however, escaped these restrictions, which the authorities did not think it worthwhile to apply to them. Consequently these banks were able to grow unhampered, often picking up lucrative lending business, such as property financing, which was turned away by the clearers.

The clearers also found themselves handicapped in another way. These were still governed by long-standing operating conventions, notably the interest rate cartel which prescribed broadly common bases of interest rates for deposits and advances, geared to Bank Rate, which in turn was fixed by the monetary authorities. The 2 per cent-below-Bank Rate paid on clearing bank deposit accounts was generally lower than the rates that could be obtained in the wholesale markets, which began to attract away some of the clearers' traditional deposit business. Under another convention, the clearing banks kept at least 28 per cent of their assets in cash, call money with the discount market, Treasury bills and other liquid, but, low yielding, holdings.

In the mid-1960s the clearers, spurred on by some of the smaller groups among them which were keener than the larger brethren to bid competitively for deposits, set up a committee under Sir (then Mr) John Thomson, chairman of Barclays Bank to re-examine their conventions in the light of the growing competitive challenge to their deposit business from participants in the new money markets. The conclusion was, however, that if interest rates were left to the free play of market forces, the clearers, as still the main takers of deposits, would find themselves paying more for much the same money; prevailing lending curbs would allow them little scope for expanding their advances business, so there would be little point in their competing for deposits with higher rates. The High Street banks did nonetheless eventually operate in the wholesale markets to some extent through subsidiaries or associates teasingly known as 'clearers' cheaters'.

The clearers' interest rate cartel and other conventions were strongly challenged in 1967 by the National Board for Prices and Incomes' report on bank charges.[5] The Board wanted the agreement on interest rates abolished, since it thought that the cartel on lending rates operated against the most efficient allocation of credit. It also suggested the sweeping away of the clearers' 28 per cent liquidity ratio and the introduction of reserve ratios for all banks. In addition, the Board wanted the big banks to drop their collective agreements on charges, to publish their tariffs of charges and to reveal their profits and reserves in full. These recommendations encouraged re-examination of existing arrangements and led on to full profits disclosure. But the report had little other immediate effect, except in one respect. This was that it triggered off a rush of mergers among several clearers – notably the creation of the National Westminster Bank – by stating that the authorities had withdrawn their earlier objections to such amalgamations.

Towards the end of the 1960s, discontent with the existing monetary control arrangements grew. Tightened curbs placed on the clearers' lending after sterling's devaluation in November 1967 proved increasingly irksome and prompted open questioning. 'The kind of reduction now demanded must either involve severe restriction of the manufacturing companies or put some smaller men out of business', Sir John Thomson, Barclays' chairman, wrote early in 1969.[6]

The result of all these trends was a fall in the share of the market held by the large banks. Between 1959 and 1968, the English, Scottish and Northern Ireland clearing banks saw their proportion of the total sterling deposits with all UK banks drop from 85 per cent to 75 per cent; over the same period, the accepting houses, overseas banks and other banks (broadly, the wholesale banking sector) trebled their sterling deposits.[7]

By the end of the decade the monetary authorities were giving a good deal of critical thought to the objectives and mechanisms of monetary control of the economy. The Treasury was anxious, in the post-devaluation era of disappointment with the economy's showing in the 1960s, to achieve a clearer concept of how the monetary, fiscal and other aspects of policy should fit together in overall economic strategy, and in particular to consider how the increasingly discussed question of the treatment of money supply should be related to other facets of policy. The Bank of England, equally concerned with these matters, was, in addition, acutely conscious of the need to relieve the various growing strains and distortions in the banking industry.

A high-level Treasury-Bank of England Committee was set up in 1969, in the latter days of the Labour Government, to re-examine the fundamentals of monetary and related economic policy. But it was not until some months after Mr Edward Heath's Conservative Government took office in June 1970 that an initiative of far-reaching importance on the subject was launched in the shape of major proposals by the Bank of England.

The Bank's plan, which became known as Competition and Credit Control (C and CC), was designed as a comprehensive solution to the various problems which had grown up. Its essence was the scrapping of the controversial ceilings on lending of the larger banks and finance houses, the abolition of certain of the conventional restraints, and the placing of the different parts of the banking community on an even footing with a view to their competing on fairer terms. The clearing banks' interest rate cartel would be dropped, so that each bank would fix its own rates in the context of market conditions. The clearers' 28 per cent liquidity minimum would also be discarded and all banks would observe a standard 12.5 per cent minimum ratio of reserve assets, such as balances with the Bank of England, Treasury Bills, short bonds and other near-cash items (but not till money) to liabilities. The Bank of England was to be able to call on all banks (not just the clearers) to place a proportion of their assets with it as Special Deposits; this was seen as a measure to influence their capacity to lend. A parallel system was planned for finance houses and complementary arrangements were proposed for the discount market. Another aspect of the proposals was that the Government Broker should become less ready to pay prevailing market prices for Government (gilt-edged) stock which holders wished to sell; this was to make the gilt-edged market more quickly responsive to changes in interest rates.

Later public comments by Lord O'Brien, then the Governor of the Bank of England, made it clear that the Bank envisaged changes in interest rates as the chief method, under the proposed arrangements, for influencing the less directly controlled monetary system. 'What we have in mind is a system under which the allocation of credit is primarily determined by its cost'[8] he said. Thus, the idea was that market forces would operate more freely, subject to broad official influence on interest rates. The reserve assets base appears to have been seen as a prudential 'cushion' of liquid assets of the kind on which the Bank of England could operate through its market operations aimed at enforcing interest rate changes.

The competitive aspect was also unmistakeable. The scheme aimed at the 'development of new techniques of monetary policy, with the objective of combining an effective measure of control over credit conditions with greater scope for competition and innovation'. This reference,[9] in the consultative plan afterwards published, was a reminder that the Bank of England was far from hostile to newcomers on the banking scene – including the multiplying band of secondary banks – doubtless seeing them as desirable rivals to the oligarchy of the large clearers.

The scheme was unfolded by Lord O'Brien to Lord Barber, Chancellor of the Exchequer, at a private dinner in January 1971 at which both were accompanied by senior advisers. It received an interested initial response from the Chancellor: the Bank had not overlooked the fact that the proposals accorded with the competitive ideology of the new Conservative Government. The plan had been taking shape earlier in the minds of senior Bank staff, led by Mr John Fforde, the executive director who was the senior official concerned with its preparation. But the change of Government had created a decidedly more welcoming environment for the proposed new deal, with its stress on reduction in controls, freer competition and fuller play for market forces.

There are some signs that the Treasury's top officials would have been glad to have been consulted even earlier than they were about the C and CC plan. But the Bank evidently felt – and this is understandable – that it would be best to bring forward an already fully considered project, the more so since some previous thoughts about altered methods of restraining bank and finance house lending, put to the Treasury three months before, in October 1970, had not made any apparent headway.

Top Treasury officials were far from sure that they liked the idea of abandoning loan ceilings – which, whatever their drawbacks, were an effective weapon for squeezing credit – and relying on interest rates as the essential instrument of monetary control. They were also concerned that a switch to a 12.5 per cent reserve assets ratio for the whole banking industry, when the big clearing banks had hitherto worked to a 28 per cent liquidity ratio (admittedly somewhat differently composed), would release large funds for extra lending and so be inflationary. The latter point was partly met in due course by an arrangement whereby, before the new system was introduced, the London clearing banks invested £750 m of their cash in three new gilt-edged stocks, the bulk maturing in two to three years. This mopped up some of the clearers' cash but still left them, after they had received repayment of £415 m of Special Deposits, with several hundred million pounds of resources freed for lending.

It seems reasonable to suppose that, in submitting the C and CC scheme to ministers, the Treasury concentrated on the point that the discarding of loan ceilings would mean that interest rates would have to take the main strain in the operation of future monetary policy. Thus, approval of the scheme would have to imply a willingness to raise interest rates sufficiently far to curb any future boom. While doubtless emphasising the fact that the effective operation of the scheme would mean using the interest rate weapon energetically as a control, the top Treasury officials were evidently willing to give the project a fair wind, despite any unhappiness that the proposals should have been developed to such an advanced degree in the Bank before they were consulted. The Permanent Secretary, Lord Croham (then Sir Douglas Allen), felt that the advice to ministers on the scheme should not be dictated by pique.

Some ministers, it seems, afterwards felt that it had never been brought home to them that it might be necessary to increase interest rates above the then politically sensitive level of 10 per cent to get an adequate grip on a later upsurge in credit. If this was so, it is hardly surprising, since, in the autumn of 1971, when the final decision was taken, the economy was sluggish and interest rates were low, Bank Rate standing at only 5 per cent.

The C and CC scheme was approved by the Government and launched in September 1971, the Government Broker having earlier become a less ready buyer of gilt-edged stock at prevailing prices, in line with one part of the proposals.

At the time, no requests were made to the banks about priorities to be observed among different types of borrowers in the management of their lending, although the scheme did reserve to the authorities the right to give this kind of 'qualitative guidance'. There was consequently no official pressure at the time to deter banks from briskly stepping up their lending to such normally non-priority categories as property concerns and individuals. The scheme thus provided a framework within which a money boom of remarkable proportions was able to blow up, under expansive economic policies, in the succeeding two-and-a-half years, contributing strongly to the massive growth in the secondary banking sector which preceded the crisis. But before these developments are examined, it is now necessary to assess further the point to which the newer fringe and secondary banks had grown by the early years of the 1970s when C and CC was in full operation.

4 Debut of the Secondary Banks

> A man of large wealth . . . always thinks . . . "I have a great income . . . If things go on as they are I shall certainly keep it; but if they change, I *may* not keep it". Consequently, he considers every change of circumstance a "bore". . . . But a new man, who has his way to make . . . knows that such changes are his opportunity; he is always on the look-out for them, and always heeds them when he finds them. The rough and vulgar structure of English commerce is the secret of its life.
>
> Walter Bagehot, *Lombard Street*, 1873

Opportunities for money making were so evident in the fifteen years up to 1973 that it is scarcely surprising that a new generation of financial enterprises grew up to take advantage of them.

Recovery in the stock markets from the mid-1950s revived scope, at least at times, for profitable investment in industrial and commercial shares. The era also produced the new business concept of the take-over, the successful bid by one company for another to extract better value from the latter's assets. Moreover, the rising standard of living not only generated the demand for profitable consumer credit services referred to in the previous chapter. It also led to increased savings, and to a revival in the business, first seen in the 1930s, of management of those savings through unit trusts and in other ways.

Britain's large High Street clearing banks have traditionally eschewed investment in the equity shares of other companies, preferring to concentrate most of their assets on purchases of Government stock and, latterly, to a considerably greater extent on lending. But the new financiers of the late-1950s and afterwards felt no such inhibitions. They responded to the fact that holding and dealing in shares, participation in take-over activities, and investment management afforded plentiful scope for profitable activity. In addition, the prolonged loan curbs on the big banks provided rewarding opportunities for lending by unrestricted smaller and newer banking concerns to those not fully accommodated by the clearers, such as some of the property companies involved in the booms of the late-1960s and early 1970s and individuals. Add to this the growth of the new money markets which, as noted in the last chapter, facilitated the raising of deposit finance by all the 'wholesale' banks operating outside the 'retail' sector of the big High Street groups, and it is clear that financial opportunities were broadening significantly. In short, the climate was unusually propitious for alert and energetic entrepreneurs to build up new enterprises.

Many took the tide at its flood in a way which led on to fortune and the fast-growing new ventures which developed to seize the opportunities came to be known as secondary or fringe banks. Some of their activities – certain lending and share investments, for instance – were not dissimilar from those of old-established merchant banks. But their speed of expansion, style of management and, often, degree of risk-taking which was to cause problems in the later crisis, tended to distinguish many of them, even in their most prosperous days, from staider members of the banking community.

Growth in the new secondary banking sector was so swift that no adequate development of generally accepted and codified standards of prudential management for such a varied and novel range of enterprises – including appropriate concepts of matching – took place in step with it. Nor was there any significant growth at the time in the supervisory capacity of the Bank of England. The rest of this chapter will briefly glance at a number of the new banking and financial enterprises which grew up in the years before the crisis and note some aspects of them which are relevant to later events. It will then look at the structure of the British banking industry as it stood in late-1973, after a new category of banking enterprises had been created under section 123 of the Companies Act 1967.

The new secondary banks and financial concerns whose rise and rise, and later troubles, culminated in the upheaval of the mid-1970s were so highly individualistic, with such a diversity of interests, that it is not easy to classify them neatly. Before a number are mentioned, it is worth noting that some were originally built mainly on the basis of a hire purchase or other lending business, while others grew largely from various forms of stock market activity.

Mr Jim Slater, the best known of the new financiers, followed the latter route in the development, from 1964, of Slater Walker Securities (SWS), originally in association with Mr Peter Walker MP, who was a non-executive director and deputy chairman until he joined Mr Heath's Conservative Government as a Cabinet Minister in 1970. The two men's names were combined in the title of this prominent group.

SWS was active from its early days in investment dealing and management and in the purchase of control of industrial concerns in the hope of substantially improving their performance, though Mr Charles Raw, in his book *Slater Walker*[1] has questioned the group's success in the latter role. Before long SWS won backing from the big property company Great Portland Estates and from certain City of London merchant banks and institutions. After some years, the group gave less emphasis to its role as a conglomerate running a number of industrial ventures and concentrated more on 'investment banking', not only in Britain but abroad. In particular, it took sizeable share stakes in a range of 'satellite' companies, often run by former Slater Walker men. Insurance was a new activity added in due course.

In 1968, SWS acquired half, and the following year the other half, of Ralli Brothers (Bankers), a banking company whose authorised status the Bank of England allowed SWS to retain and whose name was changed to Slater Walker Ltd (SWL). This bank was to play a central role in the eventual development of the SWS group's troubles and in the Bank of England's burdens in handling the secondary banking crisis. In the booming early 1970s, the SWS group, which contained numerous separate companies, bought various property assets. It also, in 1972/73, expanded the lending of its bank in a way Mr Slater later acknowledged to have been a mistake.[2] At its peak in the early 1970s, SWS was one of the fifty biggest companies in Britain, with a stock market value of more than £200 m.

Almost as large as SWS was First National Finance Corporation, whose origins lay rather on the consumer finance side. In 1963, Mr Pat Matthews injected his two hire purchase companies and a small banking concern into Birmingham Railway Carriage and Wagon (BRCW) – which was renamed Birmingham Wagon and later First National Finance Corporation (FNFC) – at the same time taking a sizeable share stake. The Ionian Bank, a long-established concern which had, in 1958, come under the control of two stockbrokers, Mr Michael Behrens and Mr John Trusted, had effectively controlled BRCW, and for a time retained a substantial share interest in FNFC. Later, Ionian, which itself went out of the banking business in the mid-1970s' crisis, ceased to be a considerable shareholder. But FNFC came to have a number of important investing institutions, including the Crown Agents, the electricity supply industry's pension fund and Hambros, a prominent merchant bank, as shareholders. The group expanded in consumer credit, including second mortgage business, in lending – one speciality was the finance of housebuilders – and through acquisitions of various share stakes; it also bought an issuing house, Birmingham Industrial Trust.

In 1964, Hungarian-born Mr Tom Whyte, previously in the plastics industry, bought into the concern which he was to build up, as Triumph Investment Trust, into a diversified group with some £200 m of banking, hire purchase, insurance, property and other interests. Mr Herbert Despard, previously a Slater Walker man, moved in in the late-1960s as a director, and afterwards chairman, of Cannon Street Investments (CSI), an investment concern which had once been a rubber company. In 1971 CSI purchased (from FNFC) a lending concern, Goulston Finance, which was later called Cannon Street Acceptances. Goulston had been part of Goulston Discount which had earlier been run by Mr Sidney Davidson, a solicitor. In 1969 Mr Davidson set up the private banking concern Sterling Industrial Securities, in partnership with the Crown Agents and another financier, Mr Sidney Finley.

In 1968 three young financiers, Mr David Stark, Mr Jeremy Pinckney and Mr Gervase Thomas, bought sizeable shareholdings in the J. H. Vavasseur commodity business. They afterwards developed it as a financial group with interests in foreign exchange broking (through Harlow Meyer), banking (Vavasseur Trust), money management, property and films. Sir Gordon Newton, the former editor of the *Financial Times*, became chairman in February 1973.

Burston Group, a further prominent new financial venture, grew from a small merchant bank started in 1955 by Mr Neville Burston, who had recently left Cambridge. In 1968, the US group Texas Commerce Bank acquired a 35 per cent stake in the company, which was renamed Burston and Texas Commerce Bank. A new holding company, Burston Group, was formed in 1971; another of its subsidiaries was Burston Finance, a provider of 'medium-term facilities for development of, and investment in, freehold and leasehold property'. Burston Group's deputy chairman was Sir Bernard Waley-Cohen, once a Lord Mayor of London.

Two financial groups earlier referred to were launched in the late-1950s or soon after, like many others of the new genre. Cedar Holdings was set up in 1958 as a banking, insurance, mortgage and finance agents' business. London and County (A and D), a financial company, came under new auspices in 1961 when control of it was acquired by Mr Gerald Caplan, a barrister and judo expert; later, it expanded in banking and acquired companies engaged in share dealing, property investment and development, department store banking and second mortgage finance. The holding company for this business was renamed London and County Securities Group in September 1973.

Mounthall Securities grew up in the 1960s, with Mr John Robertshaw and Mr Dennis Barkway as key figures. In 1967, it merged with the old-established Liverpool company Edward Bates and Sons, which had been developing as a financial concern with Mr John Woollam, formerly a Conservative MP, as chairman. The joint business, Edward Bates Mounthall, was later absorbed into the Edinburgh-based Atlantic Assets investment group. Then, in 1972, after Lord (then Sir Max) Rayne's London Merchant Securities had injected £8.7 m cash into it against a 25 per cent share stake, the group, financed further with a rights issue, was launched on the Stock Exchange as Edward Bates and Sons (Holdings), Atlantic Assets retaining a large interest. The group expanded further, enlarging its banking, corporate finance, investment management and insurance business; Welfare Insurance, which was later to incur large losses, was acquired in 1973.

Another considerable concern was Northern Commercial Trust, a Manchester-based company which was started in 1969 and grew quickly. A substantial share stake in NCT was held by Authority Investments, a company in which the family of Lord Lever (previously Mr Harold Lever MP), the former Labour Cabinet Minister, has considerable holdings; Authority also wholly owned (and still owns) another private banking concern, the London-based Knowsley, whose directors include Lord Lever's brother, Mr Dennis Lever, and his cousin, Mr Brian Sandelson. British Bank of Commerce, a Scottish concern headed by Mr Alexander Stone, and with the Earl of Harewood, the Queen's cousin, on its board, was a further sizeable group. A smaller banking business was Duboff Brothers, control of which was bought in 1970 by Mr Harvey Cohen's unquoted Consolidated Finance Holdings, among whose directors was the well known solicitor Mr David Freeman. Interests of CFH, which had been founded in the 1960s by Mr Cohen, a chartered accountant, and which at first conducted a hire purchase business, included the estate agents Gross Fine and Krieger Chalfen, and a 40 per cent stake in Cardinal Homes.

Among other newer or growing financial concerns of varying sizes were Audley Holdings, a subsidiary of Cornwallis Estates; British Bangladesh Trust (later London Capital Group), set up early in the 1970s and headed by the former Labour minister Mr John Stonehouse; Corinthian Holdings, with financial and industrial interests; Cornhill

Consolidated, a bill discounting concern, run by Mr John Morris; Cripps Warburg, named after two of its directors, Mr Milo Cripps, a nephew of the post-war Labour Chancellor of the Exchequer, the late Sir Stafford Cripps, and Mr George Warburg, son of Sir Siegmund Warburg, founder of the noted accepting house, S. G. Warburg; Chancery Trust, the Manchester-based concern whose directors included Mr David Holmes, a former Liberal Party Treasurer; David Samuel Trust, where Mr Leslie Lavy and Mr Herbert Towning were directors; Dawnay Day, with unit trust and banking interests, where Sir Peter Parker, later the British Rail chairman, presided from 1974 to 1978; First Maryland, the banking company in Mr William Stern's group; Hawtin & Partners; London Scottish Finance Corporation; Moorgate Mercantile Holdings; Morris Wigram Rosenthal (later Morris Wigram); Wallace Brothers Sassoon; and Wintrust.

Many of the specialist hire purchase finance houses, some dating from much earlier days, expanded strongly in the 1960s and early 1970s and some diversified into certain of the new profitable businesses developed by the secondary banks. A number also drew heavily, as the secondary banks frequently did, on the new unsecured money markets for short-term finance. Independents in the finance house field included United Dominions Trust (UDT), Mercantile Credit, Bowmaker (which was bought by the C. T. Bowring insurance broking group in 1971), Wagon Finance Corporation, Hodge Group, F. C. Finance (in which the Co-operative movement acquired a controlling stake in 1969) and Medens Trust. These houses conducted their business in the market for instalment credit to individuals and, often, provided industrial finance, but some, notably UDT, Mercantile Credit and F. C. Finance, also built up considerable portfolios of property lending. UDT in addition amassed extensive overseas interests.

Among banks of longer standing which expanded rapidly in the years before the crisis was Keyser Ullmann Holdings (KUH), headed from 1970 to 1975 by Mr Edward du Cann, MP, a former Conservative minister who was chairman of the Public Accounts Committee from 1974 to 1978 and has been chairman of the Conservative MPs' backbench 1922 Committee since 1972.

Many secondary banks and finance houses thus grew very rapidly in the years before the crisis: the accompanying table illustrates this – and the sequel – in the case of some of the larger groups quoted on the Stock Exchange. In a number of instances, the expansion was due to a considerable extent to take-overs: SWS, FNFC, KUH, London and County Securities Group and J. H. Vavasseur were particularly active in this way.

TABLE 4.1 Trends at some of the larger secondary bank groups

Company / Year of foundation or coming under new control		1965 (unless otherwise stated)		1971		1973		1975		Share price	
		Pre-tax profit (£m)	Gross assets (£m)	Pre-tax profits (£m)	Gross assets (£m)	Pre-tax profit (£m)	Gross assets (£m)	Pre-tax profits (£m)[4] [−loss]	Gross assets (£m)	At peak in 1972 (p)	End 1974 (p)
Edward Bates and Sons (Holdings)	1967	0.02	NA	0.1	24	1.5	74[5]	−16.3	68	337	20
Burston Group	1955	0.06	NA	1.2	70	1.8	100	–	–	224	16
Cannon Street Investments	1968	0.01	0.4	0.4	3	3.5	122	0.7[6]	NA	119	5.5[1]
Cedar Holdings	1958	0.02	8	0.9	18	1.9	128	−2.7	56	99	13[1]
First National Finance Corporation	1963	0.8	20	7.5	182	18.4	543	−83.2 (10 mths)	417[7]	139	3.5
Keyser Ullmann Holdings[2]	1962	0.6 (1969)	12	0.6	13	9.0	161	−59.2	279	385	36

London and County Securities Group	1961	0.6 (1969)	3.6	0.7	15	3.6	129	–	–	358	40[1]
Mercantile Credit	1934	2.5	12	8.2	243	12.8	377	-10.8	355	146.5	11
Slater Walker Securities	1964	0.8	20	16.3	280	23.4	588	-39.9	160	309	35
Triumph Investment Trust	1964	0.05	NA	3.4	61	6.6	203	-19.4 (1974)	153	150	5[1]
United Dominions Trust	1922	5.0	265	11.1	466	24.3	896	-53.5	1095	158.5	13
J. H. Vavasseur[3]	1968	0.05	NA	1.3	12	-16.5	52	-3.9	36	400	3

NOTES

Gross Assets figures over £10 m rounded to nearest £1 m. Year is that in which financial year ends.

Gross assets at end of year or period of accounts.

NA Not available.

– Not applicable (see text).

1. Price as at previous suspension of Stock Exchange quotation.
2. Except 1975, KUH gross asset figures for holding co. only (Banking co. gross assets £65 m in 1969, £74 m in 1971 and £265 m in 1973). Banking figures included in profits which, for 1969, 1971 and 1973 are net after tax and transfer to inner reserves. Full disclosure and pfts pre-tax 1975.
3. J. H. Vavasseur Group, 1975.
4. Takes into account exceptional and extraordinary loss items as well as provisions.
5. £168 m in 1974.
6. Excludes Cannon Street Acceptances.
7. But £41 m capital deficiency.

Growth generated from within was frequently quickened in the boom years by high profits, much of which were ploughed back to build a banking company's capital base. Since the prevailing rule of thumb, approved by the Bank of England, was that liabilities could be ten – and sometimes up to about fifteen – times capital and reserves, a rapid accumulation of capital, through high retained profits or outside subscription for new shares, made possible a very strong expansion of deposits and total assets.

Profits themselves were often enlarged as a result of 'investment banking', including the purchase, holding and sale of blocks of shares in other companies, an activity more colloquially called 'wheeling and dealing'. 'Investment dealing', for instance, contributed £7 m of Slater Walker Securities' £23 m of pre-tax profits in 1973. Triumph Investment Trust's 1974 accounts referred to 'sales by investment dealing companies'. But few secondary banks can have relied as heavily on dealing profits as did London and County Securities Group. According to the Department of Trade Inspectors who afterwards investigated the group, the great bulk of the £1.9 m pre-tax profit (apart from associated companies' profit) published for the half-year to 30 September 1973 was made up of items of profit on share and property sales which the Inspectors considered should not have been included anyway. Of the group's final approach to failure, the Inspectors remarked: 'So the attempts to promote profitable deals became more feverish. But to no avail.'[3]

Rapid switches of interest around the secondary banking sector were not unknown, as one example will illustrate. In 1971, the ill-starred Spey Investments venture, set up in 1967 by the young financier Mr Charles Gordon on the then rather novel basis of shareholdings owned and finance provided jointly by several investing institutions (including Royal Insurance and the pension funds of Barclays Bank, Unilever, the nationalised electricity supply industry and Imperial Chemical Industries) established a subsidiary, Spey Finance. With the former Labour minister Lord Chalfont as its chief executive, Spey Finance acquired, in April 1971, three financial companies, Goulston Finance, Graham Finance and Twentieth Century Banking Corporation. Mr Gordon was quoted as saying that it was only a matter of time before Spey Finance was the biggest merchant bank in Britain.

But these hopes were not realised, nor did Spey Finance long remain in the controversial Spey Investments, which soon experienced problems and incurred large losses: Mr Gordon departed and control of Spey Investments eventually passed to Brandts, which was itself to suffer major losses in the mid-1970s crisis. (Spey Investments' holding in Spey Westmoreland, a property company later known as Westmoreland Investments (WI), was bought by its main partner in that venture, Mr Boris Marmor, and his family interests, who thus emerged with control. WI was to receive major backing in the later crisis years from its minority shareholder, the electricity supply industry's pension fund which ultimately, in a controversial deal in 1979, acquired the whole of WI).

In August 1971, First National Finance Corporation (FNFC), the large secondary banking and financial group, took over Spey Finance, with its three financial companies, Goulston, Graham and Twentieth Century.

But the three companies acquired were not to be long under their new ownership. Within a few months FNFC had sold them on. All three were later to be caught up in the secondary banking crisis. Goulston Finance, as noted already, passed to Cannon Street Investments, was renamed Cannon Street Acceptances and, after a period of strong growth, collapsed in 1974. Graham Finance was sold to Moorgate Mercantile Holdings, a financial group which was to be refused a rescue operation in December 1973 but which later struggled back to recovery. Twentieth Century Banking was sold to Bovis, which was to be so threatened by its new offshoot's loss of deposits and other troubles in the crisis that it became, with the whole of Bovis, the subject of a take-over in 1974 by the big P&O shipping group, under which it continues in active business.

The significance for the study of banking of the practice of holding and dealing in share stakes in other companies was that considerable risk could be involved. If the share market were to fall away, the result could be a loss which would be particularly dangerous if there were not an ample buffer of free capital. This was just the hazard to which various secondary and fringe bankers were exposed after the storms blew from December 1973.

Likewise, the dangers on the frequently substantial commercial loan side of secondary banks, which in many cases concentrated on property financing, were often not recognised in the early 1970s. There was a widespread belief that property was the perfect inflation hedge and could only rise in value: 'they're not manufacturing land' was a dictum confidently quoted in some secondary bankers' parlours. But if the value of the security were to fall severely, the lending bank financing property could be left as exposed to loss as from a fall in the values of blocks of shares which it held. This danger too was to become a harsh reality as the property crisis from 1974 onwards accompanied, and deepened, that in secondary banking.

Various secondary banks which made venturesome share investments and loans financed these assets to a substantial extent from short-term funds raised in the inter-bank market, which generally became a far more important source of finance for them than the personal deposits from the public on which some partly relied. But dependence on short-term finance made the risks more acute when the cash was committed to assets of vulnerable value.

An instructive illustration of this can be seen in a forward glimpse at an account by Mr Slater, the chairman of Slater Walker Securities, of the situation in late-1973 in his group which, however, did not reach its own crisis for another two years. 'Slater Walker was not particularly highly geared [borrowed] in relation to most merchant banks, but its assets were invested comparatively aggressively, and in large lumps. . . . The approximate position at the end of 1973 was that our gross assets totalled about £550 m and that our net assets totalled £85 m taking quoted investments at market values. The difference of £465 m was made up of £130 m of *long-term* loans and about £335 m of *short-term* borrowings. . . . In other words our gross assets were more than six times our net assets and a 20 per cent fall in our gross assets would have cost us over £100 m and made the company insolvent. . . . . I had begun to realise too late that not only shares were dangerous assets to hold, but that in a real blizzard properties and loans were also very vulnerable'.[4]

One profitable activity of some secondary banking concerns was the management of personal savings, particularly through unit trusts; this of course placed substantial investment funds in their hands. Slater Walker Securities, Vavasseur and Jessel Securities – which also had insurance and industrial interests – were among those active in this area. Ownership of some unit trust management companies was however to change hands in the crisis years.

The expansive financial era of the 1960s and early 1970s brought inventive variations on existing investment themes and new refinements of investment media for personal savers, including bonds – usually of a life of ten years for the sake of tax advantages – which were often geared to investment in property, equity shares or a mixture of several types of assets. This concept found an important place in the long-term armoury of instruments of personal investment, but not before there had been some upsets in the mid-1970s' crisis.

One of the pioneers of the property bond idea was the young financier Mr David Rowland, who formed the Fordham Life insurance concern.

Fordham was afterwards sold to Ralli Brothers (Bankers) (later the Slater Walker bank) and from there it passed to a partnership of the Freshwater property interests and Sterling Industrial Securities. The Freshwater stake went on to the interests of Mr Osias Freshwater's son-in-law, Mr William Stern, who, with the help of borrowings from Sterling Industrial Securities, bought full control of Fordham, changing its name to Nation Life. This company was to fail in the crisis of 1974, when Mr Stern's property empire also crumbled.

A considerable number of the newer banking and financial businesses enjoyed the presence on their boards of well-known public figures and often the considerable backing of prominent investing institutions. This underlines how much the newcomer concerns became an accepted part of the financial scene during these years. In addition to those already mentioned, Sir John Foster QC, the former Conservative MP, for some years chaired Northern Commercial Trust and is still chairman of Knowsley and of its parent, Authority Investments. Lord Mais, a Labour peer and former Lord Mayor of London, was chairman of the unquoted Sterling Industrial Securities, and Mr Jocelyn Hambro, chairman of Hambros, the accepting house group, was a director of FNFC, in which his group had a considerable holding.

The fast-growing character of the secondary banks and their buoyant share prices proved attractive to a number of major investing institutions, which sometimes directly subscribed for share and loan capital in these concerns.

For instance, Prudential Assurance, Britain's largest insurance group, which had a significant stake of long standing in Dawnay Day, the banking and unit trust concern, considerably extended its interests in the banking and finance industry in 1972. In that year it bought from Barclays Bank a sizeable holding in United Dominions Trust (UDT), raising its stake in that group to some 26.5 per cent, and acquired an interest of about a fifth in the rapidly expanding Keyser Ullmann Holdings, into which it injected new capital. It also took a stake in the smaller Wintrust banking business.

Eagle Star Insurance acquired some 10 per cent of UDT. In addition it had a shareholding in the private Sterling Industrial Securities (SIS). N. M. Rothschild and Sons, one of the City's old-established merchant banks, also had a holding in SIS, as did Franklin National Bank, the US bank associated with the Italian financier Signor Michele Sindona, whose empire was to crumble in 1974. Eagle Star was a shareholder too in London and County Securities Group. Outside the institutional investment world there were several companies with dominant stakes in banking concerns. These included the Co-operative Bank, which long controlled and now fully owns F. C. Finance, and Northern Foods, which until 1978 owned Beverley Bentinck, a consumer credit business later renamed British Credit Trust whose own subsidiaries included the Bear Securities banking concern.

Undoubtedly the most unusual institution in the secondary banking near-tragedy was the Crown Agents organisation, a British State body, then of undefined status, dating from 1837, which provides purchasing and investment services for some hundred overseas governments. From 1967, the Agents embarked on an investment venture on their own account, FINVEST, the plan for which was described by a later report on the Agents as 'the prospectus for a sizeable fringe bank'.[5] To obtain funds for FINVEST, the Agents drew on sums deposited with them by their 'principals' – overseas governments (some so investing their national reserves) and other authorities – and also borrowed substantially in the money markets. These resources the Agents deployed in various assets which, at the end of 1973 included £188 m of 'advances to secondary banks, property companies and others', £61 m of 'own account' property investment and £39 m of other investments.[6]

The Agents, who apparently did not consider it would be feasible to link up with any of the top-flight accepting house merchant banks, took equity shareholdings in several secondary and fringe banks. They had substantial stakes in Sterling Industrial Securities[7] and in E. D. Sassoon Banking,[8] later part of Wallace Brothers Sassoon, and smaller interests in FNFC,[9] London and County Securities,[10] Moorgate Mercantile,[10] Northern Commercial Trust,[11] and London Capital Group.[12] Recipients of the much larger sums of the Agents' lending included FNFC,[13] London and County Securities,[10] Cedar Holdings,[10] Triumph Investment Trust,[14] Burston[15] and Israel-British Bank.[16] All these concerns were to face at least severe difficulties in the later crisis. In addition, the Agents owned 51 per cent of the English and Continental private property company,[17] the rest being owned by Mr Jack Walker, a solicitor, and Mr Ramon Greene, a property man. Major loans, and support for outside borrowings, were provided by the Agents to E and C, whose vicissitudes will be mentioned later. Very large further sums were committed by the Agents to property ventures in Australia,[18] while other loans, which were to result in probable heavy losses, were made, as will be related, to Mr William Stern's property companies.[19]

It is a curious fact that the Agents, although a State body, do not appear to have been able to borrow in the money markets at the cheapest rates available to the most high-ranking borrowers; this obliged them to go 'down market' by lending on to concerns of less than the highest standing, which would pay enough to allow the Agents a margin of profit.[20]

Personality was always important in the secondary banks, which were frequently directed to a major extent by one prominent entrepreneur who had done much to build up the business and customarily had a large shareholding. For instance, Mr Jim Slater had shares in SWS worth some £6 m at their peak, while Mr Pat Matthews, the deputy chairman and managing director of FNFC, controlled a stake valued, at its highest, at nearly £10 m in that company. Others owned holdings running into millions of pounds in the early 1970s.

The principal entrepreneurs tended often to dominate their banks. To a leading clearing banker, looking back afterwards, they appeared as 'one-man bands', by contrast with the big High Street groups which were run by teams of managers. Mr Slater implied his own supremacy, at least earlier, at SWS, by acknowledging that by 1973 his underlying objective was not to dominate any more.[21] The atmosphere in the boardroom of London and County Securities was described in evidence to the Department of Trade Inspectors as 'like the court of a medieval king'.[22]

The central financier was generally surrounded by a group of younger executives who were frequently 'head-hunted' from more traditional and sedate banking houses with the offer of high salaries and other incentives. The 1966 Finance Act diminished the attractions of conventional share option schemes, but other methods of providing incentives to directors were devised and were particularly attractive when shares were rising as fast as were those of secondary banks in the early 1970s. Likewise they naturally gave the management a strong interest in the performance of the share price.

One system adopted by many quoted companies, including a number of secondary banks, was the executive (partly paid) share incentive scheme. This allowed executives to buy new shares in their companies at the current market price when a small initial downpayment, usually of only two or three pence, was made; the much greater remaining balance was then due to be paid up some time within the succeeding few years. The idea was that during this period the share price would have risen further, so that when the executive paid the rest of the agreed price he would find himself with a holding showing a profit. The steep tumble in secondary bank share prices during the later crisis years, however, meant that, so far from gaining, participants often had an onerous obligation to pay up on shares which had largely lost their value. Stop-loss schemes were introduced by Slater Walker Securities[23] and some other groups to lighten this burden.

Executives of one bank sometimes borrowed from other banks to buy their own company's shares. For instance, Mr Matthews, it was reported,[24] arranged for Hambros Bank to finance certain senior members of the FNFC staff in buying FNFC shares on the market. The FNFC accounts show certain executive directors as having very substantial shareholdings: Mr John Black, the property specialist among the directors, held 1,771,970 shares at 1 January 1973,[25] when they were worth over £1 m, as well as substantial shareholdings in associate companies of FNFC.[26] A number of other FNFC executive directors also had holdings worth several hundred thousand pounds. It is not known to what extent, if at all, any particular individual's holding was financed by credit. One published example of an executive director's large shareholdings being held in parallel with borrowed funds was at J. H. Vavasseur. The 1973 accounts of the company, which was to receive Lifeboat help and be reconstructed several times in the crisis, show that the shareholding of Mr Jeremy Pinckney was reduced from 438,121 to 172,456 shares during 1973: 'the shares were sold in order to reduce borrowings at the request of his personal bankers', the directors' report recorded.[27]

A number of secondary and fringe banks also made substantial loans to their own directors, under the proviso in Section 190 of the Companies Act 1948 which permitted lending to directors in the ordinary course of business, despite a general prohibition on companies' loans to their directors. Further reference will be made later to certain instances of such loans.

After this brief survey of the secondary banks by reference to origin, activity and size, it is now appropriate to consider how they stood in the somewhat complex structure of official ranking of banks. At the top had long been the big High Street clearers, the senior merchant banks, the discount houses and a few others, all treated as banks under Schedule VIII of the Companies Act 1948 and so allowed certain privileges. Chief among these privileges was the right – which the clearers no longer used by 1973 – to keep hidden reserves and not fully to disclose trading results. A large number of further banks, many foreign-owned, were authorised by the Bank of England, on behalf of the Treasury, under the Exchange Control Act 1947 to carry out foreign exchange business but did not have the more prestigious Schedule VIII status.

Until the late-1960s, the banking system consisted largely of these categories. But then many more newcomers crowded on to the scene, helped by a provision of the Companies Act 1967, the notorious Section 123. This section, allowing the Board of Trade (later the Department of Trade and Industry, and then of Trade) to certify that particular companies were carrying on the business of banking, although they came into neither of the categories of bank just described, contributed to the crisis by admitting a new class of companies with a 'junior' form of banking status into the field. An understanding of this development will be helped by a glance at the legal case, *United Dominions Trust* v. *Kirkwood*, which led to section 123's enactment.

Mr Kirkwood, the owner of a private garage business which had collapsed, had challenged the right of UDT to enforce a debt against him, claiming that this finance house group neither had the status of a bank (although it described itself as 'bankers') nor held a licence under the Moneylenders Acts which would have entitled it to claim repayment of finance provided on the terms involved. The case went to the Court of Appeal where Lord Denning, the Master of the Rolls, giving the two-to-one majority judgment,[28] noted that existing legislation did not define the term 'bank' and stated that, under a number of criteria, UDT did not rank as a bank. In particular he referred to UDT's acceptance of sums of money on deposit, chiefly from institutions in the City or from trustees and repayable, if not renewed, at a fixed time after three, six or nine months, with interest. He remarked that 'these deposits are not the sort of deposit accounts which are characteristic of bankers . . . they are short-term investments. Bankers may on occasion accept deposits of this kind but they do not become bankers on that account'.

Lord Denning, however, continued that four of the (then) Big Five banks had given evidence that they regarded UDT as a bank. He added that it was a maxim of English law to give effect to anything which appeared to have been established for a considerable course of time and to presume that what had been done was of right. 'This maxim is of particular force here where innumerable transactions have been effected on the faith of UDT being a banker' he said. 'UDT has itself made loans of millions of pounds which are recoverable if its claim to be a banker is correct; but irrecoverable if it is not. Are we to throw all these over?' He concluded: 'In view of the long period of time in which [UDT] has been accepted as a banker I would hold it to be such and not a moneylender.'

He also made this recommendation: 'If any other concern should wish to be regarded by the Courts as a banker it ought to ask the Board of Trade for a certificate that it should be treated as a banker.' Lord Justice Diplock, who agreed with Lord Denning (Lord Justice Harman dissenting) said that it did not follow that in some other case, if the evidence were more complete or more closely probed, the result would be the same. The authorities sighed with relief and moved rapidly to ensure that a different decision in another case should not put at risk the security of hundreds of millions of pounds of consumer credit business.

When the Companies Act 1967, including section 123, had been passed, UDT quickly obtained a certificate that it was carrying on the business of banking. Many other concerns followed suit. No fewer than 87 certificates had been issued to financial companies by 1970; by 1973 the number had grown to 133. While many holders were, or were subsidiaries of, banking groups of high standing, others were of less strength and of these quite a number were to be vulnerable to the subsequent crisis. The Bank of England later remarked: 'A large number of companies which were not of sufficient size or quality to warrant the more advanced banking recognitions . . . felt the need (not least because they could not otherwise safely make personal loans) to obtain the protection of a section 123 certificate, the criteria for which they were fairly readily able to satisfy. Revocation of a certificate once granted is difficult, since the Department [of Trade] must "cease to be satisfied" that a company is bona fide in the business of banking. . . . The possession of the certificate . . . allowed the impression to be created that the companies concerned were recognised by the responsible Government department as carrying on a banking business, without drawing attention to the fact that they were only so recognised for one narrow purpose.'[29] A senior police officer engaged in a later investigation said more succinctly: 'They just dished the certificates out to all and sundry.'

The Companies Act 1967 also included section 127, which became the provision through which status parallel to that under Schedule VIII of the 1948 Act was newly accorded; no more names were then added to the Schedule VIII list. It is worth noting that in 1972 the banking companies of five large groups, United Dominions Trust, First National Finance Corporation, Mercantile Credit, Julian S. Hodge and Lombard North Central, were among those receiving this prestigious section 127 status; the first three, then all independent companies, were nonetheless strongly buffeted in the secondary bank crisis which soon followed and made very heavy calls on the Lifeboat.

The banking industry proper on the eve of the crisis thus consisted of: the groups treated as banks under Schedule VIII of the Companies Act, 1948; the few concerns more recently given full bank status under section 127 of the Companies Act, 1967; and the wider category of banks, often foreign-owned, which did not hold these rankings but were authorised under the Exchange Control Act 1947. All these, numbering 323 in the autumn of 1973, were listed[30] by the Bank of England as the contributors to the published banking statistics and will be broadly referred to hereafter as 'listed banks'. In addition, there were the 133 companies holding section 123 certificates that they were carrying on a banking business.

The Bank of England liked to refer to the gradations of ranking as a 'status ladder' of recognitions, up which a company could climb rung by rung as its performance and standing merited. But this was a game of snakes and ladders without the snakes: a banking concern could move up but it almost never moved down. There were the difficulties noted above about removing recognitions, once given. Moreover, the new provisions of the Companies Act 1967 did not provide for continuing surveillance of companies holding either the lower-ranking section 123 status or the higher-grade section 127 recognition. The Bank of England was consulted before any banking concern was given section 127 recognition or a certificate under section 123, but the statutory responsibility for such decisions rested with the Board of Trade (later the Department of Trade).

Thus, responsibility for watching over the health of a vastly increased banking community, whose members varied greatly in size, age, standing and activity and which numbered, with the section 123 concerns, over 450, became awkwardly split between the Bank of England, the Department of Trade and the Treasury. Laissez-faire was the prevailing atmosphere, based on the view that banks were run by a group of gentlemen who were personally known to the Bank of England's senior officials and could be depended on to conduct the banking game according to the unwritten rules. But by 1973 there were, amid the far more crowded London banking fraternity, not only gentlemen but players, sometimes ruthless professionals who competed to the limits the law allowed, on occasion taking legal counsel's opinion as to where precisely those limits lay. As history has now shown, in a few cases the boundaries between the legal and the illegal were overstepped.

Even had it been desired, which it was not before 1974, that there should be close official monitoring of the prudence of banks' conduct of their businesses, the Bank of England's Discount Office, which then acted as the 'eyes and ears' of the Governor in keeping in touch with the banking industry, was not of a size which could possibly have undertaken this task over the whole field, active as was the contact kept with the senior strata and others in the banking pyramid. Nor had the

Department of Trade sufficient manpower with the requisite deep financial expertise for the task.

The present study is mainly concered with the secondary sector of the whole British banking industry, which, to generalise somewhat, was mainly made up of many of those in the banking sector proper which were classed as 'other banks in the UK' – chiefly listed banks outside the principal British banks and foreign banks – and the section 123 companies which were not subsidiaries of the primary banks, British or foreign.

Leaving aside subsidiaries or associates of British clearing banks and of accepting houses, subsidiaries or branches of overseas banks, consortium banks and subsidiaries of sizeable British companies outside banking, the remaining 'other UK banks' listed at the end of September 1973 numbered twenty-three (of which the three in the Hodge Group were shortly to be absorbed into a large primary bank group, Standard Chartered). They were of varying size, age and nature, and the majority, although, as will be explained later, certainly not all, of them were to feel the sharp impact of the crisis. They were: Henry Ansbacher and Co.; Henry Ansbacher and Co. (C I); Edward Bates and Sons; Cripps Warburg; First National Finance Corporation; Ionian Bank; Julian S. Hodge and Co.; Julian S. Hodge Bank (Jersey); Julian S. Hodge Bank (Guernesy); Leopold Joseph and Sons; Leopold Joseph and Sons (Guernsey); Keyser Ullmann; Mercantile Credit; Morris Wigram; Old Broad Street Securities; Slater Walker; Slater Walker (Guernsey); Slater Walker (Isle of Man); Slater Walker (Jersey); United Dominions Trust (Channel Islands); United Dominions Trust; G. T. Whyte (subsidiary of Triumph Investment Trust); and Wintrust Securities.

Of the listed banks classed as finance houses, three were controlled by major banking groups and one (Ford Motor Credit) by a major international industrial group. The others were: Beverley Bentinck; Bowmaker; F. C. Finance; Moorgate Mercantile Holdings; Wagon Finance Corporation; Western Credit Group. The following narrative will indicate that none of these finance house concerns was uninfluenced by the crisis in the mid-1970s.

A list of the section 123 companies at the end of September 1973 appears as the appendix to this chapter.

In addition to the ladder of legal rankings, banks were – and are – also grouped by their membership of various associations. Those achieving authorised status customarily joined the wide-ranging British

Bankers Association, as did others in the higher rankings which also had – and still have – their own specialist groupings. The clearers, for example, belong to the Committee of London Clearing Bankers or its regional counterparts, while foreign banks have their own clubs. The top-flight merchant banks make up the Accepting Houses Committee (AHC), which had eighteen members at the end of 1973. In the previous two years the Bank of England had given some encouragement to an enlargement of the élite AHC, apparently favouring its being made more representative of the growing banking industry. One or two new members were elected, but some other aspirants – including three later caught up in the crisis – were not. The AHC was not satisfied that these concerns would meet their exacting criteria – fortunately as it turned out, or the later crisis could have invaded the upper reaches of the banking system.

So was the scene set for the secondary banking upheaval of the mid-1970s. But its prelude, the 1971–3 monetary boom, must first be considered.

APPENDIX   Section 123 Banking Concerns at 30 September 1973*

African Continental Bank
Allied Bank International
Anglo-Eastern Bank
Astley Acceptances
Audley Holdings

Banco de Estado de Sao Paulo
Bank of Europe
Bank Hapoalim Nivi
Bank of New Providence
Bank of New South Wales Savings Bank
Bank of Scotland Finance Co.
Bank of Tokyo Trust
Barclays Bank Trust Co.
Barnett Christie
Bear Securities
Beverley Acceptances
Bowmaker
British Bank of Commerce
Brook Securities and Co.
Brown Harriman & International Banks
Burlington Investments
Burston Finance

Cannon Street Acceptances
Castle Finance
C. E. Coates and Co.
Cedar Holdings
Chancery Trust
Citibank Trust
Citicorp International Bank
Cleveland Guaranty
Clydesdale Bank Finance Corporation
Commercial Bank of Malawi
Commercial Bank of Wales
Commonwealth Savings Bank of Australia
Commonwealth Trading Bank of Australia
Concorde Trust
Consolidated Credits & Discounts

* Those holding certificates under section 123 of the Companies Act 1967 that they had satisfied the Department of Trade and Industry that they could properly be treated for the purposes of the Moneylenders Acts 1900 to 1927 as being persons bona fide carrying on the business of banking. (Source: *Trade and Industry*, 11 October 1973, pp. 97–8). "Ltd" etc omitted from names.

Continental Bankers Agents
Co-operative Commercial Bank
Copleys Bank
Corinthian Securities
Credito Italiano
Cripps Warburg

Dalton Barton and Co.
Dalton Barton (Scotland)
David Samuel Trust
Dawnay Day and Co.
Drayton Corporation
Duboff Brothers
Dunbar and Co.

Eagil Trust
Edward Bates & Sons
Erwin Brecher and Co.
E. S. Schwab and Co.
European Brazilian Bank

First Chicago
First Maryland
First National Bank in Dallas
First National Securities

Gray Dawes and Co.
Greyhound Guaranty
G. R. Dawes and Co.
G. T. Whyte and Co.
Gresham Trust
Grindlays (London) Finance Co.

Havana International Bank
Hawtin & Partners
Henry Ansbacher and Co.
Heritable & General Investment Bank
Hume Corporation

Industrial Bank of Japan
Investitions-Und Handels-Bank
Italian International Bank

Jacobs Kroll
Janata Bank
Japan International Bank
Julian S. Hodge and Co.
Julius Baer International

Knowsley and Co.

Lloyds Associated Banking Co.
Lloyds and Scottish Trust
Lombard North Central
London and County (A & D)
London and County Investments
London and North British Trust

Medens Trust
Mercantile Credit Finance
Merrill Lynch-Brown Shipley Bank
Midland Bank Finance Corporation
Mitsubishi Bank
Morris Wigram Rosenthal

National Union Bank
N. H. Woolley and Co.
Nordic Bank
North Carolina Bank
Northern Commercial Trust
Northern Trust

Old Broad Street Securities
Overseas Financial Trust

People's Bank
Philipp Brothers & Joseph
Pubali Bank

Raphael Robinson & Glyn
Red Dragon Securities
Republic National Bank of Dallas
Robert Fraser and Partners
Rothschild Intercontinental Bank
Royal Bank of Canada Trust Corporation
Royal Trust Company of Canada

St Margarets Finance
Security Trust Company of Birmingham
Slater Walker Finance Corporation
Societé Générale (France) Bank
Standard Bank (Inc. in Pakistan)
Sterling Guarantee
Sterling Credit
Sterling Industrial Securities

Thames Guaranty
Trade Development Bank

Trucanda Trusts
Twentieth Century Banking Corporation

UDT Finance
United Dominions Trust
United International Bank

Vavasseur Trust

Wallace Brothers Sassoon Bank
Wells Fargo
Western Bank
Western Trust and Savings
White Weld and Co.
Whiteaway Laidlaw and Co.
Williams Glyn and Co.
Wintrust Securities

5 The Boom which Got Out of Hand

> We lived in a tremendous, a most optimistic world at that time [1973]. What you bought for a million pounds one day you sold for two the next, and that person sold for three the day after. I am exaggerating, but it is just to try to get to my point.
>
> Mr Stanley Van Gelder, former Managing Director of Keyser Ullmann Holdings.[1]

Shortly after the introduction in September 1971 of Competition and Credit Control (C and CC), the liberating new deal for the banking world, Mr Edward Heath's Conservative Government adopted an economic growth strategy which implied an expansionary monetary policy. The combination of these two developments provided the signal for Britain to embark on a major financial spree. C and CC had removed various discriminatory restrictions on the bigger banks and, in the buoyant climate, no adequate new restraints were imposed instead. The way was thus clear for competition across the banking board in a euphoric atmosphere. All banks, large and small, were looking for business and it became increasingly tantalising to the slower-moving to see the rich profits made by the swifter-footed. Competition was free, but there seemed plentiful room for all: any idea that, because the larger banks had freer scope to expand, the fringe concerns would wither away was proved false while the boom lasted. Increasing fortunes were made by many with large stakes in the newer entrepreneurial banking ventures, though whether they were fully retained depended on later events.

It was a remarkable era, as both recollections and statistics attest. Mr William Stern, whose rapidly expanded private property group crumbled in the later crisis of 1974, leaving him with debts of well over £100 m arising from his guarantees of his companies' borrowing, recalled afterwards to the Crown Agents Tribunal: 'Starting from September 1971, Sir, when the Bank of England's well-known Competition and

Credit Control paper was published, the money markets which had operated under the limitations of a fairly savage corset for the previous four years suddenly changed, virtually overnight, and money for property development, which was one of the least recommended categories of lending until September 1971, became freely available, not merely from the merchant banks but from the clearers. . . . [In 1973] money in the tens of millions was being offered and made available by a number of first class banks'.[2] Mr Ronald Lyon, whose private property empire also crumbled in 1974, remembered in 1978: 'In my company it is no exaggeration to say that we were having bank money thrust at us from all directions'.[3]

Long-established restrictive attitudes within the High Street clearing banks were abandoned in the tussle for new lending business. Sedate bank managers from the big High Street clearers shed their didactic 'no-man' image and became like salesmen, actively marketing that commodity then in plentiful supply, money. New personal loan schemes, packages for small firms and longer-term loans for industry abounded, while managers became more open-handed with overdrafts to individuals, who borrowed heavily to play the stock market boom which was well under way. Personal borrowing from the banks, which rose very strongly in the two years to November 1973, got a boost when the Budget in March 1972 made interest above £35 a year offsettable against tax, a very valuable concession for high-rate taxpayers. Newspaper stories a few days later quoted Cannon Street Acceptances as saying that there had been a rush by professional men seeking to borrow sums mainly between £20,000 and £100,000, while demands from stockbroking firms wanting finance for clients could go up to £250,000.[4] *The Economist* urged readers who fancied their touch with equities and believed a firm stock market lay ahead to 'go to your bank manager and demand a loan with which to flutter in the City'.[5] Above all, loans to cash-hungry and active property companies expanded dramatically— from the clearing banks and, even more, from secondary and fringe banks.

No longer curbed by loan ceilings, conventional restrictions or priorities requests, the big clearing banks began the C and C C regime with plentiful funds available for lending. Moreover, these could be added to, as required, since under the new system the clearers became free to, and could afford to, tap the wholesale money markets for additional 'bought' funds. 'Almost for the first time in the whole history of banking, you found your lending business and then scurried round for deposits', a senior clearing banker afterwards recalled of this period.

So developed a major fresh impetus to the modern practice of liabilities management, whereby the banks 'buy' deposits in the wholesale markets to supplement the natural inflow of retail deposits through their branches. Altogether, the big London clearers tapped the wholesale market so actively that these wholesale deposits rose to 34.7 per cent of their much enlarged total sterling deposits by November 1972 and to a peak 45.6 per cent in November 1973, before easing away to around 40 per cent in 1975/76.[6]

Secondary and fringe banks were far more heavily reliant on the wholesale markets. As the Bank of England afterwards remarked: 'The bulk of the fringe's deposit requirements was met from the money markets. . . . The ambiguity of section 123 recognition . . . encouraged a further blurring of the distinction between bank and non-bank in the inter-bank markets'.[7]

Some figures will illustrate how amazingly expansive for the clearers, and still more for the secondary banks, was the 1971–3 period, with its 'go for growth' strategy, mellow atmosphere of easy money and, until the second half of 1973, modest interest rates.

In the two-and-a-quarter years between September 1971, when C and CC was launched, and December 1973, when the secondary banking crisis broke out, the supply of money, according to the most widely accepted measure, sterling M3, which includes bank deposit accounts, rose by 73 per cent to £33,200 m.[8] More striking and ominous was the much stronger upsurge in bank lending. By December 1973, total sterling bank advances to UK resident borrowers had risen to two-and-a-half times their October 1971 level, a climb of 148 per cent to £20,057 m. The clearing banks were no slouches, since they raised their lending by 112 per cent to £11,379 m, while foreign banks in Britain, also liberated from lending ceilings, sharply increased their advances too. But 'other UK banks', broadly the secondary sector of listed banks, as distinct from the 'junior' section 123 concerns, boosted their lending many times over, from £395 m to £3366 m.[9] Even adjusting for the fact that five sizeable finance houses or secondary banks were included in the statistics after being re-designated as part of the banking system on receiving section 127 status in January 1972, the level of lending by 'other banks' probably more than trebled.

The pattern of the lending was striking. In the two years to November 1973 active and aggressive borrowers in the property and financial sector more than quadrupled their bank loans to £6347 m. It is a remarkable fact that by then these categories owed more to the banks than the whole of manufacturing industry, whose advances had risen to £6337 m[9] over the same period, an increase of 73 per cent. Individuals almost trebled their borrowing to £4076 m, spurred on by the tax concession on interest and the boom to a stock market peak in 1972 (when the *Financial Times* 30 share index reached a record 543.6 on May 19). Another factor stimulating bank borrowing by individuals was the opportunity for rich pickings through stagging – seeking short-term profits on – new share issues.

Not only the clearing banks but other parts of the banking sector, notably the secondary banks and some American banks in London, as well as merchant banks, were prominent sources of lending to property and financial borrowers, up to ten or more banks sometimes lending to the same borrower. The Committee of London Clearing Bankers noted later that by far the larger part of the increase in bank advances to the property sector from £343 m in November 1970 to £2834 m in November 1974 was accounted for by non-clearing banks.[10] The Royal Institution of Chartered Surveyors, whose members, as valuers and surveyors, were always close to the property scene, said that 'the secondary banks had, by the end of 1973, overtaken the clearing banks as the main lenders for property development'.[11]

Of the large figure of £4495 m loans outstanding by listed non-clearing banks to the property and financial sector in November 1973, £1399 m was to property companies but still more – £2034 m – was to 'other financial' borrowers, excluding hire purchase finance houses.[12] It seems plain from this that various wholesale banks were making large funds available to the rapidly growing fringe of section 123 and other financial companies which fell outside the banking sector proper.

But even these banking figures do not tell anything like the whole story of what finance was available to the secondary and fringe banking sector altogether, since they exclude funds raised by that sector as deposits from the wholesale money markets. Figures from two companies will illustrate the magnitude of the dependence which there could be on these markets for funds. In the two years to mid-1973, London and County Securities' deposits multiplied nearly ten times from £9 m to £88 m, while those of Cedar Holdings rose from £3 m to £67 m in the three years to mid-1973. In both cases much the greater part of these deposits (which in turn constituted the bulk of the group's resources by 1973) was drawn from the wholesale markets rather than from individual depositors.

The expansion in the wholesale sterling money markets, which was thus such an important source of finance for the fringe banking system, was certainly dramatic. While, in October 1971, there was £2000 m outstanding in unsecured loans through the inter-bank market and £1860 m against sterling certificates of deposit (CDs), these figures had climbed to £5500 m and £5000 m respectively by the time a Bank of England survey was made in April 1973.[13] This study showed the somewhat alarming fact that the average life of the borrowings was relatively short, only nineteen days for the inter-bank market, a situation which carried obvious risks of just those rapid panic withdrawals which were, in the event, to take place and precipitate the secondary banking crisis within a few months. Expansion of the wholesale market continued unabated until the end of 1973 when there was £7700 m outstanding in inter-bank loans and some £6000 m against CDs.[14]

Since a great deal of lending by the secondary and fringe banks went to the property world, a brief glance at it is now appropriate. The start of the boom in late-1971 found the property community already in a buoyant mood. The Conservatives, on their return to office in June 1970, had abolished Labour's Land Commission and system of betterment levies and had lightened burdens on the property market in other ways, such as by relaxing planning procedures.[15] These moves, coupled with the hope, and then the reality, of a new expansion in the supply of relatively cheap money set off an upsurge in property shares, which virtually doubled in the year to May 1972. The property world had meanwhile become more fully populated since the late-1950s, when such major enterprises as Lord Samuel's Land Securities Investment Trust and Mr Joe Levy's Stock Conversion became powerfully entrenched. By the early-1970s there was a new wave of energetic newcomers including Mr John Ritblat, head of British Land, Mr Robert Potel, chairman of Star (Great Britain) Holdings (later English Property Corporation), and the late Mr Gabriel Harrison, who presided over Amalgamated Investment and Property.

Property activity in the 1971–3 boom included development – the building, mainly of new commercial blocks on sites assembled for the purpose; investment in existing commercial buildings, such as through the purchase of reversionary leases in the hope that revenue from them could be significantly increased through the raising of rents; investment in residential blocks, often with a view to their 'break up' into individual flats for sale; and house-building. All required large amounts of borrowed cash. In the euphoria of the time, the increasingly prevalent view was that property values could only go up; the result was that various property concerns had a keenness to borrow which matched the banks' enthusiasm to lend and little hesitation about shouldering interest rate and other commitments which were in the event often to prove massively burdensome in the much altered conditions of the later crisis.

The optimism of developers was the greater in 1971–3 because of the usual British method of valuing properties which, in simple terms, involves applying to rent income a multiple of a number of years' purchase which is the obverse of a given yield. Thus, with a going yield of 5 per cent and income of £100,000, the value derived would be £100,000 × 100/5 = £2 m. Low prevailing yields and rising rent levels therefore boost asset values, and in the buoyant atmosphere of much of 1971–3 yields were low (along with interest rates) and rents rising; the increase in prime shop, office and industrial rents in 1972 was 13.4 per cent (the average annual rate since 1969) and in 1973 as much as 41.6 per cent. Capital values thus swung sharply upwards and, on average, the yearly increase in property prices accelerated from 11 per cent in 1971 to 24 per cent in 1972 and 26 per cent in 1973.[16]

The freer atmosphere, the plentiful availability of loans and the rich gains in prospect when local authorities gave permission for the existing use of a site to be changed – for instance to clear away old housing and shops and to build an office block – all quickened the momentum of activity by property developers. Property revaluations often led to big surpluses being written into companies' balance sheets, so enlarging the size of shareholders' funds as the basis for more borrowing, as well as increasing share prices and the fortunes of large shareholders. As *The Economist* observed in its property survey in March 1972: 'More millionaires have been thrown up by the property business in Britain since the war than by any other industry. Office rents are higher in London than in New York, Paris, Brussels and just about anywhere else. Rents have risen much faster than inflation. . . . Every year the revaluations of property company assets effortlessly create gargantuan surpluses. Through economic boom and recession the men of property have been turning stone into gold. Can it last?'[17]

Some remarkable profits were made on a number of deals, bringing home to the public how much the development of, or the mere dealing in, property had become the new alchemy. Keyser Ullmann Holdings, the banking concern, whose chairman was Mr Edward du Cann MP, took over Central and District Properties, also chaired by Mr du Cann, in April 1972 for some £69 m, largely met by the issue of new shares, and in

September 1973 sold it on to Town and City Properties for £97 m cash.

A highly profitable deal came at the beginning of 1973, when the private English and Continental Property Holdings (E and C) concern, in which the Crown Agents had a 51 per cent share stake – the other 49 per cent being owned by Mr Jack Walker and Mr Ramon Greene – was sold in January 1973 to the Post Office Superannuation Fund for some £34 m. The original equity capital had been small and the sale showed a profit of approaching £17 m to the Crown Agents, which had put up large loans for the venture, and one of some £16 m (£8 m each)[18] for Mr Walker and Mr Greene. Subsequently, however, the Agents re-invested in a new English and Continental venture, also involving Mr Walker and Mr Greene, on which they were ultimately to face losses put at over £42 m,[19] not only on their own loans to the venture but through their issue of 'comfort letters' covering its other borrowings.

An interesting sidelight on some attitudes to valuation at this time was afterwards given to the Crown Agents Tribunal by Mr Walker, in describing how he arranged for the big Bush House – bought by E and C for £22 m – to be valued at a higher figure as four separate blocks than as a single entity. 'I asked them (the valuers) to value the buildings as independent buildings since there was a greater market for buildings having a value of, say, £7 m than one building at £22 m. By virtue of this exercise [they] were able to value the four properties at £28 m. This was not alchemy. It was a matter of creative thinking on my part and demonstrates why differences in valuation can come about.'[20]

An instance of the irresistible appeal of the property market which led to a secondary bank making a highly venturesome investment as early as 1969 can be seen in the spending of £6 m by the newly-formed Sterling Industrial Securities – set up by Mr Sidney Davidson, formerly of Goulston Discount, Mr Sidney Finley and the Crown Agents – on a building at 11 Belgrave Road, London, with the aim of selling it at a profit. The purchase absorbed a very high proportion of all the resources available to the bank which, at 31 October 1969, had deposits of £7.5 m from the Agents and of £1.4 m from elsewhere. The building was later sold, just making a profit. 'It was a narrow squeeze?', Mr Peter Scott QC, one of the Tribunal's Counsel, asked Mr Davidson at the Tribunal's hearings. 'Hindsight, Mr Scott', was the first answer. 'It was a narrow squeeze, was it not?' 'Yes, but may I say at the time we did that the objective was limited. I admit it was inappropriate.'[21]

An example of a deal in land and property done on the basis of a value multiplied seven times in a year-and-a-half emerged in a case in which Singer and Friedlander, the merchant bank and accepting house, later

sued the valuers John D. Wood for an allegedly excessive valuation of
some building land in Gloucestershire on which the bank had made a
loan to a company in Mr Ronald Lyon's group. Singer and Friedlander
had lent £1.5 m – which was not repaid because of the Lyon group's
later crumbling – to Lyon Homes, on the strength of a valuation of £2 m
for 131 acres made by the respondents in December 1972. The plaintiff
claimed that the valuation was excessive by about £600,000. The land,
or rather a slightly larger 140 acres, had been purchased early in 1972 for
£620,000 on a valuation made in December 1971; earlier, in mid-1971,
nearly a third of it had been valued at only £100,000. The Judge, Mr
Justice Watkins, referring to these fast-changing figures, observed that,
assuming the original mid-1971 valuation had been right, 'Manor Farm
in 18 months had become about seven times more valuable by Christmas
1972. In the light of that, may it not be apt to remind oneself of what a
redoubtable and eminent personage said on a famous occasion "This is
an ill-conceived world, but not as ill-conceived as that".'[22] The
plaintiffs, Singer and Friedlander, won their case, receiving judgment
against the defendants for almost £0.5 m. Later there were other cases of
valuers being sued for allegedly excessive valuations during the boom.[23]

There were various practices within the property world in the boom
time which were to prove danger points when the storm broke in 1974. In
the first place, property companies then tended, as they still frequently
do, to have a high proportion of their gross income going out in interest
charges; one result of this is that profit is limited, benefit often accruing
to shareholders more significantly through increases in values of the
properties. In the boom period borrowings were pushed to the point
where, on average, the proportion of property companies' gross income
going on interest was a half in 1972, two-thirds in 1973 and perhaps 90
per cent in 1974. In many cases it was far above 100 per cent. This was to
prove a dangerously high (in some cases fatal) degree of reliance on
borrowed funds after interest rates had risen sharply.[24]

It was not unusual for property companies to operate 'deficit
financing' – meeting interest charges on new developments from income
from letting existing properties or sometimes from dealing profits or
from the proceeds of selling properties. Other concerns got their banks
to 'roll up' interest on developments – postpone payment of it until the
new building was finished and let.

Many banking concerns which financed property in 1971–3 took
risks in lending a very high proportion – 75 or 80 per cent – of the

value of the land or buildings charged to them as security; if the lender was taking an equity stake in the project ('a slice of the action'), as secondary banks often did, up to 90 or 100 per cent of the value was often advanced. These thin or non-existent margins left the banks with no adequate protection when property values crashed severely in 1974.

Subsequent assessments agree about the riskiness of much of the secondary and fringe banks' financing of property during the boom. The Royal Institution of Chartered Surveyors noted that 'during the (property) boom of 1968–73, lenders too often abandoned normal standards of commercial prudence'.[25] The clearing banks, while defending their own lending in this field as 'not unduly high in relation to their resources and their ability to take a long-term view . . . ', roundly condemned 'a number of secondary banks which had indulged the appetite of property companies with loans and advances, financed by short-term deposits, beyond the limits of banking prudence.'[26] The Bank of England noted that the nature of demand in the two years before the crisis 'encouraged the fringe to extend their position in property lending, particularly at the speculative end of the market'.[27]

The widespread practice has been for new property development to be financed initially with short-term borrowing, to be replaced, when the building is finished, by longer-term finance from investment institutions, such insurance companies and pension funds. But an ominous trend which developed in 1971–3 was the growing tendency for some property companies to finance operations through bank loans without having first fixed up longer-term funds to replace them. In late-1973, when interest rates rose sharply, there was a particular temptation, as the big banks later pointed out, for property companies to postpone longer-term financing arrangements in the hope that rates would fall.[28]

Sir Kenneth Cork estimates that properties being developed in the boom were worth about three times the amount allocated by the institutional investors to finance such assets, leaving a gap which carried a clear threat of disaster. 'Everybody was developing for somebody else – and the somebody else was not there'. Sir Kenneth is also critical about the extent to which many property companies were taking on interest commitments exceeding current income, sometimes he believes by about three times. 'They were developing property and paying interest out of sales – and that's the kiss of death' he remarks.[29]

The secondary banking sector was not only backing new commercial property development in 1971–3. It was also financing, or investing in, purchases of existing commercial property to obtain the 'reversionary' right to increase rents when the next time for re-negotiation came. Some calculations were, however, somewhat upset by the commercial rents freeze introduced as part of the prices and incomes standstill in November 1972. House-building was a further area attracting large lending, often combined with investment, from the secondary banks in 1971–3. This, and the pressure on the capacity of the building industry, had a sharply inflationary effect on house prices: the average price of a new house rose by 52 per cent between June 1972 and June 1973.[30] In the hope of gaining consequently high profits, house-building companies themselves rapidly expanded their stock of sites, often relying heavily on credit, in this period.

The purchase of big blocks of flats and their 'break up' into individual dwellings for sale was yet another activity heavily financed by the secondary and fringe banks. A huge deal which at first appeared highly profitable but which did not turn out as intended, arose from the purchase in September 1971 by First National Finance Corporation (FNFC), partly in association with Mr William Stern's group, of 114 blocks of flats from the large MEPC (then Metropolitan Estates and Property Company), for some £33 m. The acquisition included many well-known blocks of 'Key Flats' in London. Some of the price was paid in cash at the time of purchase, but the majority of it was left outstanding as a debt from FNFC to MEPC, which took mortgages over the relevant blocks as security. A quarter of the blocks was acquired by the Stern group, with finance from FNFC; a half was equally owned by FNFC and the Stern group, and FNFC itself held the last quarter, from which it sold off a number of flats.

In June 1972, FNFC, which, having recently become a section 127 banking company, wished to withdraw from the flat-owning business, and announced that arrangements had been made for all the blocks then held to be sold; the total proceeds would be some £76 m, giving rise to a pre-tax profit of £24 m after minorities. Completion of the disposals and the realisation of profits would be spread over a number of years. Particulars were given of one disposal: blocks worth £22.25 m were to be purchased from FNFC and its associates by Regalian Properties, in which FNFC itself held a stake of 30.5 per cent. The arrangement was that Regalian would complete the acquisition over the period 1975–80, as it itself sold off the flats in question. The purchase price was meanwhile to be owing from Regalian to FNFC, with an entitlement for interest to be rolled up. (In this way, the profits from the deal, and similar ones, would have accrued to FNFC over a period of years).

The sale of another, larger, collection of blocks to the interests of the late Mr Gerson Berger, the millionaire recluse who was one of London's largest residential landlords, was also fixed up.

With the arrival of the secondary banking and property crisis less than two years later, the major flats sale project largely went awry. Following the crumbling of the Stern empire, its share of the flats, financed by FNFC, came back under the latter's control. Arrangements were also in due course concluded under which flats sold to the Berger interests reverted to FNFC. A new agreement was made in 1976 under which Regalian (which incurred heavy losses from 1974 to 1978) charged the assets of its relevant flat-owning subsidiaries to FNFC, while it continued to manage the property. The large funds left outstanding on mortgage from MEPC to FNFC under the original 1971 flats purchase were duly discharged by FNFC with the help of funds financed through the Lifeboat.

The episode is an illustration, not only of the highly profitable deals which could be arranged during the 1971–3 boom, but of the drastic reversal of fortunes which could prevent the implementation of those not finalised before the crisis.

The financial environment in 1971–3 was generally highly favourable for profit-making. Pre-tax profits of the Big Four clearing banks rose from £278 m in 1971 to £580 m in 1973, and, as Table 4.1 on pages 40–1 shows, similar if not proportionately greater increases took place in the profits of secondary banks. For a time share prices of the latter rose swiftly and plans were made to launch several newer concerns on the stock market.

But some clouds began to gather and by mid-1973, when economic worries were gaining ground, the shares of quoted secondary banks had dropped to far below their 1972 peaks. The ominous trend brought declines of as much as a half in Keyser Ullmann Holdings, at 198p in June 1973 against a 385p high, and in J. H. Vavasseur to 200p from 400p; FNFC had dropped to 74p from its 139p peak, Slater Walker to 196p from 309p and Cedar to 46p from 99p.

This downward trend meant that those senior executives and directors who had heavily invested in their companies' shares with borrowed money risked losing their profit and perhaps being left owing large sums not covered by the value of the related asset.

Such fears in some cases inspired further hectic activity to generate more earnings, often by big deals, in order to keep the profit trend pointing upward, so that it helped the share price. It became necessary to run ever faster to keep the share price even standing still.

This situation has been vividly remembered by a leading City of London accountant, Mr Richard Langdon, who from his vantage point in the City was well able to observe the scene clearly. Mr Langdon was, and is, a director, and has, since 1975, been deputy chairman, of FNFC, in which however he has never held shares; he is also the liquidator of London and County Securities Group.

'By 1973', he recalls, 'the game seemed to be coming to an end. There were signs of developers over-extending themselves. The writing was on the wall. But you had created a high earnings capacity in these secondary banks and if you said you were going to put your balance sheet right by going for cash, it was withdrawing from the race, going into port. People said you couldn't do this. Because of the Government's destruction of share options people had borrowed money from a third party who would lend it (who might be a friend of the employer) to buy shares in the company they were working for. It happened when you expanded a bank and needed to get senior staff. Then people couldn't face the fall in the share value. I became aware in 1973 that . . . people had borrowed money to take up offers to buy shares and the fall in the value of the shares would be a personal disaster to them. They said "We can only go forward; we can't go back". People who have known success don't believe in less success. If some advised going slow, people argued that you had to stay with it. When it was realised that the music was going to stop, they were locked into shares against which they had borrowed money and which were now crashing'.[31]

At this point, when the pattern of rapid over-expansion has been reviewed, it is desirable to pause and look at the attitude to events taken by the Government and its advisers while the boom was mounting with little check and then to observe the final approach to the crisis.

6 The Dash for Growth – and its Consequences

'No stopping: no U-turns'.

Sign at the entrance to motorways.

Although the money boom which helped to fuel the secondary banking crisis seems astonishing in retrospect, it can be better understood against the background of the economic scene in the early 1970s. By the autumn of 1971, fifteen months after the Conservatives under Mr Heath had won the General Election of June 1970, Britain's economy was in the doldrums; unemployment was at what was then regarded as a high level of 800,000, and was heading for the politically ominous one million mark which it was to reach in January 1972. Total output remained subdued and, worst still, manufacturing industry's investment was forecast to fall, by 6–8 per cent, in 1971 as a whole. In July, the Chancellor, Lord Barber, had cut purchase tax and certain other taxes and had introduced more public works, but with little apparent reviving effect on activity. In these circumstances, it is scarcely surprising that interest rates were low – Bank Rate being only 5 per cent – and were to drop further to reach, in January 1972, their lowest since 1964.

Against this background, Mr Heath's administration, so far from being alarmed about the danger of over-heating the economy by allowing too much cash to be pumped into the system, was primarily concerned to boost activity. The Prime Minister also wished to see Britain's industry in better competitive shape before the country joined the European Economic Community (EEC) on 1 January 1973. These considerations led to top level discussions in the winter of 1971/72, as a result of which there was a decisive shift towards a more expansionary economic policy, a by-product of which was the money boom. The Government also sought the powers embodied in the Industry Act 1972 to enable it to provide financial assistance to strengthen the position of certain industries in preparation for Britain's entry to the EEC.

It is clear that Mr Heath, who was closely interested in the health of the economy, did not want his contacts with commerce and industry to be only with the heads of the industrial organisations. Consequently, on occasion, he met and canvassed the views of some of the newer and younger bankers and entrepreneurs in the City. He already knew Mr Jim Slater, from whom he had, Mr Slater has said, received personal financial advice.[1] On 3 January 1972, at a New Year dinner at Chequers,[1] Mr Heath entertained a party including Mr Slater, Mr Malcolm Horsman, a former board colleague of Mr Slater's, Mr Nigel Broackes, millionaire creator of the Trafalgar House Investments property and shipping empire, and Mr Jacob Rothschild, a director of N.M. Rothschild & Sons, the merchant bank. Mr Rothschild is the son of Lord Rothschild, then the head of the Government's 'Think Tank', the Central Policy Review Staff. Lord Rothschild was also at the dinner, as was the late Lord Armstrong, the former Permanent Secretary to the Treasury and, at that time, Head of the Civil Service, who was to play an increasing role as an adviser to Mr Heath.

Mr Broackes afterwards recalled, of the dinner, that Mr Heath's Government 'wanted to encourage an investment boom with an abundance of easy credit'.[2] How far, if at all, the Prime Minister may have been impressed by the views of the newer bankers is unknown. But Mr Heath invited Mr Slater, then at the height of his fame, to social gatherings more than once. On one such occasion, the 'whizz kid' entrepreneur met Lee Kuan Yew,[3] the Prime Minister of Singapore, an encounter which was to be of interest in relation to later chapters of the Slater story. Mr Heath also encouraged a meeting between Mr Slater and Lord Armstrong, who in 1972–1973 went to see Mr Slater and some of his colleagues. Lord Armstrong later remarked: 'I wondered if I could learn anything about "oomph" ',[4] but he does not appear to have gained any illumination from the meeting. Indeed, a somewhat amusing misapprehension occurred when Lord Armstrong, then an archetypal Whitehall mandarin, and afterwards chairman of the Midland Bank, misunderstood Mr Slater's references to the need to 'give the boys a piece of the action' – Slater Walker house jargon for assisting executives to have shareholdings in companies with which the group was concerned. Lord Armstrong appears to have taken the expression as referring to active participation in management – and anyway to have come away feeling he had learned no new truths about management skills.

An early public manifestation of the new economic growth policy – one of whose objectives was to halve the unemployment level of one million – was the highly reflationary Budget in March 1972. A target rate of 5 per cent annual increase in national output – much higher than Britain had achieved for many years – was established for the period up to mid-1973, Government spending was sharply boosted, personal taxes were cut and concessions were introduced to encourage industrial investment. Important structural changes in the tax system were also announced. The overall deficit, the public sector borrowing requirement, for 1972/73 was put at £3360 m, which was at that time, as the Bank of England subsequently recorded, 'an unprecedentedly large figure and nearly three times as much as the estimated actual amount of £1159 m required in 1971/72'.[5] In his speech unfolding this 'dash for growth' Budget, the Chancellor, Lord Barber said: 'the high growth of output which I intend to sustain with this Budget will entail a growth of money supply that is also high by the standards of past years, in order that adequate finance is available for the extra output'.[6]

All the signs are that the shape of the 1972 Budget was the subject of important differences behind the scenes. The size of the stimulus injected into the economy by the public spending increases must have been greater than the Chancellor and the Treasury would themselves have wanted, to judge by clear later indications. The official view probably was that there were already forces in the economy making for growth. But it seems certain that the more expansionary views of the Prime Minister, and the Cabinet generally, prevailed, so that the Budget boost was of record size.

The episode must have caused Lord Barber some disquiet and, in conjunction with the Cabinet pressure for higher public expenditure, probably led him to consider resigning, though any such idea was put aside as unacceptable and in any case unlikely to achieve anything except the removal of an advocate of caution. One or two glimpses of the affair survive in published form, notably in the following paragraph by Mr Brendon Sewill, Special Assistant to Lord Barber, in the book *British Economic Policy 1970–4: Two Views*[7]: 'It may well be that the unemployment statistics are misleading: what is undeniable is the pressure they create from the Press, Parliament and Cabinet colleagues for further reflationary action. It is easy to say that Chancellors should resist such pressure and, if necessary, resign. But these issues are always ones not of principle but of judgment; resignation at a time of economic difficulty can be construed as unpatriotic in that it may shake industrial and foreign confidence. Moreover, as the example of Mr Peter (now Lord) Thorneycroft (or earlier of Lord Randolph Churchill) showed, it only leaves in command those who are in favour of higher expenditure.'

This paragraph is believed to have been written with the knowledge and approval of Lord Barber. Some years afterwards Lord Barber himself wrote: 'It was certainly the view of the Treasury (and, I might add, myself) that the level of public expenditure was too high.'[8]

Mr Heath was evidently one of history's more interventionist Prime Ministers in the economic decision-making process and the indications are that, from early 1972, the ultimate word in key economic decisions rested with him more than with his Chancellor. Lord Barber had not originally been placed in the latter office, to which he succeeded on the sudden death in July 1970 of Mr Iain Macleod. This may well have meant that, although he presided effectively over the fiscal aspect of his task, on some key issues of economic policy he perhaps lacked the political weight to prevail in the Cabinet, particularly on occasions when he did not receive full support from the Prime Minister.

It also appears that Mr Heath consulted senior Treasury advisers more frequently in 1972/73 than many Prime Ministers had in the past. Equally it seems clear that this relationship was by no means always easy. While there was doubtless mutual respect between the Prime Minister and top Treasury officials headed by Lord Croham, the Permanent Secretary, the Prime Minister's well-known stubbornness led to the impression that he was sometimes unreceptive to advice. At the same time, Lord Croham's astringent style, and his scepticism about the benefits of British membership of the Common Market, perhaps did not endear him to Mr Heath. There may be some hint of all this in the remark of Mr Douglas Hurd MP, at that time Political Secretary to the Prime Minister, that officials who worked closely with Mr Heath would laugh ruefully at the notion that civil servants shaped his ideas. Referring to one meeting in 1973 Mr Hurd comments that nobody there could have considered that civil servants run the country.[9] The relevance of this is that the desire, first to restrict public expenditure in the 1972 Budget and, later, to raise interest rates as a means of curbing the developing boom, which appears to have existed in the Treasury in 1972 and 1973, stood little chance of prevailing over the cheap money and growth policies of a Prime Minister and colleagues preoccupied with economic expansion.

As the boom in bank lending and in the stock market became unmistakeable in the summer of 1972, public attention began to focus increasingly on the expansion of the money supply, and the case for a restraining rise in interest rates began to be more discussed, but with little immediate result.

At the time of the major sterling crisis in June 1972 which led to the floating of the pound, Bank Rate was raised just 1 per cent to 6 per cent, no higher than a year earlier, and Lord Barber made it clear that the crisis was not altering the Government's expansion policy. 'It would be quite wrong', he told the Commons shortly afterwards, 'to restrict the rate of growth of the money supply in a way which would hinder the rate of economic growth at which we are aiming.'[10] When Mr Reginald (later Lord) Paget asked whether the Chancellor of the Exchequer realised that the rewards of ownership of land, shares and empty office buildings had been rising by three times earnings, Lord Barber acknowledged the sense of discomfort on the subject of property and land gains which the Heath Government displayed throughout, and remarked 'I, and I think my Right Honourable friends, find some of the profits made in land dealings offensive.'

It cannot have been Lord Barber's happiest day, for Mr Emlyn Hooson, a Liberal MP (later Lord Hooson), went on to point to another product of the surging money supply, the upswing of the *Financial Times* 30 share index over the previous two years to a (near-peak) 537.6, 'accompanied by galloping inflation'. Mr Hooson warned prophetically 'The atmosphere of the country is all wrong for a voluntary prices and incomes policy to succeed'. And Sir (then Mr) Harold Wilson, the former and future Labour Prime Minister, rubbed salt in the wound with the remark that 'with all the money they have poured out, investment remains stagnant'.

As inflation and sterling worries continued, it was decided, in October 1972, that Bank Rate, the discount rate which had hitherto been directly fixed by the Bank of England, and which influenced so many interest rates, should be replaced by a Minimum Lending Rate, which was normally to reflect certain short-term market rates (Treasury Bill rates), although the Bank retained the right itself to fix the MLR, should it wish to do so. The change was seen as making it easier for interest rates to adjust – particularly upward – away from the limelight.

Then, in November 1972, the Heath Government executed a major U-turn by adopting a statutory anti-inflationary prices and incomes policy. Its earlier 'N–1' policy of pressing for each pay settlement to show rather less increase than the last had effectively been torpedoed by the big 20 per cent-plus wage awards to the miners and power workers in the spring of 1972. The new legally backed approach was, however, decided on after prolonged discussions with the unions as well as with industry representatives and left Ministers as closely committed as ever to the growth policy. This policy was the more firmly held to since it was a sweetener to the unions, whose goodwill and co-operation Mr Heath needed for the success of his incomes policy. The new anti-inflation approach therefore did not pave the way for a substantial toughening in monetary policy to curb the boom then proceeding in the secondary banking and property sectors. A limited tightening up did, however, take place at this stage, MLR edging up to 7.5 per cent in late October and touching 9 per cent at the end of 1972 before easing back to 7.5 per cent by late-June 1973. A call was also made for the banks to lodge 3 per cent of their deposits with the Bank of England, a move designed to squeeze their resources available for lending, though it did not effectively do so, since they obtained funds in other ways, such as by selling gilts and borrowing in the wholesale markets.[11]

Early in March 1973 the Government's devotion to its growth policy was again demonstrated with another Budget which accepted the target rate of 5 per cent yearly expansion as valid up to the middle of 1974, fixed as the end of the special 'dash for growth' period; unemployment had by then fallen to near 600,000 and some growth in output was visible, partly stimulated by a consumer boomlet. The Budget boosted the prospective public sector borrowing requirement for 1973/74 to a new high, £4.420 m; this surprised many at a time when there was already a good deal of uncertainty about the wisdom of continuing with fast expansion policies: Sir (then Mr) Michael Clapham, President of the Confederation of British Industry, had not very long before told Conservative backbench MPs that the Government's 5 per cent growth target was open to some doubt.[12] Meanwhile, the deficit in the balance of payments, which had gone into the red in the second half of 1972, was increasing again.

By the spring of 1973, some market pressure on interest rates was beginning to make itself felt and the question arose of the building societies lifting their mortgage rate to a new record of 10 per cent. But the Government, against the background of the incomes policy, could not stomach the idea of families who were buying their own homes having to pay a double-digit interest rate. In April 1973, therefore, it announced a special 'bridging grant' to the building societies so that the mortgage rate which these bodies were planning to raise from 8.5 per cent to 10 per cent could be held down to 9.5 per cent. This move to resist the upward trend of interest rates was decided on by the Cabinet against the strong resistance of the Chancellor, Lord Barber, who was by this stage fighting very hard for allowing interest rates to go up. Lord Barber afterwards wrote, of this issue: 'I warned my colleagues of the folly of subsidising a particular interest rate but my views did not prevail – for perhaps understandable reasons.'[13]

The Bank of England had been growing increasingly worried for some time at the Government's unwillingness to see interest rates increased as a means of restraining the gathering money boom. 'We little knew that Ted Heath would lose his head and bolt for wildly exorbitant expansion just after C and CC started', a former top Bank of England man afterwards observed. 'The system was meant to rely on interest rate movements and we were going to be allowed to use that instrument as required. Against the background of enormous expansion in the economy and with the banks, just released from their shackles, bolting for business, the end result was very different from what we had hoped.' Lord O'Brien, Governor until June 1973, later recalled: 'I admired Mr Heath very much as a man of extraordinary integrity . . . he listened, but was not easily deflected from what he felt he wanted to do.'[14]

There is no doubt that the Bank of England wished interest rates to be a higher than they were in 1972, though some key members of the Heath Government had the impression that the Bank pressed the need for control of public expenditure and for an incomes policy more strongly than the importance of higher interest rates. Various gentle hints about the need for dearer money were dropped publicly by the Bank's Governors,[15] but although they conveyed a meaning to sophisticated City listeners they were hardly the table-thumping oratory which makes headlines and brings significant pressure on Governments.

As the money boom went on, it brought constant stories of soaring housing land prices and multi-million pound gains on City property deals of the kind already referred to. The protests at 'land speculators' and 'windfall property profits' mounted, with comment often querying the justification for the big overnight profit which the mere granting of planning permission for altered land use dropped into the laps of development firms.

There was also recurrent criticism about office buildings being left empty for long periods. The Centre Point skyscraper, which was put up in the early 1960s by Oldham Estates near Tottenham Court Road Station in London and which remained largely unoccupied for years aroused considerable controversy.

Criticism of multi-million pound untaxed property profits soon became a persistent embarrassment to the Cabinet, especially since every working person in the country had, in November 1972, to accept a pay freeze.

The Government appears to have desired that the property boom should be tackled directly, since it did not wish to endanger the sacrosanct growth policy by a general tightening of credit. But how was the alarmingly effective profit-making property machine to be controlled?

Various types of forceful action were doubtless considered, but were not taken in the boom period. Some tentative moves were made, but with comparatively little restrictive result. An initial attempt to limit credit for property borrowers was made in a letter from Lord O'Brien to the banking system in August 1972 which said that there were signs of demand for bank finance for industry growing more broadly than in recent months and asked that banks should 'as necessary make credit less readily available to property companies and for financial transactions.' . . .[16] The Governor added that he understood the London clearing banks were already taking steps in this direction. This request, the first priorities-type guidance issued since C and CC was introduced in the previous year, was, however, couched in mild terms and does not seem to have had a great deal of effect. Indeed, lending to property companies by all banks included in the Bank of England's statistics showed a larger rise, of £746 m, in the year after August 1972, than the increase of £550 m in the year up to that month.

Mr Heath's stop on rises in wages, prices and dividends in November 1972 did temporarily freeze commercial rents, causing some worries for property companies which had invested in reversionary leases, hoping quickly to push up rents. Land prices were untouched, but the White Paper which followed in January 1973 promised that, before the next stage of the incomes policy came into operation, the Government would 'bring forward proposals which will increase the availability of building land and reduce the extent to which it is possible for people to make disproportionately high profits from transactions in land'. It was also stated that the standstill on business rents would be continued in the next stage.[17]

This caused apprehension about possible drastic measures and property shares took a tumble. It may well be that early measures to control or tax property profits as such were considered by the Government. But if they were, problems must have arisen. For when the Budget of 6 March 1973 was opened it contained neither the widely feared special tax on development gains nor restrictions on keeping office space vacant: 'One of Mr Barber's poodles that did not bark was the doggie that has been snapping at the heels of the property men', observed *The Economist*.[18]

Nevertheless, as expectations of an ultimate crackdown on development gains persisted, a number of big take-overs of property companies by investing institutions occurred, the effect of which was to allow shareholders to get profits safely home. These deals included the Prudential Assurance's £24.6 m acquisition in September 1973 of Edger Investments and the larger £45 m acquisition by Legal and General Assurance in October of Cavendish Land. The sale of Cavendish Land brought its key figure and largest shareholder, Mr David Lewis, proceeds of £11 m gross, representing a profit in the region of £7–8 m; part of the proceeds were placed in family trusts outside his ownership. Mr Lewis also had a large private property business, which absorbed a significant part of the cash from the Cavendish take-over but which was destined to hit the rocks in the coming storm. Only a few weeks before these big property take-overs in the autumn of 1973, the large Town and City Properties, which was to have its own problems after a period of vast expansion, had bought the Sterling Land group for £28 m and made its take-over of Central and District Properties from Keyser Ullmann Holdings for £97 m.

At length, the Government was forced by a new deterioration in the balance of payments and the pound to resort to a substantial levering up of interest rates to levels which finally broke through the 10 per cent barrier. Minimum Lending Rate (MLR) went up from 7.5 per cent to 9 per cent on 20 July and by another 2.5 per cent to 11.5 per cent a week later. The rapid two-step leap, making the rate more than half as much higher again within eight days, left the gilt-edged market and the discount houses, which held many assets whose value was hard hit by such an unprecedented jump in interest rates, in a state of shock. This was going into double digits with a vengeance, though none too soon, as credit had been expanding increasingly swiftly; indeed the action came too late to curb the damaging money boom in good time.

In retrospect, many people date the beginning of the end of the property boom from these very sharp interest boosts. The banks soon raised their own base lending rates to 11 per cent, making costs to borrowers often up to 14 per cent or more and upsetting the calculations that had been made for many property projects.

However, the Government, which had by now seen a noticeable rise in national output and investment and a reduction in unemployment, did not consider that it had changed course fundamentally or abandoned its growth policy. Even at this stage, the effect of the rapidly expanded money supply in over-inflating the secondary banking and property industries does not seem to have been a major influence in the

Government's thinking, which remained focused chiefly on counter-inflation, growth and employment-boosting objectives. Much of the monetary expansion was also explained away in some quarters as due to distortions caused by 'round-tripping' arbitrage, in which bank customers drew down their overdrafts to lend at higher rates in the money markets.

At a press conference for financial journalists at the end of July 1973 Mr Heath was asked whether, in view of the deteriorating balance of payments trend, it was not time to restrain home demand by more restriction on borrowing. He replied without hesitation 'That is not our intention.'

This press conference, whose holding, along with at least two other larger such gatherings under TV lights, in November 1972 and October 1973, showed how anxious the Prime Minister was that his policies should be put across and understood, had a small sequel which can only be described as bathos. After a time, perhaps because of the impending summer holiday, journalists ran out of economic questions and discussion turned to the Government's recent policy of imposing charges for admission to museums and galleries. Challenged about these, Mr Heath said he had never been able to understand why they were so much objected to, adding, in an allusion to the practice at major Continental galleries, 'after all, you expect to pay for going into the Louvre and the Prado'. These words appeared in the following day's *Times* as 'you expect to pay for going into the loos'.[19]

The next move by the financial authorities was a fresh and tougher request to the banks in September 1973 from the new Governor of the Bank of England, Mr Richardson, which went further than the letter a year earlier in reimposing the concept of officially-blessed lending priorities – and their opposite. Underlining the need for adequate finance for exports, industrial investment and other essential purposes, the Governor added: 'This will involve significant restraint on the provision of credit for persons . . . and further restraint on lending for property development and financial transactions.'[20]

An ominous episode which provided a curtain raiser to the as yet unforeseen secondary banking crisis and the Lifeboat rescue occurred in the spring of 1973 when the Scottish Co-operative Wholesale Society's banking department, classified as a listed bank, got into very deep waters through dealing in a particularly sophisticated sector of the far-away City of London, the forward market in sterling certificates of deposit (CDs). In effect, the Scottish Co-op – to be known for ever to top bankers, perhaps inappropriately, as Scoop – had undertaken to lend at pre-fixed rates by taking up CDs in future years, hoping to borrow more cheaply to finance the deals and so to make a profit. Instead, interest rates shot up and the Scottish Co-op was left committed to putting up over the succeeding five years large sums which it could only finance at rates much dearer than those it would receive.

With this disaster looming, the Bank of England and the big English and Scottish clearing banks mounted, with the Co-operative Wholesale Society, a rescue operation in which they agreed to share the costs of the commitment over the years. (The Bank of England at first wanted the three Scottish clearers alone to shoulder the responsibility for the rescue, but this, which could have sharply hit their profits, was strongly resisted). The total bill finally proved to be some £29 m, of which the Co-op carried about £17 m and the banks £12 m; the Bank of England contributed a small share of the clearers' proportion.

As the economic atmosphere became increasingly thundery in the autumn of 1973, bankers became more uneasy. Sir Julian Hodge, the Welsh financier who had built up Hodge Group, sensed the disquiet when he attended the International Monetary Fund's annual meeting in Nairobi in October. 'After the first day there, I thought I had never seen so many strained faces', he recalls. 'I had an acute sense of foreboding which troubled me, so I said to my wife while we were dressing for dinner: "You know, Standard Chartered Bank [which already had a sizeable interest in Hodge Group] would like a bigger stake, and I have a good mind to let them have it. Indeed, I would not mind selling them the lot as I think things are going to become very difficult." She replied: "I am surprised that you haven't done it before", to which I rejoined, "If you really mean that, I will sell the whole lot before Christmas." ' He did and Hodge Group went at a price valuing it at well over £40 m to Standard and Chartered (now Standard Chartered) Bank – afterwards chaired by Lord Barber – just before the crisis broke, in what was one of the best-timed multi-million pound sales in history. 'I feel it must have been my guardian angel', Sir Julian adds.[21]

In a number of financial concerns the feeling that the party was nearly over led at least to debate whether to quieten down activities and in others to positive decisions to follow a defensive strategy. On the national policy front, there was less sign of awareness of impending crisis. The White Paper in October on Stage 3 of the counter-inflation policy produced no significant tightening of policy and property shares enjoyed a new Indian summer.

After a new widening in the trade gap and a sharp further rise in bank lending, MLR was pushed up in mid-November to a record 13 per cent, clearly a crisis rate, and another 2 per cent was called up from the banks in special deposits with the Bank of England, making a total of 6 per cent. The country was also moving towards such new emergencies as the Government's showdown with the miners, three day working, and the related State of Emergency, as well as the oil price upsurge, which was to have repercussions on banking internationally.

The sense of foreboding gradually spread and there began to be speculation that restrictive measures, going beyond the belated rise in interest rates and modest cuts which had by now been made in Government spending plans, would be necessary. Talk about an autumn Budget developed. On 15 November, Mr James Prior, the Lord President of the Council and Leader of the House of Commons, was confronted, after making his regular Commons statement on the coming week's Parliamentary business, with a question from the Opposition Leader, Sir Harold Wilson: was there going to be an autumn Budget? Mr Heath, the Prime Minister, who was seated next to Mr Prior and who would occasionally prompt the reply to such an unexpected query, remained silent. Mr Prior answered that there was no question of an autumn Budget. Not long after this exchange, Mr Prior, walking along a corridor in the Houses of Parliament, met Lord Barber, the Chancellor, who asked 'How long does autumn last?' In the event, a tough Mini Budget was destined to be forced on the Heath Government only a few weeks later.

By now nervousness was swiftly spreading among those who had lent money through the wholesale money markets to the secondary and fringe bank sectors. 'The secondary banks had a variety of maturities and had in the past been able to renew, say, a three month deposit, when it matured', recalls a leading City money broker about this period. 'But now, when a three month deposit matured, the fringe could only get one month, one week or overnight money. The next day more matured and the same thing happened. Their books got shorter and shorter. And the shorter the book, the greater the demand that was seen in the market. Velocity increased enormously and this began to alarm people; the cannier lenders started to withdraw their limits.' The top was spinning more dizzily, but could it stay up?

Another ominous development concerned interest rate differentials. Until the autumn of 1973 secondary and fringe banks had been able to borrow at a relatively narrow margin of about 0.5 per cent (between 0.25 and 0.625 per cent) above the basic inter-bank rate payable by top banks. But now the margin widened out to 1–2 per cent, a differential which for a time allowed some less well judging brokers to tempt equally incautious lenders to place loans more willingly with the fringe. 'The broker had an awesome responsibility for seeing the lamb was not put to the slaughter', a leading broker recalled afterwards.

Even before the crisis loomed, many fringe banks paid higher commission rates to brokers who got them deposits than the standard 0.031 per cent charged to borrower and lender for deposits with listed banks. The extra was obviously an incentive to brokers specialising in finding deposits for the secondary banks, and indeed the tertiary, to use a term which became more popular at this time to describe the more down-market borrowers. As fringe concerns cast round more desperately for funds, they sometimes offered a richer commission bait still. There are recollections in the market that in late-1973 one fringe concern, not now operating, was saying to brokers: 'I will pay X per cent interest, and if you can get the money for X minus 1 per cent or more, you can keep the difference.' This would have meant much larger than usual commission – and scarcely justice to the lender as to interest, let alone risk of loss.

After the new jump in interest rates in mid-November, the position became more serious all round and many fringe banks saw an alarming gap emerging between the suddenly much higher cost of their borrowings (if they could get the money at all) and the now lower interest due in from their earlier lending operations. Even larger finance houses were feeling some of the same squeeze.

So mounted the tensions which were to culminate in the major event at the end of November which precipitated the beginnings of the December crisis with which the reader came in. This event was the effective collapse, as an independent viable entity, of the hugely expanded fringe banking concern, London and County Securities Group. The crunch came with the announcement that Mr Donald Bardsley, a former merchant banker who had been on the company's board for less than five months, had resigned.

London and County Securities Group (L and C), which operated largely with deposits from the wholesale money markets, was, by the end of September 1973, in a 'desperate financial position',[22] according to the Department of Trade Inspectors who later investigated it. When the group's half-year statement was issued on 23 November, its liquidity position was acute and its share price was collapsing,[23] having virtually halved from 200p at the beginning of the month; this was despite a major share-support operation financed with almost £5m loans by the group's

A & D subsidiary[24] which the Inspectors concluded were 'not in the ordinary course of business'.[25]

The L and C group tried to ease its difficulties by arranging £12.5 m of loan facilities from Keyser Ullmann, a listed bank which was then a ready lender following its big property deal; in November £10 m of L and C's loan book was transferred to Keyser Ullmann.

However, at the time, many of these developments, particularly those later most criticised by the Inspectors, were not generally known, nor were various alleged transactions reported on by the Inspectors which led to police enquiries and subsequent charges.

The final slide of L and C towards disaster followed the announcement on Monday 26 November of the resignation of Mr Bardsley four days earlier. The shares tumbled afresh and the company – whose motto, ironically, was 'with every step we gather strength' – was hit by the usual development which gives the coup de grâce to a financial institution, loss of confidence causing inability to withstand a run on the bank.[26] The shaky concern simply could not get its money market deposits renewed.

On the night of Thursday 29 November, an emergency meeting about L and C's predicament was held at the Knightsbridge offices of Keyser Ullmann, whose deputy chairman, Mr Jack Dellal, was among those present, along with Mr Caplan and various L and C colleagues. Representatives of Eagle Star, the insurance company, including its then chairman, the late Sir Brian Mountain, were also there: Eagle Star had a share stake in L and C and Mr F. A. Davies, one of its senior officers, was on the L and C board as a non-executive director. United Drapery Stores, whose pension fund was a shareholder in L and C, was represented too.

Mr James Keogh, head of the Bank of England's Discount Office, who had been kept in touch with the increasingly disturbing developments by Mr Bardsley at times in October and November, was called to the gathering between 11 p m and midnight; he telephoned in the small hours to Mr Alex Dibbs, the chief executive of the National Westminster, L and C's main clearing bank. Another meeting between Mr Dibbs, Mr Keogh and representatives of the shareholdings institutions and of KU, but not of L and C, was held at 8 o'clock the next morning at the National Westminster Bank headquarters to consider further how the problem should be grappled with. L and C's shares continued to be traded on the Stock Exchange at first but after they had crashed away from 80p to 40p their quotation was suspended, never to be resumed.

The Bank of England, faced with the threatened collapse of a by then very sizeable banking concern – though it was not a listed bank, but only the holder of a section 123 certificate – wanted the crisis to be handled through a rescue operation mounted by, or with, those closely concerned. Anxiety at this stage focused predominantly on the potential risks to the many thousands of small savers to whom the group owed some £15 m at its 23 banks-in-stores throughout the country. The dangers of more general blows to confidence in the wholesale money markets, where L and C had raised a much larger £65 m or so of its deposits, were less discussed, at least publicly. To lead the rescue operation the Bank of England invited in the large First National Finance Corporation, by then a listed bank, whose own business included lending, second mortgage financing and investment banking, fields in which L and C operated. FNFC undertook the task after a day or two of hesitation; this was a decision which the Bank of England was not to forget and which was doubtless to stand FNFC in good stead when the secondary banking crisis drastically buffeted that company itself.

On 3 December it was announced that a consortium headed by FNFC had arranged for substantial financial support which would fully protect depositors and that FNFC was assuming the complete management of L and C. The consortium of FNFC, Keyser Ullmann, Eagle Star and United Drapery put up £20 m of new loans to L and C, while National Westminster Bank remained closely in touch with the situation. A shake-up of L and C's board, with the blessing of the Bank of England, followed, Mr Caplan resigning, along with all the other L and C group directors except Mr Davies of Eagle Star and Mr Jeremy Thorpe, the Liberal Party leader. Mr Thorpe resigned soon afterwards, on 17 December.

The revamped board, chaired by Mr Richard Langdon, soon afterwards requested the Department of Trade and Industry to appoint Inspectors under the Companies Act 1948 to investigate the company, and this was done on 11 January 1974. Furthermore, on 7 January 1974 the new board disclosed that substantial additional provisions would be needed against losses on L and C's loans and investments, a warning which must have been taken to heart by markets already nervous about other fringe banks.

The L and C crisis, with the shocks to confidence it generated, against an already darkening economic background, was followed in the third week of December by a new blow – the harsh Mini Budget which threw so many previous Government policies into reverse. On 17 December,[27] the Chancellor, Lord Barber, unveiled drastic plans for cutting Government spending and, in a move very unwelcome to Conservative backbenchers, placed 10 per cent addition on surtax, the upper tier of personal income tax which was due shortly to be abolished. The freedoms of C and C C were much qualified by a strict new 'supplementary special deposits' system of control – the so-called 'corset' – over the banks. This effectively restricted their capacity to lend by imposing penalties if their 'bought' money – their interest-bearing eligible liabilities – increased at more than a prescribed slow pace.

In addition, the Chancellor announced the long-feared crackdown on the property business, remarking that 'With land, an owner can make huge windfall gains simply as a result of decisions by planning authorities acting on behalf of the community as a whole. It is the huge gains due to this development value – or even to potential development value – which people find offensive.' He foreshadowed the introduction of a development gains tax to apply to disposals and first lettings.

These moves were heavily to hit the property industry, just as it was already beginning to totter under the impact of the crisis in the secondary banking sector, an important source of its finance. Still more immediately, the Budget, with its tight money policy, worsened the situation of the secondary and fringe bank community itself.

Within two days, on 19 December, matters reached the critical situation to which the reader was introduced in Chapter 1. The sequel to that, in the further unfolding of the crisis and the management of the Lifeboat operation, is now to be described.

Part III HOW THE RESCUE WAS MANAGED

7 The Lifeboat Embarks on its Mission

The downfall of Overend and Gurney, and of many other houses, must be traced to the policy which they adopted of paying interest on deposits at call, while they were themselves tempted to invest the money so received in speculations in Ireland or in America, or at the bottom of the sea, where it was not available when a moment of pressure arrived.

> Launcelot Holland,
> Governor of the Bank of England, 1866

Once the chiefs of the Bank of England and the big banks had decided on a combined rescue mission for vulnerable secondary and fringe banks, the operation was launched with speed. From the time when the Lifeboat committee, chaired by Sir Jasper Hollom, the Bank of England's Deputy Governor, went into action on 28 December 1973, it met almost daily for many months to consider and deal with applications for support and to monitor the development of events. The committee was drawn from some of Britain's most senior clearing bankers, notably Mr Jim Dyson, a general manager and director of Barclays Bank; Mr Stuart Graham, a general manager and later a chief general manager and director of Midland Bank; Mr Alec Ritchie, then an executive director of Williams and Glyn's Bank and afterwards deputy chairman of Grindlays Bank; the late Mr Evan Vaughan, a general manager and director of Lloyds Bank; Mr Sidney Wild, then deputy chief executive of National Westminster Bank; and representatives of the Scottish clearing banks.

A lengthy list of banking concerns came under the watchful eye of the committee, which itself advanced support loans to many and satisfied itself that others had received backing from their large shareholders or banks or that they were surviving unaided. As Mr George Blunden, a Bank of England director who was one of the most important personalities in the rescue programme from mid-1974, afterwards recalled: 'In the first eight months of 1974 about thirty secondary banks had to be taken into communal support by the Lifeboat . . . and outside the Lifeboat at least as many more required support under individual arrangements from their clearing bankers or from the Bank of England itself or from parent companies and other large shareholders. Without these supporting operations virtually all of them would have collapsed and the cumulative effect of those collapses would have spread much more widely through the banking system. Undoubtedly many of the primary banks would have been swept away in the maelstrom. As it was, by protecting the secondary banks the Bank of England and the clearing banks ensured that not one of the inner ring of primary banks had to be supported.'[1]

Support loans soon totalling hundreds of millions of pounds were provided fairly liberally in line with the principle of recycling funds to banking concerns which conformed with certain requirements. One was that they had, at least, the status of section 123 certificate holders and had consequently been accorded a degree of official recognition. Another necessity was that the company should appear likely to remain solvent, given the aid, and that it was not in a position to command adequate assistance from other parties, such as large shareholders. But inevitably it was sometimes a case of aid first and question later, so complex and, on occasion, opaque, were some companies. Sir Jasper Hollom later told a House of Commons committee: 'In the case of a company under real pressure one had to make one's decisions very quickly or the decision would be taken out of one's hands by events. . . . I can recall one group which had no less than 149 companies more or less inextricably intermingled. . . . So one had to look at the totality in deciding whether there was a reasonable basis for support or not.' On the same occasion, the Governor, Mr Richardson, remarked: 'We had to support some institutions which did not themselves deserve support on their merits . . . because collapse there was capable of letting the wave come on to [the main banking system].[2]

Help was not unconditional. Quick preliminary investigations were made, or arranged for, by the clearing ('related') bank most closely connected with an applicant to check, as far as was possible in a short time, that the concern fulfilled the requirement that it must be viable to merit help.[3] Borrowing secondary banks, certain of which were considered, even at this stage, to have been over-trading, were sometimes expected to curb the taking on of new business and to sell off certain of their assets; the hope was that this would improve their own situation and ease the burden on the Lifeboat. Interest, typically at

1.5–2 per cent over the relevant inter-bank rate, was charged on the support loans and there were commitment fees on any unused approved loans. To protect the Lifeboat as far as possible, security was often sought, sometimes in a form giving the rescuers the right to appoint a receiver if they wished; in certain cases, however, the beleaguered fringe concern was already heavily mortgaged and could give little or no valuable security. Loans were for stipulated periods, after which the position was subject to review. The exact conditions imposed, and the degree of continuing surveillance, varied a good deal according to the nature and standing of the assisted concern. Among those brought within the ambit of the Lifeboat operation were two large banking concerns which, as noted in Part I, had already been supported – London and County Securities Group and Cedar Holdings.

One of the initial tasks of the Lifeboat committee was to sort out applicant banks into four categories. The first grouping, A, was made up of those approved for support loans with the financing, and the risks of loss, shared out among the Lifeboat's member banks. The great majority of the secondary banking and finance house companies which were assisted on a continuing basis fell into this class. The second category, B, comprised a much smaller number of about half a dozen concerns whose support borrowings were financed, or in some way backed, by the Lifeboat, but where the risk of loss was carried by the related clearing bank concerned.[4] In certain instances, a case was in category B because the clearer continued to shoulder the risk of loss on borrowing facilities it had granted a customer before the Lifeboat's launching. In others, a clearer agreed to carry the full risk, perhaps recognising that it might have done more in the boom days to discourage over-expansion by a fringe bank to which it had been the principal banker. Some category B companies eventually failed, leaving a substantial burden – in which in two or three cases the Bank of England significantly shared – on the clearer concerned.[4]

Category C was an interim class in which applicants were sometimes placed until it was settled how they should be handled. Category D was composed of those concerns which, because they were not banking businesses or for other reasons, were refused support. One for which no rescue was mounted was Cornhill Consolidated, a sizeable unquoted financial business with extensive share links, whose failure early in January 1974 was one of the first resounding signs of the crisis. This concern was afterwards investigated by Department of Trade Inspectors, who noted that the Cornhill Consolidated Group's employed funds had risen from £35,000 to over £20 m in its life of less than five years; they described it as, from its early days, 'no more than a huge speculation with borrowed money'.[5]

In December 1973, before the Lifeboat's launch, the big banks had decided against a support operation for Moorgate Mercantile Holdings, a small quoted finance company, since it was considered too far from the centre of the banking system for its troubles to be a matter of acute concern. In the event, this company avoided collapse through arrangements with its creditors; it was placed under the control of a receiver and special manager (Mr Rupert Nicholson, the accountant who had so successfully handled the old Rolls-Royce group after its collapse in 1971) and in due course staged a good recovery.

Reports of the Lifeboat support operation were steadily confirmed in the early months of 1974 by a flow of announcements, revealing the widespread new problems in the secondary bank sector and sometimes disclosing swift moves, through take-overs or otherwise, to solve them. For example, Twentieth Century Banking, a section 123 company which after various changes of control was now owned by the Bovis building group, suffered a run on its deposits that created difficulties for itself and for Bovis, which had guaranteed £45 m of its deposits. Twentieth Century had the additional problem that it had made considerable loans to what was soon to be the troubled field of property.

This led in January 1974 to agreement on a £25 m takeover by the big P & O shipping group of the whole of Bovis, in which it already held a near-10 per cent stake and which it had, ironically, earlier made an abortive move to buy at a much higher price in a celebrated bid battle in 1972. A glimpse of the Lifeboat's approach at this stage was given in P & O's announcement of its offer.[6] After referring to the 'unexpected and unprecedented withdrawal' from Twentieth Century of money market deposits, beyond the means of Bovis, as guarantor, to meet – and to the help urgently provided through the National Westminster Bank, and then through the Lifeboat, to stave off collapse – this statement added that the help was 'for a limited period only whilst Bovis sought an association with a financially stronger partner'.

In February, a remarkable move demonstrating its commitment to the control of the crisis was made by the Bank of England, which in December had called in the large First National Finance Corporation (FNFC) to take on the management of the tottering London and County Securities Group. The Bank said it was taking ownership of L and C's banking business jointly with FNFC on a 50:50 basis. But already FNFC, with large short-term borrowings, was being hit by the crisis and acknowledging publicly that it shared in the 'widespread problems'. FNFC, with an ultimate £350 m extended to it in support loans, eventually became one of the Lifeboat's two largest borrowers and was to experience severe falls in the value of its assets. In view of the large support loans which were already being provided to FNFC, Mr John Glyn, a well-known City figure, was appointed in the spring of 1974 to the group's board in response to the Lifeboat committee's wishes and became a deputy chairman. It was also arranged that Mr Douglas Horner, then a regional general manager and later senior general manager and a director of Barclays Bank, should keep in close touch and spend time at the company on the Lifeboat's behalf. But at this point there was no question of any other changes in the board, headed by Lord De L'Isle, the chairman, and Mr Pat Matthews, a deputy chairman and managing director.

Other disclosures continued of the pressures affecting secondary banks. The Scottish-based British Bank of Commerce revealed that it had received support through its clearing bank – this was financed through the Lifeboat – to meet withdrawals of deposits, that £2 m of provisions had been made against possible losses and that profits had slumped from £1.5 m to only £35,000. Burston Group, whose Burston Finance – a recipient of Lifeboat support loans – financed property extensively and had a number of joint companies with property developers, pointed to its policy of curtailing investment and accepting new business only on a selective basis. Texas Commerce Bank, the US group which was a minority partner in its Burston and Texas Commerce Bank, helped put in £1 m against subordinated loan notes and postponed for four years its entitlement to require Burston Group to buy out its interest.

Northern Commercial Trust, the previously fast-growing unquoted Manchester-based concern in which a substantial share stake was owned by Authority Investments, received access to up to £40 m of loans financed through the Lifeboat support group, of which some £30 m was drawn. In the altered circumstances, plans to launch the shares on the Stock Exchange were abandoned and a highly cautious lending policy was followed.

For the smaller Duboff Brothers, in the unlisted Consolidated Finance Holdings (CFH) group, the abrupt change of climate was a considerable blow. Plans had been well advanced in late-1973 for CFH's shares to be launched on the stock market but these were shelved in the altered circumstances and Duboff experienced a significant withdrawal of deposits, some of which had come from major finance houses. A

£2.5 m secured loan facility was provided to Duboff by the National
Westminster Bank in the first half of December 1973; it afterwards, for a
time, came under the aegis of the Lifeboat group.

The Morris Wigram quoted banking concern, whose directors
included Mr David Heimann, son-in-law of the late Iain Macleod, who
was Conservative Chancellor of the Exchequer briefly before his death
in July 1970, received some £10 m of support loans. In 1974 it was
bought, for a nominal price, by the then South African-linked Schlesinger Organisation, which subsequently repaid the loans. Morris
Wigram's name was changed in 1975 to Schlesinger. In 1980, when the
Schlesinger group was disposing of several interests, the Schlesinger
banking company was sold to the well-known Dutch group
Slavenburg's Bank.

In due course, it emerged that a wide range of prominent finance
houses, including Mercantile Credit, Bowmaker and Wagon Finance
Corporation, as well as various other secondary banks of different sizes,
were receiving help from the Lifeboat through support loans.

In the early months of 1974, the big banks still hoped that the crisis
they were fighting was essentially one of liquidity which could be solved
by re-cycling loans to banking concerns which had suffered a flight of
deposits. But almost from the very start of the Lifeboat operation there
were signs that the problems were in some cases more deep-seated and
that various secondary banks faced losses in the value of their assets
through having committed too much money against property and
shares, both now declining in the darker economic atmosphere. Major
problems of this kind at three quite prominent groups took much of the
Lifeboat committee's attention early in 1974. It is instructive to look at
these groups because they illustrate the manner in which a previously
fast-growing financial company could, in a harsher climate, quickly
suffer not only severe cash problems but a dangerous crumbling in the
value of its assets; they also show the Lifeboat's ways of tackling such
situations which later became much more widespread.

One such case was that of J. H. Vavasseur, the former commodity
group which had been built up as a financial, investment and property
business after coming under new direction in 1968. This group had
previously been highly expansionary; its report and accounts for 1973
listed some twenty deals in that year. The largest had been the £17 m
acquisition early in 1973 of Barclay Securities, the conglomerate with a
reputation for asset-stripping run by a former Slater Walker man, Mr
John Bentley, whose own shareholding was worth millions of pounds
under the take-over deal. Mr Bentley's 'Vava-who?' query on hearing of

the bid offer had earned him a niche in history. Other Vavasseur transactions in 1973 included overseas purchases in Canada, Holland, South Africa, Australia and elsewhere. The group had attempted in November 1973, as the atmosphere darkened, to sell its controlling stake in Roeday Properties, but this deal had fallen through and more money had had to be put in to finance Roeday's developments.

The tide turned dramatically against Vavasseur in the winter of 1973/74; its business was just the kind that became most vulnerable to tighter, dearer money conditions and tumbling share and property markets. A swathe was cut through the value of its properties and its shareholdings in other companies, and millions of pounds of write-offs and provisions produced a £17.6 m net loss for 1973, against a 1972 profit of £1.3 m. In particular, a very large amount had to be written off against the investment in Barclay Securities. Then, the banking subsidiary, Vavasseur Trust, a section 123 company, had to fix up large-scale borrowing facilities through its bankers, Hambros and Lloyds Bank, while a further facility was arranged for the rest of the group. Much of this was taken over by the Lifeboat.

To obtain cash, the group began a sequence of sell-offs. Its half-share in Trident Investors Life Assurance was disposed of in January 1974 to Schlesinger Organisation, and in the following month its Vavasseur Life Assurance was sold for a nominal price to the big Prudential Assurance. A Canadian acquisition was sold and a Luxembourg subsidiary was placed in liquidation. Other sales followed.

Firm conditions were imposed by the Lifeboat committee and the big banks. The loan facilities were, according to a note in the accounts, 'made available on the basis that the [parent] company would warrant the collectability of certain advances made by [Vavasseur Trust], that the facility for the Group would be secured on shares in certain subsidiaries and that Sir Ian Morrow and other personnel introduced by Hambros Bank . . . would act as advisers to the Board'.[7]

But disposals and large-scale support loans could not stave off a drastic moment of truth. As the directors told shareholders: 'In the depressed state of the stock market and in the virtual absence of a property market, assets cannot be sold quickly enough or at sufficiently good prices to reduce the Group's indebtedness to the level permitted under the Trust Deed constituting the [partly convertible stock issued against the Barclay Securities acquisition] calculated on the basis of the reduced asset values'.[7] This breach of the Trust Deed triggered a crisis. A major reconstruction, involving the cancellation of this stock and its replacement with ordinary shares and some loan stock in a new holding company, J. H. Vavasseur Group, became necessary as the only way of enabling the business to continue and avoid being forced into liquidation. It was approved in June 1974, and the original Vavasseur ordinary shareholders ended up with only 20 per cent of the revamped group's equity. Slater Walker Securities emerged with 29 per cent of the new ordinary shares, through exchanging the stock it had received on the take-over of its Barclay Securities 'satellite'; it also helped to underwrite a £1 m rights issue by the new holding company.

In the changed circumstances, alterations of management became appropriate. The Scottish chartered accountant Sir Ian Morrow, a Hambros director, moved into the chairmanship of the fresh holding company and Mr Clive Hollick, from Hambros Bank, became managing director. Banking activities were much reduced and a programme of property sales was embarked upon. Afterwards additional large losses were incurred and Vavasseur underwent further reconstruction and a merger which will be noted later; however, with continued Lifeboat support it avoided a collapse.

Triumph Investment Trust, the sizeable group with extensive home and overseas interests, including banking, insurance, unit trust management and metals – as well as a 27 per cent stake in the Scotia Investments hotel and gaming concern – was another large and diversified financial concern where the crisis soon struck hard. It became known as early as February 1974 that support loans were being provided by the Lifeboat: up to some £30 m was made available. As will be noted later, considerable backing was also mobilised by the Bank of England from the Crown Agents in the attempt to rescue Triumph and its G. T. Whyte banking subsidiary, which had just graduated, in 1973, from the status of a section 123 company to that of a listed bank.

By the time Triumph's results for the year to March 1974 were revealed, it was seen that large write-offs and loss provisions had produced an overall loss of £19.5 m, compared with a £4 m profit in 1972/73. Major sums which had had to be set aside included £4.8 m of provisions against losses on the investments of the insurance and investment trust subsidiaries, £3.0 m against losses on investments in associates, £2.4 m against losses on the banking company's advances and £2.0 m to cover falls in the value of overseas property developments.

Under board changes in early August, Mr Tom Whyte, until then executive chairman, handed over the chair to Lord Chelmer, a former Treasurer of the Conservative Party, and already a director, but remained chief executive; four directors resigned. The Lifeboat support loans, aimed at giving the group a breathing space for recovery, were subject to security being provided. In remarks sombrely reflecting the prevailing stresses, the former and new chairmen told shareholders: 'Help was given but on very stringent conditions. The plain fact is that practically all deposits are withdrawn as they mature and no new ones are placed and even in the best of economic conditions there can be very few banks, if any, who could unwind their affairs sufficiently fast to meet an almost total withdrawal of funds on due dates.'[8] The position of G. T. Whyte and the other group companies involved in merchant banking, property and investment activities had 'clouded and threatened the existence of the entire group'. It was necessary to dispose of assets to raise funds to reduce dependence on bank borrowings. The future of the company was much bound up with the country's economic and political future and 'both are as presently uncertain as the group's'. Disaster, however, eventually overtook Triumph, which failed later in 1974, with an estimated deficiency of £48 m,[9] the Lifeboat men having by then decided they could not carry it any longer. Mr Whyte went to live in the United States. In November 1980, it was reported that, through a Bermudan company, he had played a significant role in the acquisition of interests in the quoted London money broking group R. P. Martin and that he held a stake in the company himself.

Another case with which the Lifeboat was much occupied early on was Cannon Street Investments (CSI), an investment and banking company which was headed by the former Slater Walker man Mr Herbert Despard and which owned the section 123 banking subsidiary, Cannon Street Acceptances (CSA). CSI had grown swiftly at home and abroad in the early 1970s. As many as twelve acquisitions were made by CSI in Britain, Holland, Belgium and Switzerland in the eleven months to October 1973. When the crisis hit CSA, a £20 m line of credit was arranged from the National Westminster Bank, its financing being backed by the Lifeboat; it was conditional on a floating charge over the business, property and assets of CSA, which undertook to curtail its lending, and on a guarantee up to £20 m from the parent CSI. Heavy drawings on the credit took place and a programme of disposals of CSI group investments was adopted to raise cash. However, these measures did not save the situation and in September 1974 a receiver was appointed to CSA; CSI's UK banking interests were sold to the National Westminster Bank for the nominal sum of £10 and CSA was later reported to have a deficiency of £24 m.[10] A reorganisation of the CSI parent was then proposed as the only alternative to the winding up of the group and the forced realisation of its assets; this was carried through, leaving the National Westminster Bank with 63.6 per cent of the capital. These instances show how the Lifeboat allowed secondary banks considerable time to seek solutions to their problems, even if the ultimate outcome was failure or a major scaling down of business.

A high priority on the agenda of the Lifeboat committee was to consider what other parties could be asked to assist in the support moves to deal with the pressure on the secondary banks. After all, it had been a term of the original agreement of 27 December 1973 that the possibility of drawing in other suitable financial institutions was to be explored.

No attempt was made to rope in as co-rescuers the accepting houses, the eighteen top merchant banks which, with the clearers and the discount houses, form the inner heart of the commercial banking system. The accepting houses are much smaller than the clearers and, so far from having resources to back a general support operation, could conceivably themselves have been vulnerable to any more wide-ranging crisis. Generally, thanks to prudent management, the accepting houses fared well, with few worries and no acute ones, in the crisis years. If there were any isolated cases of accepting house finance being committed to hard-pressed secondary banks, repayment was taken care of by the Lifeboat operation. However one house, Brandts, which saw its reserves wiped out by £14 m provisions mainly on its property, left the Accepting Houses Committee after its parent, Grindlays Bank, had strengthened its management control in a way considered incompatible with the management independence characteristic of accepting houses.

The event proved that none of the accepting houses needed Lifeboat help; on the other hand, they were probably glad at such a troubled time not to be asked to carry further burdens and, like all in the City of London, they certainly gained indirectly from the Lifeboat's stabilising effects. The accepting houses, whose importance in relation to the clearers tended to diminish somewhat for a few years after the crisis, must at least count themselves fortunate that in the crisis they benefited from the Lifeboat operation without having to contribute to it.

The main type of back-up sought by the Lifeboat committee was the provision of finance from related interests, notably controlling or large shareholders, of the affected fringe banks. This is how the policy was described by Sir Jasper Hollom, the Lifeboat chairman, to the Fay Committee on the Crown Agents: 'If there were responsible institutional investors who had put their money in and lent the support of their name as well as their money to a fringe banking organisation we pressed upon them the argument that they therefore had a responsibility to rectify the problem, and not just leave it to the support group [the Lifeboat] to step in and, as it were, to relieve them of responsibility.'[11] In blunter terms, the message was: 'You were involved with them in good times, now help them out in bad.'

A number of large shareholders found it quite natural to follow up earlier investments in secondary and fringe banks by providing further finance, when the Lifeboat was not being called on; some helped Lifeboat passengers with additional loans and credits, encouraged, on occasion, by the Bank of England's persuasions. In certain cases, this aid developed into that full-scale take-over of a fringe bank which soon emerged as the ultimate solution much favoured by the Lifeboat for dealing with the future of over-exposed financial concerns. In some instances, however, large shareholders proved disappointingly reluctant to shoulder any of the burden.

Several examples of institutional activity can be found. For instance, Prudential Assurance, Britain's largest investing institution, which had built up stakes in a number of financial concerns, rallied round in various ways. Since the secondary banking sector in which it had enlarged its investment during the boom years was going through an unexpectedly difficult time, it was as well that it could take the long view. The Prudential provided a £10 m borrowing facility to Dawnay Day, a section 123 banking company with unit trust interests, in which it had a 19.5 per cent holding. Dawnay Day followed the general trend of the time by cutting back various of its activities, particularly by realising a large part of the portfolio on its investment banking side, where losses were incurred, and by cutting its banking activity right back. In 1980 it was taken over by Hume Holdings, a recently acquired subsidiary of Rothschild Investment Trust (now RIT).

F C Finance, the Co-operative Bank-controlled finance house which had branched out into lending to the property and house-building sector, experienced a marked outflow of deposits, which fell in 1974 from £36.5 m to £11.0 m. It accordingly received increased backing and advances from its holding, and fellow-subsidiary, companies in the Co-operative movement, whose advances to it rose from £8.2 m to £34.0 m. In the following year the deposit position had largely reverted to normal, but a £2 m loan was made by a fellow subsidiary. In 1980, Co-operative Bank bid to buy out the 18 per cent publicly-held minority shares in F C Finance for £1.4 m.

Beverley Bentinck, the instalment credit business whose name was changed to British Credit Trust, improved its position in the difficult year 1973/74 by withdrawing from medium- and long-term financing. It was provided with £2.5 m of increased support from its parent company, Northern Foods, and it also received some help from its bankers. Part of the latter came under the aegis of the Lifeboat support group for a time. In 1975/76 the Bear Securities banking arm was sold. Afterwards, in 1978, British Credit Trust was acquired by the large Dublin-based Bank of Ireland in an £11 m take-over.

Much the biggest and most widely discussed amount of back-up finance for the Lifeboat support operation came from the Crown Agents. By April 1974, the Agents, who were heavy lenders to and investors in the fringe banking sector, had – according to a letter from their then chairman, Sir Claude Hayes – provided £45 m of 'passive support' by the continuing of loans due for repayment. Later, there was, according to the same letter, 'rather more active support', to Keyser Ullmann and to two concerns in which the Agents had large share stakes, Sterling Industrial Securities and Wallace Brothers.[12]

An insight into what happened in one case was given by a witness to the Crown Agents Tribunal about his organisation's contribution to the attempted rescue of Triumph Investment Trust. On 2 January 1974 the Bank of England called the Agents and other institutions to a meeting at which the Agents apparently agreed to roll over at least some existing deposits and to put up another £5 m. When a report by a former colleague, the late Mr Bernard Wheatley, was read, saying that 'the Bank of England suggested very strongly that the shareholding institutions covered should mount a rescue operation for Triumph because the Bank is naturally very reluctant to see a listed bank fail', the witness, Mr Eric Osgodby, then the Agents' Deputy Head, and afterwards Head, of Banking, remarked 'we were leant upon by the Bank of England who used their authority to draw us into the rescue consortium'.[13] It seems that the Crown Agents eventually left £5 m of deposits in the Triumph group and provided the promised further £5 m.

Sterling Industrial Securities, the unquoted banking concern in which the Crown Agents had a stake of about a quarter, received £2 m of loans through the Lifeboat but was largely supported by the Agents, whose loans to it reached £12.2 m in 1974.[14] SIS's result for the troubled year 1973/74 was a loss of some £8.5 m after more than £4 m of provisions for bad and doubtful debts; this caused a deficiency of a few million pounds. The company was afterwards the subject of a managed run-down operation presided over by the Agents and was eventually sold. The Lifeboat loan was repaid in 1976, the Agents ensuring that there was no loss to the Lifeboat. Board changes had taken place from late in 1974, when Mr Wheatley, the Crown Agents' representative on the board, resigned. Mr Davidson, the managing director and a major shareholder, resigned in January 1975, as did Mr Finley, another director and shareholder. Mr Finley was afterwards convicted of corruption concerning loans to Mr Wheatley, against whom charges were brought, but no case was heard, before his death in 1977. Mr Finley was sentenced to one year's imprisonment.

As a result of a civil action brought by the Crown Agents, Mr Davidson was ordered by a High Court judge in 1980 to repay £250,000 to the Agents, who had said the money in question reached Mr Davidson as an unsecured loan as a result of improper and unauthorised actions by Mr Wheatley.[15]

Among other concerns helped by the Agents was Burston Group. Mr Norman Hewins, the Agents' Director of Finance for a time from late-1973, told the Tribunal: 'our lending to the Burston Group . . . was influenced by the fact that we were receiving a nod and a wink from the Bank of England to take part in the support operations of fringe banks'.[16] The Fay Committee afterwards put the Agents' total losses on Burston at £5.2 m and those on SIS at £10 m.[17]

The total amount committed by all non-bank parties to back up the direct support operation by the Lifeboat for the secondary and fringe banks is not known, but it may have been approaching £200 m, including the contributions of the Crown Agents, of the institutions behind the rescue of Cedar Holdings and of various other parties. The total seemed pretty modest to the clearing banks which were themselves ultimately to provide nearly £1200 m. However, the investing institutions were to play a larger role in helping out the property industry, as will be seen.

By the end of March 1974, the loans outstanding from the Lifeboat support group itself were still less than a third of their ultimate size, but 21 storm-tossed secondary banks, the great majority of the 26 ultimately helped in this way, were already in receipt of Lifeboat loans totalling £390 m[18]. The atmosphere in the banking industry had also become less dangerous than in December 1973. It was still disturbed but the tension had been held below emergency point by the support arrangements and the quietness of the whole operation. However, hopes that the rescue operation could be kept to no more than its then existing scale were disappointed as two further developments, the property crisis in Britain and the outbreak of new troubles on the international banking scene, darkened the climate in which Britain's secondary banks were struggling. These two events must now be glanced at before the chronicle of the UK banking crisis is resumed.

8 The Property Crisis

Because of the attractions of the property market, a large proportion of the funds flowing into the fringe institutions was employed in that market

Bank of England, 1978[1]

Scarcely had the initial, acute, crisis among the fringe banks been brought under control than another loomed up to vex the harrassed top bankers. This was the emergency which got under way in the spring of 1974 in the property world, where values began to slide under the impact of the development tax and the tight – and then unprecedentedly dear – money policies announced in the winter's Mini Budget. Within a few months, the values of commercial property had often fallen by between a quarter and a half while, with the prevailing scarcity of finance, there was virtually no market in such development sites as holes in the ground and clusters of old shops awaiting demolition. Never since the South Sea Bubble had there been such a massive evaporation of speculators' expectations as at that time in the previously euphoric property market.

There was to be constant and important interaction between the new property crisis and that among the secondary banks. The latter's troubles had cut off a major source of finance for property ventures, while investing institutions which had cash to deploy saw little point in lending it to problem-ridden property concerns when they could safely earn upto 15 per cent or so in the money markets. At the same time, the collapse in property values as the speculative froth faded meant that more and more fringe banks saw the security, in the form of property, behind their lending melting day by day while, on the other side of their accounts, they owed large debts, often at rising interest cost.

By March 1974, too, a Labour Government had just replaced the Tory one which had for most of its term been so mellow towards the property industry. While the change of Government did not inhibit the creation, under the Bank of England's sponsorship, of certain informal protective arrangements – which are shortly to be discussed – for troubled property companies, it may have made for a greater willingness to tolerate the collapse of some large private property interests whose difficulties were acute. State-sponsored rescues of over-ambitious property tycoons would hardly have been a popular point of Labour policy.

In the first quarter of 1974, property values remained in a state of suspended animation, after peaking in late-1973 before the banking crisis, but thereafter the adverse factors had increasing effect and values started on their long tumble. The decline was accentuated by the extension, in the early summer, of the existing freeze on commercial rents.

By March Guardian Properties, the quoted company headed by Mr Harry Soning which had multiplied its profits rapidly and which, like so many British property groups, had branched out on to the Continent, admitted that it had liquidity problems. It had lost money market deposits and had, from early on, been brought into the Lifeboat for a relatively modest amount of help. This proved a somewhat anomalous arrangement which was not repeated for other property companies, but it gave the Lifeboat committee and the Bank of England an occasion to keep in touch from its start with the property crisis. By June the company's difficulties were more acute, the Lifeboat would no longer keep the business afloat and, after a project for a joint rescue by larger property groups had been deeply considered but had come to nothing, a receiver was called in to Guardian in June 1974.

Another, larger, casualty was a private property business of Mr Ronald Lyon, who had built up a group under Ronald Lyon Holdings which concentrated on industrial property and housing development. Latterly, more of the industrial property was retained for investment and some resources were channelled into office development. Short-term borrowing was considerable. The group proved vulnerable to the sharp financial squeeze and the severe break in property values in the early summer of 1974 and insufficient further finance was forthcoming to fend off a crisis. The Ronald Lyon Holdings group called a moratorium in May 1974 and some time afterwards went into liquidation with an estimated deficiency for the group in the region of £50 m. Mr Lyon, who had personally guaranteed many of the group's borrowings, entered into a deed of arrangement with his personal creditors.

There was no Lifeboat for the property industry in the sense of a combined rescue operation by the banks or the larger and stronger property groups. But as the property crisis mounted, the Bank of England encouraged the banks, as far as possible, to temper the wind to certain of their more vulnerable property customers and to hold off from pushing them into collapse by appointing receivers as they would have been entitled to do when the borrowers could not pay interest or principal due. The banks concerned generally complied and frequently rolled up (deferred) interest, often also channelling in major additional loans to give hard-pressed property concerns the means of completing and selling developments. Retrenchment, of course, had to be the keynote for problem-vexed property companies, as for secondary banks, and this meant their selling off many existing and newly-completed properties to repay debt.

To encourage a market for all this bricks and mortar, the Bank of England did much to bring information about available properties to the attention of the big institutional investors – the insurance groups and pension funds – whom they aimed to coax into giving this type of purchase a good place in their portfolios, in order to relieve the scarcity of long-term financing for the heavy programme of property development begun in the boom years. Altogether in the four years from 1975 to 1978 inclusive, the big institutions invested in property to the tune of £4392 m; this was £2276 m greater than the £2116 m which they spent in this way in the previous four years.[2] Thus were property companies which had previously raced to expand, and secondary banks to which property had accrued as security for unrepaid loans, able over time to divest themselves of major property assets in exchange for cash. The institutions naturally looked for good buys and they picked up some valuable properties. The National Coal Board pension funds, for instance, which had been investing £30–40 m in property each year, stepped this figure up to £100 m of property acquisitions in the year from June 1974 and is now showing good gains on those purchases.

The reasoning behind this quietly-conducted campaign to ease the worst stresses in the property field – one inspiration of which was an appraisal by Sir Kenneth Cork – was that a widespread collapse of property companies and the resounding crash from the unloading of their assets on to the market by liquidators would have wrecked the already tottering property market, with further dire consequences, too, for the fringe banks.

Nor would the damage have stopped there, for such a catastrophe would have undermined the value of the investing institutions' existing holdings of property. It might also have threatened insurance companies' solvency margins. As it was, some smaller insurance concerns must have been precious near to the danger level at the end of 1974 – which was to be the nadir of the crisis – given the slide which had by then taken place in share, as well as property, values; it is perhaps as well that some smaller insurance concerns' valuations for balance sheet purposes were not made until after share prices had bounced up sharply early in 1975. Given the prevailing atmosphere, it is thus scarcely surprising that, from early December 1974, Prudential Assurance and five other large insurance companies should have undertaken an exceptional pump-priming stock market share-buying operation[3] which certainly had a dramatic sequel after a short interval: in the fifteen business days after touching a 20-year low of 6 January 1975, the *Financial Times* 30 share index had rallied by no less than 64 per cent.

The thinking which prompted the Bank of England-sponsored moves by the larger banks and financial institutions to help the property world over the crisis also led to the 'Cork's dam' scheme, which Sir Kenneth Cork conducted, with the Bank of England's blessing, to handle the selling off of the properties in the large property empire of Mr William Stern after it had crumbled in May 1974. Again, the principle was that there should not be an uncontrolled off-loading of properties on to a fragile market: its translation into practice involved the creditors clubbing together in an agreement under which the numerous Stern companies were held back from immediate liquidation and the sale of the properties was, broadly, restricted to the current demand so that they only flowed on to the market at such a rate as to fetch acceptable prices.

Hungarian-born Mr Stern, a lawyer who was educated in the USA (of which he is a citizen) but lives in London, epitomised the many who in the early 1970s thought property would hold its value and the bold few who backed this belief with expansion on a major scale. The private group he built up after parting company in business terms in 1971 with his stepfather-in-law, Mr Osias Freshwater – one of London's largest private landlords – consisted in May 1974 of about 180 companies, including some abroad, one of them a large house-building concern in Israel. Some 40 of the 180 were active, 25 being engaged in property development. The group also included the Nation Life Insurance concern, specialising in property bonds, and the First Maryland fringe bank, a section 123 company, which was for a time helped through the Lifeboat.

Assets of the Stern group had been put at £163 m in draft accounts for mid-1973 of the holding company, Wilstar Securities. They afterwards increased to an apparent £200 m or more, though by May 1974 there was a huge question mark over all values. On the other side of the account, there were heavy borrowings. There was some £180 m on loan from about 40 banks and financial institutions, including some of the largest British and American banks, the Crown Agents and a number of secondary and other banks. Many borrowings were secured on properties of the Stern empire, and had been advanced by major British and American banks, including International Marine (part of the US group Marine Midland Banks), which lent £10 m and was accorded a floating debenture over the Stern group assets. More than £100 m of the loans were personally guaranteed by Mr Stern. Some of the loans thus guaranteed were very substantial ones owing to secondary and certain other smaller banks. They included[4] £11.48 m owed to A. P. Bank (formerly Anglo-Portuguese Bank), £9.80 m to First National Finance Corporation, £1.98 m to Grindlays Brandts, £1.75 m to Grindlays Bank (Scotland) (formerly British Bank of Commerce), £20.5 m to Keyser Ullmann, £1.96 m to Knowsley, £1.75 m to Sterling Industrial Securities, £4.44 m to Trade Development Bank and £3.95 m to Whiteaway Laidlaw, part of Sir Isaac Wolfson's interests, as Anglo-Portuguese Bank also was at that time.

When the Stern group foundered with the collapse in the value of properties, Mr Stern's basic assumptions had been exploded. 'I believed property would hold its value and I was geared (borrowed) up to, in round terms, £180 m', he remarked some years later. Of the general property slump in 1974 he added, 'It was equivalent to walking out of the house and, before you reach the corner, there is an earthquake. It was not capable of being foreseen. Some buildings were sold afterwards at 40 per cent of their previous values and sites for only 20 per cent or so.'[5]

The effective crumbling of the Stern empire in May 1974 came only after many millions of pounds of further loans had been vainly poured in in efforts to save it. Interest on the Stern borrowings was running at about three times the group's income, excluding surpluses on sales, and, with the property market and financial markets going sour, some creditors were, by early 1974, getting nervous about their security. Support loans of £13 m were provided by the Crown Agents, already a lender to the Stern companies, and £7 m more was put up by the National Westminster Bank, making some £27 m from that group. By April 1974, the Agents had £35 m on loan to the Stern group, the argument within the Agents' organisation having been that they were so deeply committed as to be in danger of themselves being dragged down by the Stern group's downfall. By May–June, the figure had reached £40 m; this debt afterwards rose, with unpaid interest, to the remarkable figure of £54 m by 1978.

By the spring of 1974, other Stern creditors were getting restive and in early April Mr Stern consulted the Bank of England, then frantically monitoring the general property emergency. The Bank at first 'used its persuasive powers to assist' according to the Fay committee.[6] Both the Agents and the National Westminster Bank gave a limited amount more credit, but at the same time the City accountants Peat Marwick Mitchell were called in to look at the Stern group. Peats reported on 6 May, and on 9 May Mr Stern was referred to W. H. Cork Gully, the conclusion by then being that the creditors would not channel in the further large sums needed to keep the group afloat. Wilstar Securities was put into liquidation on 6 June; the hour had struck for the urgent construction of 'Cork's dam'.

The dam-building went ahead rapidly. In July 1974 some 50 Stern creditors were called by Sir Kenneth Cork to a meeting and asked to back a moratorium 'so that their affairs could be dealt with and their assets realised for the common benefit of all . . . in an orderly and economical manner'. A large majority agreed. In the following year the pact was incorporated more formally into a scheme of arrangement, imposing 'control and restraint'.[7] Its key features were that the participating creditors agreed not to call in receivers to Stern companies on whose property they held charges, nor to charge penal interest rates, as they would have been entitled to; they also agreed to give the scheme's administrator prior notice of any intended sales of property charged to them and, generally, suitable provision was also included to encourage the channelling in of more funds to complete developments left part-finished by the crash. A special fund to finance the scheme was to be financed from levies of 10 per cent of rent receipts and 1.5 per cent of sales proceeds. In the arrangements the special position of International Marine as the holder of a floating debenture was recognised. Again, the great majority of the creditors agreed.

The purpose of the prior consultation on sales was to give Sir Kenneth Cork, as administrator of the scheme, the right to say if a proposed sale price was too low, and likely to depress the market. The fragile condition of the property market at the time was illustrated by the opinion in April 1975 of the chartered surveyors quoted in the relevant documents that, since a valuation of May 1974, 'the completed properties held as investments may generally have fallen in value by amounts of the order of 30 per cent', while 'no substantial market exists today for the development properties'. Mr Stern later recalled, to the author, that an earlier valuation at the time of his group's crisis in the spring of 1974 had shown that the commercial property and sites in the group had by then already fallen by 20 per cent compared with 1973 boom values.

Sir Kenneth reflected afterwards about 'Cork's dam': 'It was the only scheme of its kind ever produced. The idea was that if you have £200 m of property to dispose of in those conditions, you can sell £1 m if £199 m is held off the market. The properties weren't put on the market with a price. At that time, if a building was offered at £1m, it went down to £0.75 m or £0.5 m. The arrangement was that, if there was an offer, the mortgagee could accept it but he could not offer the property publicly on the market with a price tag. The mortgagees never gave up their right of sale. All we had the right to do was to say that, if the price was wrong, they should wait a month or two.'[8]

Most of the sales made subsequently were carried out in close consultation with Cork Gully. By 1979 some 90 per cent of the properties had been disposed of, those remaining chiefly being undeveloped sites. But secured creditors had generally only got some 50 per cent of what was owed them, because of sales made earlier at less favourable prices than were obtainable after the property market's rally in the late-1970s.

Following a petition by one large creditor, Keyser Ullmann, Mr Stern was declared bankrupt in 1978 with debts of more than £104 m, the overwhelmingly greater part of which had arisen from his guarantees of his companies' borrowings.

As the property industry went through the traumatic years 1974–6, when the market was so fragile and in parts hardly existent, several larger, quoted property companies in due course came to grief – some after special efforts had been made to save them – though most struggled through the worst crisis ever known with greater or less difficulty. For a number of those which had expanded most swiftly, a lengthy process of de-gearing – reducing borrowings by cash sales of assets – took place over several years as an eventually reviving market made this possible. In this process the investing institutions, with their more active buying of property, helped greatly, as already noted, and the big banks continued to give important support by renewing and increasing their loans, and often deferring interest; this enabled buildings to be finished and held until sales could be made, and the long climb back to recovery ultimately achieved. The sums thus deployed by financial institutions in ways not expected before the crisis ran into many hundreds of millions of pounds.

In some property companies capital was reorganised to reduce the debt burden and so make continued operation and recovery possible. Not infrequently the existence of large foreign currency loans which had been raised to finance British property companies' major invasion of the continent of Europe in the early 1970s meant yet further burdens on property companies as the pound fell heavily in the mid-1970s.

One company which went under, being put into voluntary liquidation in late-1976 after lengthy struggles to survive, was Town and Commercial Properties. A big stake in the company had been held by Charles Spreckley Industries, the quoted group of which control was acquired around the end of 1973 by Cambourne Securities, the private company of Mr Jack Walker and Mr Ramon Greene, who had made £16 m profit some months earlier from their first English and Continental property venture with the Crown Agents. Charles Spreckley Industries itself, which had borrowed more than £15 m from Slater Walker – which was obliged to make heavy provisions on this debt – had had a receiver appointed to it in February 1976.

Another, larger, concern, Amalgamated Investment and Property, whose assets had been put at £220 m near the height of the money boom, failed in 1976 after more credit had been pumped in by its bankers in 1975; its deficiency, after large guarantees, was estimated at £198 m. The Senior Official Receiver's later report with the AIP statement of affairs is worth pausing over, for it vividly highlights some of the problems of the era. 'In the opinion of the Official Receiver the failure was due primarily to misjudged investments in the property sector, largely on borrowed money, exacerbated by the recession in the property market which led in many cases to mortgage advances being not fully covered by assets', says the report.[9] The following, quoted as the observations of senior company officers, explains the position further and encapsulates much of the trouble in the hardest hit part of the property sector. 'From 1971 onwards credit became very much easier and money for property investment was freely available from the institutions. . . . Most of the money borrowed . . . was for terms of up to 5 years and it was anticipated that within the 5 year period it would be possible to arrange alternative longer term finance.' Reference is then made to the company's having, in 1972/73, undertaken three developments, estimated to cost £20 m in Paris, including a 35-storey office block, but to the market there having become depressed, while costs had escalated; the consequence had been that the company's liability under its guarantee of its subsidiary's borrowings from French banks could be very substantial. Then, as to the British business, the report says that: 'in November 1973 there was a sudden collapse of confidence in the property market and it became impossible to replace the company's short-term finance with longer term finance . . . and it even became difficult to draw on the existing short-term facilities because property values fell drastically. . . . It was necessary to "top up" existing security and the institutions would not accept new development projects . . . there was also a very rapid rise in interest rates and in building costs and the investment yield which the institutions sought to achieve rose from 4.5 per cent in some cases to 8 per cent or 9 per cent. . . . The solvency of the company was brought into question because so much depended on property values and . . . it was impossible to be sure about valuations when there were no buyers'.

A further large business to which receivers were appointed, in June 1975, after additional bank credit had been provided in the crisis years, was Northern Developments Holdings, which was one of Britain's largest house-builders and which was chaired by the former Blackburn Rovers footballer Mr Derek Barnes, a large shareholder.

The collapse of the property market also brought down the unquoted David Lewis group, which had large borrowings of over £60 m, against assets which had been put at the height of the boom at a total value of some £90 m but which were not to prove worth anything like that figure in the slump. The assets included a few sites but consisted mostly of a number of considerable London buildings. Of the borrowings, £20 m was long-term and at fixed interest, but a great deal was bank money, geared to interest rates which had soared. 'We had intended, as was our standard policy, to get long-term institutional finance to refinance this', Mr Lewis afterwards recalled.[10] But by 1974, the investing institutions had become very shy about their lending. A combination of optimistically high borrowing, soaring interest rates which left current outgoings well below income, and crumbling property values precipitated the crisis in a way which exemplified what happened at some other companies. 'One had not been cool enough to recognise that values had gone too high and one had been tempted to borrow at two-thirds or 70 per cent of values', Mr Lewis remembered. 'Cash flow became so negative we had to start selling properties. But with the rent freeze extension in May 1974 the market became paralysed. By the last quarter of 1974 we couldn't pay bank interest and by then the market was such that you couldn't sell at any price. Your traditional safety-valve – to sell assets – was extinguished'.[11]

As to the general position of the David Lewis group, 'the minus quantity was substantial', says Mr Lewis: it was probably around £20 m. The assets were gradually sold off, Mr Lewis playing a significant part in this process as agent of the creditor banks. 'My personal obligations were resolved with each bank when the majority of the realisations were completed', he said later. Inevitably, as in a number of other cases, the lending banks were substantial losers. A document issued in 1979 by Estates & Agency Holdings, into which family interests of Mr Lewis later injected some properties against a sizeable shareholding, noted, after referring to his role in the build-up of the successful Cavendish Land and its subsequent sale (in 1973): 'His [Mr Lewis's] own private property investments were however lost as a result of the financial and property crisis in 1974 and certain lending banks incurred very substantial losses.' The family trusts holding part of the profit from the Cavendish Land sale, being outside Mr Lewis's ownership, were not called on for the settlements with the banks; from 1975 to 1976 these contributed capital for new property ventures by Mr Lewis on behalf of his family interests.

A big property company which went through a lengthy process of de-gearing was Capital and Counties Property which, from the difficult days of the mid-1970s, reversed an earlier growth trend and reduced its debt from some £271 m in 1975 to £43 m in 1978 following a programme of disposals including the sale of the major Knightsbridge Estate to British Petroleum's pension fund for £45 m. It is interesting to note that C & C had been the Crown Agents' partner in their controversial move into the Australian property world. That venture turned sour when the property recession also struck 'down under' and the Agents were estimated in 1977 to be facing losses of more than £33 m on their Australian property business where they were responsible for providing the bulk of the finance.

A property group which fought its way through a period of financial difficulties is British Land. It carried out £40 m of sales in 1975–7 but avoided the need to sell the bulk of its holdings, including the big Plantation House in the City of London, because of a refinancing package in 1977. A limited watering down of existing shareholders' interest was involved. Backing the refinancing plan, the chairman, Mr John Ritblat, remarked that the alternative of liquidation would involve massive forced sales of the whole portfolio. In 1978/79 the group again made profits after five years of losses.

The biggest of all the property companies hard pressed by the crisis was the rapidly-expanded Town and City (T & C) with wide interests including the Arndale centres and many other properties. Town and City's assets following its growth phase were some £600 m, but when property values crumbled in 1974 the company's large borrowings posed severe problems. These were accentuated by the fact that long-term

funds were not already fixed up to replace short-term bank financing of
some developments. In the boom it had sometimes been assumed by
property people that long-term funding would always be readily
obtainable, a supposition which the crisis of 1974 invalidated. T & C was
also suffering a revenue deficit, mainly because the cost of its borrowings
to finance the £97 m acquisition of Central and District Properties from
Keyser Ullmann Holdings was higher than the income from that
company's low-yielding reversionary properties.

In 1974 T & C acquired Mr Jeffrey Sterling's Sterling Guarantee Trust
and Mr Sterling became chairman of the combined group in the same
year, afterwards presiding over a long haul back towards recovery. In
1975, Barclays Bank and Prudential Assurance channelled £25 m into T
& C, against convertible loan stock, and in 1978 a further major
refinancing operation was carried through, with Barclays and the
Prudential again participating. De-gearing on a massive scale gradually
took place, with sales of £375 m between April 1974 and July 1980
leading to big reductions in borrowings, which, net of cash balances, fell
from £318 m in 1976 to £188 m in 1980.

In the harsh climate, there was also some shifting of property interests
from individuals to the large investing institutions. For instance,
towards the end of 1974 the millionaire property man Mr Harry Hyams
sold a major holding in his private Oldham Estates to the Co-operative
Insurance Society, a subsidiary of the Co-operative Wholesale Society,
for an estimated £27 m.[12] The deal raised Co-operative Insurance's
stake to above the controlling 50 per cent level and reduced that of Mr
Hyams' to around 32 per cent.

In such ways were the troubles in the property industry to be
painstakingly handled over the years ahead, after the crisis struck in the
spring of 1974. The impact of that upheaval on the secondary banks is,
however, the chief point of significance for this narrative, which will
return to events in the secondary banking world as the tension mounted
there. First, however, a brief glance is to be taken at the shocks which
were running through the banking community internationally, and the
response to them, in the summer of that troubled year, 1974.

9 The Lifeboat Idea Internationally

The Bank [of England] was simultaneously coping, together with its partner central banks in other countries, with an unrelated crisis among international banks operating in the Euro-currency markets. That crisis had its seeds in malpractices or inefficiencies in banks adapting themselves to foreign exchange dealing in a sea of floating rates. It was basically a crisis of confidence, not of bad lending, and was more quickly overcome.

Mr George Blunden,
Director of the Bank of England,
discussing the recent crises, in 1976.[1]

While Britain was grappling with her secondary bank and property crises, the international banking world experienced some shocks which called for remedial action and led to closer and lasting co-operation among central banks in monitoring the health of the worldwide financial system. The difficulties were partly attributable to the problems of adjustment to floating exchange rates in the early 1970s and to strains in the Euromarkets in the harsher economic climate following the major round of oil price increases. But sometimes the trouble was more fundamental and lay in problems at individual banks.

One of the first symptoms of difficulties outside Britain came late in 1973 at the West German Hessische Landesbank, which incurred large losses and was set on the path of subsequent strong recovery by its shareholders, the State of Hesse and the Hesse Savings banks association, the latter in turn receiving backing from other West German savings banks.

The collapse in the autumn of 1973 of the US National Bank of San Diego, run by President Nixon's friend, Mr C. Arnholt Smith, caused concern to the many international banks with loans outstanding to it. Then, Franklin National Bank, the American group which had a stake in the Crown Agents-backed British fringe bank Sterling Industrial

Securities, hit a crisis from the early summer of 1974, along with the related Italian empire of the controversial financier Signor Michele Sindona, who was later to be convicted in the US of fraud in connection with Franklin National's affairs.

Shocks of a different kind arose when large losses on foreign exchange business were also reported in 1974 by three leading European banks, Union Bank of Switzerland, one of the Swiss Big Three, Westdeutsche Landesbank, of West Germany, and Lloyds Bank of Britain, through a Swiss branch. All these major banks, however, had the size and strength to absorb the blows satisfactorily.

This fraught summer and autumn of 1974 also brought crises at two secondary banks with Israeli connections. One was the Swiss-based International Credit Bank (ICB) of Geneva. The other was Israel-British Bank, a concern based in Tel Aviv but with a British subsidiary, Israel-British Bank (London), an authorised bank, which in turn controlled two insurance companies and had a stake of nearly 30 per cent in a property concern, London City & Westcliff Properties.

ICB was headed by Hungarian-born Mr Tibor Rosenbaum (a brother-in-law of the British property tycoon Mr William Stern), who was treasurer of the World Jewish Congress and a director of the millionaire-backed Israel Corporation, set up to finance Israel's industrial development. Mr Rosenbaum was respected for his activities in helping fellow-Jews to escape from the Nazis in the Second World War; he also arranged deals for the Israeli Government.[2] However, his bank was regarded as going in for high-risk investments. A 36.4 per cent stake in ICB was held by Hessische Landesbank, which was hardly helped at the time by the connection.

Israel-British Bank (IBB) was run by the two sons-in-law of the late Walter Nathan Williams, the Israeli parent company by Mr Joshua Bension and the British subsidiary by Mr Harry Landy, a former vice-president of the Board of Deputies of British Jews.

The parent company reached a crisis early in July 1974 and was placed in liquidation not long afterwards. Israel-British Bank (London) suspended payments on 11 July. The Israeli authorities prosecuted Mr Bension, who was convicted and imprisoned in Israel. In 1979, Mr Landy was jailed in Britain after being found guilty of conspiracy to defraud and of conspiracy to utter forged documents. However, in January 1981 the appeals of Mr Landy and of two others sentenced with him were allowed by the Court of Appeal and their convictions quashed.

In his Appeal judgment, Lord Justice Lawton said that when IBB (London) had stopped payments in July 1974, it owed £37.1 m to eighty-five banks, £4 m to members of the Williams family and to companies in the Williams group and £1.8 m to other depositors. Most of the debts owed to IBB (London) by companies in Leichtenstein, which had been formed by the late Mr Williams, and other debts from members of the Williams family and companies in the Williams group, proved to have little value. The deficit in July 1974 was about £38 m but since then considerable sums had been obtained from Mr Landy and the Williams interests. All small depositors and charities had been repaid in full; the larger creditors were likely to be paid a dividend of about 40p in the £.

The foreign-owned Israel-British Bank (London) was not in the Lifeboat, so its depositors were not protected like those of other fringe banks. But, in order somewhat to increase the limited sum available for creditors after the crash of the IBB group, the Bank of England contributed £3 m to the pool for distribution by the liquidators to the creditors of the twin Israeli and British concerns, while the Bank of Israel subordinated (effectively wiped out) a claim it had in respect of a DM30 m (£7.5 m) deposit with IBB(L). In this case the crash came before central banks had accepted the principle of 'parental responsibility' shortly to be described.

By far the most resounding crash in 1974 was the collapse in June of the prominent West German private bank Bankhaus I.D.Herstatt. Great was the fall of the house of Herstatt and greater still were the repercussions of the collapse. The closure of the bank by the West German authorities at 3.30 on the afternoon of 26 June – still banking hours in the US and elsewhere – left important foreign exchange deals half completed and heavy debts owing to a large number of international banks, including many leading names. Hill Samuel, the London merchant bank and accepting house, initially faced a loss of DM55 m (£9 m or $21.5 m), and other banks substantial ones. Herstatt, which had been dealing extensively in foreign exchange and precious metals, proved to have losses in the region of DM 1200 m. In the end, Herstatt's private creditors were to receive 65 per cent of their claims, and German and foreign banks and public authorities 55 per cent. Eventually, and after lengthy legal battles, Hill Samuel's net loss was no more than £1.2 m.

The collapse sent more powerful currents of shock through the international banking system than at any time since the early 1930s. It led banks to adopt a much more defensive policy on foreign exchange deals – some deciding for the time being to handle nothing but cash-down transactions – and, in the huge Euro-dollar market, prompted a precautionary flight of deposits from many banks outside the ranks of the leaders. For months afterwards the Euro-dollar market remained subdued, interest rates in it jumped sharply and the values of Euro-dollar bonds against which various British secondary banks and other second-line borrowers had raised money plummetted dramatically.

That the new Herstatt-induced crisis did not escalate into an emergency of 1930s dimensions is largely thanks to swift co-operative action taken by the world's leading central banks on the initiative to a considerable extent of the Governor of the Bank of England, Mr Richardson, who had had recent experience through the Lifeboat of just such a problem of crumbling confidence.

What Mr Richardson propounded to his fellow Governors from the world's leading industrial nations at their monthly meeting in Basle in July 1974, was, in effect, the idea of a partial internationalisation of the Lifeboat concept in its protective aspect. More specifically, the principle put forward was that parent banks should accept responsibility for the well-being of their offshoots the world over and that supervisory authorities should interest themselves in this being done.

This principle of 'parental responsibility' did not command instant acceptance by all. But, for the sake of bolstering confidence, the Governors at once let it be known that they were agreed on the idea of assisting at least sound banks within their own countries which were facing difficulties through losses in the turbulent foreign exchange markets. This was to be translated some months later into an acceptance that it was the duty of central banks to provide lender-of-last-resort facilities, if required, to their own banks to secure the safety of their operations in the Euro-currency markets.[3] It is worth noting that this understanding was to be an important factor in the Bank of England's later decision to support Slater Walker, which had £75 m of Euro-currency market borrowings.

The central bank chiefs quickly realised that, over the previous fifteen years or so, the world banking scene had become peopled with large banking groups whose tentacles stretched into many countries through subsidiary companies, branches and participations in consortium banks. The same thinking therefore led them on within the succeeding year to accept the principle 'that a bank or banking group has responsibility for its activities throughout the world – whether through branches, subsidiary companies or joint ventures – where the parent bank's name is involved'[4] as was recalled afterwards by Mr Richardson. Equally, it was 'agreed that the supervisory authority in the country where a banking group's head office is located should assume primary responsibility for monitoring the whole of that group's activities'.

The initial understandings were rather more formalised at the meeting of the governors in September 1974, though there remained differences of view about how far any less deserving prospective bank casualties should be helped; some countries were reluctant to agree to anything like blanket support of all banks, good and not so good. However, there was broad acceptance of the need to mitigate the adverse consequences of any difficulties in particular banks. While the new approach did not mean that central banks would always act to stem bank failures within their own territories, particularly where there were few international implications, it appears to have led to a fresh sensitivity on the part of several of them to the need for more positive action to sort out any domestic banking problems, in one way or another.

These important decisions can be seen both as an extension of the spirit of earlier co-operative action, through loans between central banks, to help ailing currencies in the fixed exchange rate era, and as a recognition of the need for more official surveillance of banking businesses worldwide, in view of the great growth of bank groups internationally and the vast expansion of the Euro-dollar market.

Describing his *démarche* of July 1974 three-and-a-half years later to a House of Commons Select Committee, Mr Richardson said: 'after the Herstatt collapse, when I went to Basle in July, I went thinking that what I had to do was to arrive at a system of international responsibility, to discover how the responsibility between central banks should be shared internationally, because business had become so international. . . . The principle arrived at was [that] of parental responsibility, that the parent and therefore its central bank should have responsibility for the branches and subsidiaries and I think that was accepted'.[5] That there was some detectable swing subsequently away from an attitude of laissez-faire on the part of other leading central banks was suggested by Mr Richardson's further remark that 'the attitude of the German authorities changed in consequence of Herstatt' and that in September 1974 they 'set up a special organisation to help with the liquidity of banks in difficulties'.

Sir Jasper Hollom also commented to the Select Committee that as earlier action had not prevented bank failures, 'in the very recent cases the Federal Reserve Bank (of the US) has certainly felt impelled to act in a way rather similar to ourselves'. Evidence of the depth of the stresses in the US banking system at that troubled time, but also of the close watch maintained by the American supervisory authorities, came when, in late

1974, the Comptroller of the Currency announced that as many as 150 of the country's banking institutions were under close scrutiny.[6] In the winter of 1974/75 the problems were kept on the boil by recurrent troubles among the United States' much expanded real estate investment trusts (REITS), concerns which could be seen as a kind of amalgam of those in the troubled British property and secondary bank sectors.

The central banks' new principle of parental responsibility naturally stimulated improvements in supervisory techniques. One of the first moves was the establishment under British chairmanship – that of a Bank of England director, Mr George Blunden – of the Basle-based Committee on Banking Regulations and Supervisory Practices, afterwards called the Standing Committee of Banking Supervisory Authorities, on which are represented the group of ten leading industrial countries plus the very banking-oriented Switzerland and Luxembourg. This active group of twelve, whose chairmanship later passed to Mr Peter Cooke of the Bank of England, has been the first exercise in international co-operation in banking supervision. But it does not aspire to be a supra-national authority. It studies and exchanges views on supervisory techniques, maintains an early warning system about possible impending troubles in the banking world, and arranges guidelines about the main division of responsibility among national supervisors for monitoring the health of banks.

Largely as a result of the collective approach agreed on in the summer of 1974, there were no massive uncontrolled banking crashes – such as the domino collapses of the early 1930s in the US – following the major failure of Herstatt in June 1974. Moreover, central bankers, while holding somewhat differing views about the extent of protection which is justified in cases of threatened disaster, have since been more concerned than previously to see that troubled banking situations are approached or handled with a view to limiting the damaging consequences.

It is not to be assumed that, with the vast growth of international banking and of the Euro-currency markets, the defences against new troubles are impregnable. The Governor of the Bank of England told a conference in July 1979: 'it would, I feel, be prudent for those who work in the supervisory area to be alert to the possibility that the resilience of the international banking system may be tested again in the next few years'.[7] Nonetheless, progress has been made and a preliminary framework put in place in the international context for confronting future crises.

Britain's follow-up to the international combined protection move in July 1974 was rapid. The Bank of England proceeded to seek – and get – assurances of any necessary support from the overseas parents of foreign-owned British banking companies and branches: similar 'comfort letters' were obtained from the various partner shareholders of consortium banks. Action on some of these was needed before long. In the panicky post-Herstatt atmosphere, deposits which flowed out from some such concerns were replaced by funds channelled in from overseas parent and shareholder banks. For instance, Western American Bank (Europe), whose shareholders included Hambros Bank and four foreign banks (Bank of Tokyo, and three US groups, National Bank of Detroit, Security Pacific National Bank and Wells Fargo) was hit by a flight of deposits and by troubles in its Eurobond business. Shareholder banks provided large short-term borrowing facilities and bought out £191 m of its loans. The restored company came under the control of Bank of Tokyo in 1977 and is now known as Bank of Tokyo International. Some other consortium banks had to call on parent shareholder banks for funds, sometimes running into hundreds of millions of dollars, to compensate for a widespread outflow of deposits. These calls were generally met with little hesitation, although the need for them added to the crisis atmosphere and to the dampening, for many months, of confidence in the Euro-markets.

Thus, within a few weeks, the quite alarming separate international dimension of the crisis had been brought under reasonable control. But by then, the next anxiety in the traumatic year of 1974 arose as Britain's bankers' Lifeboat suddenly faced the need to have a much heavier weight of passengers on board as the crisis waves, whipped by the Herstatt affair, swept up and threatened to overwhelm large concerns previously less harmed by them.

10 Crisis Climax and Turn of the Tide

Before the Chancellor of the Exchequer was perhaps out of his bed we had advanced one half of our reserves.

> Launcelot Holland, Governor of the Bank of England,
> on the 1866 Overend and Gurney crisis, quoted by
> Walter Bagehot in *Lombard Street*, 1873

As the property crisis developed from the early summer of 1974 and the international scene was darkened soon after by shocks such as the Herstatt crash, the scale of Britain's secondary bank problem expanded dramatically. Calls on the Lifeboat grew worryingly, with total support loans increasing by £53 m in the second quarter to £443 m and by a further £551 m to £994 m by the end of September.

Alarm touched off by the property upheaval heightened the nervousness of depositors with secondary banks which were heavily committed to the property sector, such as First National Finance Corporation. These banks looked to the Lifeboat for large additional loans to replace the market deposits they could not retain. Various other banking companies, so far from being able to win back market deposit finance, increased their Lifeboat borrowings and a few more concerns, notably Keyser Ullmann and Edward Bates, both listed banks, were obliged to seek Lifeboat help.

United Dominions Trust, then the country's largest finance house, with the status of a listed bank and £1255 m of gross assets – including large lending to housebuilders – had to turn to the Lifeboat for very big sums as the summer went on. The Bank of England, which had itself put up capital for UDT for a period of years from 1932, at first provided the group with a facility of some £10–15 m for borrowing from itself. When this was exhausted, the Lifeboat took over the financing; by October, it had about £500 m on loan to UDT.

As the clearers became more anxious about their commitments, the

Governor of the Bank of England, Mr Richardson – in line with the policy of seeking back-up support from large shareholders of affected financial concerns – called Mr Kenneth Usherwood, chairman of the large Prudential Assurance, and Mr Edward Hatchett, the Prudential's former investment chief and later a director of UDT, into consultation in July. The Prudential held 26.5 per cent of UDT, largely bought in 1972 from Barclays Bank in a deal which proved well-timed for the latter; Eagle Star Insurance owned another 10 per cent. The Governor wanted the two investing institutions to channel new capital into UDT. This was agreed and some weeks later the two institutions provided the bulk of £30 m (£20 m of it paid up immediately) against new convertible subordinated unsecured loan stock in UDT. In subscribing for this stock, whose terms avoided putting burdensome new claims on UDT, the institutions did all that was requested of them; however, some of the clearing banks felt that, in view of the mounting calls on their own organisations, still more might have been asked of them.

The growing calls of UDT and other borrowers focused the clearers' worries about the expanding scale and changing nature of the Lifeboat operation and prompted them to seek an alteration in the open-ended character of their commitment to it. By August 1974, it was clear that the combined rescue, initially conceived of as a short-term cash re-cycling exercise, was proving a far graver undertaking. It was not only that the total of support lending was rising rapidly. Property and share markets were declining and it was becoming clear that at an increasing number of secondary banks the value of property-related and other assets was shrinking to the point of raising doubts about the company's solvency.

Moreover, the big banks were discontented with the efforts so far made by many assisted secondary concerns to restore their own fortunes. True, a number had cut back or halted the taking on of new business, but management changes had been relatively few; support loans also were being taken rather too much for granted by some borrowers and there was too much an atmosphere of 'business as usual' at one or two large fringe banks to suit the feelings of the clearing groups.

The clearers looked at the £1000 m-plus deposit base of the largest passenger, UDT, and saw the possibility of the Lifeboat fund mounting, with the new calls on it, from the £1000 m which it was already nearing, to £2000 m; its commitments were already close to £1200 m, which was equivalent to two-fifths of the capital and reserves of the English and Scottish clearing banks. These large commercial banks, the main backbone of Britain's banking industry, had now to watch out that their own businesses should not be threatened; the time for a stand had come – and the moment was seized.

The clearing bank chairmen and their top officials met in August 1974 under their new chairman, Sir John Prideaux, head of the National Westminster Bank, who in April had succeeded Sir Eric Faulkner of Lloyds Bank as chairman of the Committee of London Clearing Banks. They recalled that they had recognised the need to take part in the Lifeboat operation for the sake of the whole UK banking system but were now concerned to ensure that confidence in the clearing banks themselves was not endangered nor their own depositors put in any jeopardy. Their commitment to the Lifeboat had to be kept down to a proper proportion of their capital and reserves and limited so that it did not encroach on their ordinary lending business.

On 19 August 1974 Sir John Prideaux met Sir Jasper Hollom, the Bank of England's Deputy Governor, who was receptive to the idea that a line should be drawn, in the interests of banking prudence, to the clearers' Lifeboat commitment. The figure of £1200 m was felt to be an appropriate maximum for joint support of the secondary banking system at shared risk and after a few days' further discussion, this limit was agreed on.[1] The implication was that the Bank of England, which as central bank is supremely concerned with the health of the banking system, would itself take responsibility for any necessary later rescues. Consequently, no secondary banks running into crisis for the first time were dealt with through the Lifeboat after the autumn of 1974.

The reappraisal of August 1974 not only set a limit to the size of the Lifeboat operation but led to a new toughness in the administration of the whole combined support campaign. In short, an effort was made to lighten ship: there was less readiness to provide additional help to those for whom there seemed little hope of long-term survival. Greater efforts were also made to encourage the take-over by large British or foreign banking groups of supported secondary banks along with the Lifeboat loans to them. The Lifeboat's crew of senior bankers also began to press more insistently for changes in the boards and managements of supported companies. In addition, they urged the slimming down of secondary and fringe banks' loan and investment portfolios through sales to generate cash for repayment of support loans, so far as was possible in the prevailing depressed business climate.

But it was some months before the altered policy was fully apparent. As further effects of the greatly increased world oil prices were felt, the financial atmosphere in Britain and the world became increasingly dark and confidence more fragile, creating a need for much caution in the handling of the fringe bank situation if new alarms and uncertainties were not to be created.

The last quarter of 1974 was one of the most troubled periods in recent decades for Britain's business community generally. Industrial and commercial companies suffered their worst cash squeeze for years, their troubles being accentuated by the new Labour Government's Spring Budget, which had increased Corporation Tax. All this depressed share prices, which declined to their lowest real level for 20 years; by early January 1975, the *Financial Times* 30 share index had sunk to 146.0 (1935 = 100), a tumble of 73 per cent from its 1972 peak. Property values continued their decline, bringing more acute worries not only for property companies and secondary banks which were heavily committed to property but for the major banks which themselves had large property lending and were often, as noted above, having to extend its scale and duration. At this difficult time, it was some comfort that the pound held up relatively well, helped by the inflow of deposits from the newly-rich oil nations, and that inflation had not yet soared as it was to in the following two years.

It is worth pausing here to note several remarkable events near the end of 1974 which were symptomatic of the highly disturbed atmosphere of of the time. One occurred when the National Westminster Bank, one of the Big Four clearers, became the subject of rumours that it had problems itself. In the severe stock market slump, many shares had dropped to below their nominal value, among them the £1 shares of the National Westminster which, on 29 November, fell to only 88p. A statement, which was one of the many unprecedented events of this dangerous time, was made that day by Sir John Prideaux, the National Westminster's chairman, to the effect that current rumours that the bank was receiving support from the Bank of England were without foundation.

The National Westminster Bank had been created through the merger five years earlier of two banks, the National Provincial and the Westminster, both with a large business in the City of London. Consequently the combined group was the main clearing bank to many smaller banks, including a considerable number of secondary and fringe banks. This led to some unsympathetic comment at the time about the number of hard-pressed secondary banks to which it was the principal banker. The National Westminster group had itself shown fast growth in the boom period of the early 1970s, when it was active in developing the modern trend of liabilities management by vigorous 'buying' of deposits in the wholesale markets. The bank's embarking on the construction of its massive International Westminster skyscraper in the City also looked venturesome at the end of 1974, though this building seems certain to prove a most valuable investment. The late-1974 outcrop of rumour had, however, focused particularly on suggestions of possible losses to the National Westminster Bank as an indirect result of the Sindona affair. At all events, the open denial by Sir John Prideaux put paid to the potentially dangerous rumours and by the end of January the group's shares had rebounded, in the market revival, to almost double their November low at 153p.

Looking back on the episode, Sir John afterwards recalled, in 1979: 'During 1974 there was an increasing feeling of unease in the financial world as a whole, and in London the effects of the oil crisis and the property collapse gradually soared to threaten a succession of weaker institutions. As a result the press began to look for the next crisis and rumours without foundation began to circulate concerning the National Westminster Bank, which culminated in an *Evening Standard* article of 29 November [headlined 'Bank of England denies NatWest rescue move']. These rumours had no effect on National Westminster's standing in the money markets which would most certainly have happened if the well-informed international banking community had had the slightest reason for doubt. Throughout this period the National Westminster Bank played a full part in the support operation led by the Bank of England and we were not anxious about the contingent cost of the operations to ourselves, nor did we ever doubt our strength to maintain and indeed expand our own operations. Therefore, I must emphasise that not only were the rumours concerning the (NatWest) without foundation – they were utterly surprising. My problem, therefore, was to consider whether a statement denying the rumours would have the desired effect. We were not seeking to "save ourselves" by dampening the rumours, but only to make the true position clear, namely, that there was no cause or foundation for them.'[2]

Considering that the newspaper headline was 'bound to create doubt in a domestic and international financial scene which was in a highly sensitive state', Sir John decided to issue his statement. This reiterated that the National Westminster Bank had no outstanding liabilities or losses in relation to the Sindona group of banks or from any of its own foreign exchange operations throughout the world and also dismissed as totally false a suggestion that the National Westminster Bank had received a substantial amount of support from the Bank of England on the ground, apparently, that it had been unable to make a rights issue.

The suggestion was also categorically denied by the Bank of England. 'In retrospect, I still feel that the course adopted was right, because there was an immediately favourable reaction. . . . Difficulties in the financial scene continued. . . . However the rumours particularly directed at the National Westminster ceased, and did not occur again', Sir John summed up later. The *Evening Standard* remarked shortly after the bank's statement: 'This affair emphasises the state of tension and anxiety in the City but it also raises the tricky question of when and how rumours should be denied. Most organisations are understandably reluctant to answer every rumour that is circulated, either maliciously or otherwise. There can be no general rule but in this case there is no doubt that Sir John Prideaux acted with expedition and wisdom . . . there have unfortunately been enough crashes in the past year or two to prepare fertile ground for even the most unlikely suggestions.'

Another exceptional event of this disturbed time was the disclosure on 18 December that the State-owned Crown Agents organisation was to receive an £85 m repayable grant (later raised to £175 m) from the Government, together with stand-by borrowing facilities at the Bank of England, to stave off the threat of its own collapse. The Bank of England had already made it clear that the Lifeboat could not be expected to rescue the Agents – whose losses were later estimated at up to around £200 m – and that the amounts involved were too great for the Bank of England itself to consider mounting a rescue. These points had been made by the Deputy Governor of the Bank, Sir Jasper Hollom, at the high-level Treasury meeting on 13 May 1974, according to part of the minutes of it which were read later to the Crown Agents' Tribunal. There was also the point that the Crown Agents, being probably insolvent without major aid, would not meet the Lifeboat's criterion that a recipient should have prospects of survival given help only in the form of loans.[3] This meeting had been the occasion when the Agents' plight had become known in top Whitehall circles; shortly after that gathering it had been decided to prepare to announce Government backing for the Agents, should the hazardous position emerge in public.[4] The announcement of the grant several months later followed an investigation set in train by Sir (then Mr) John Cuckney, who in October had taken over from Sir Claude Hayes, a former official of the Treasury and the Ministry of Overseas Development, as the Agents' chairman.

A further dramatic event at the turn of the year 1974/75, and the one which marked the nadir in the more general atmosphere of crisis, came when a major oil and industrial company, Burmah Oil, which had been a favourite of investing institutions, neared the rocks. It had branched out adventurously in the previous few years and its big investment in tankers had gone sour after the oil price rise, undermining the security for $650 m of borrowings partly taken a year earlier to finance the purchase of the large US group Signal Oil and Gas. When the Burmah crisis broke in the last days of 1974 (the second Christmas crisis running), the Bank of England stepped in with large guarantees and credit lines. In January 1975 it bought Burmah's 21 per cent stake of 77.8 m shares in the giant British Petroleum at the then depressed market value of £179 m. Within less than five years the shares were worth over £1000 m more and the Bank of England faced legal action, claiming the recovery of the shares (against repayment of the original purchase price, less subsequent dividends) by the new Burmah board, headed by Sir (then Mr) Alastair Down. Burmah was thus pulled back from the brink in the Bank of England's largest rescue, this time outside the banking industry. The Bank originally wanted any profit on the holdings in BP to be shared with Burmah but the Labour Government would not agree to such an arrangement.[5]

During the last few months of 1974, the load on the Lifeboat became increasingly heavy. Support loans at the shared risk of the Bank of England and the big banks rose £188 m in the last quarter of 1974 to £1182 m, only £18 m from the agreed £1200 m limit. As the call for loans mounted still higher in the opening months of 1975, the Bank of England helped out by making itself responsible for the excess above the limit: it temporarily financed part of the loans for the biggest borrower, United Dominions Trust which, at the peak, was drawing some £500 m. This action allowed the Lifeboat total to rise to £1285 m in March 1975, but thereafter the figure began slowly to decline. These figures exclude the few category B cases, in which individual clearers were at this stage carrying the risk of support and, sometimes it seems, the financing as well.

The first weeks of 1975 saw the beginnings of a return to a more stable atmosphere after the previous shocks. The cash situation of companies generally was improved by a Mini Budget in November which eased the burden of Corporation Tax through concessions concerning stock appreciation. The exceptional share buying operation briefly referred to above which was set in train from December by agreement among five large insurance companies – Prudential Assurance, Commercial Union Assurance, Equity and Law Life, Legal and General Assurance, and Sun Alliance and London Assurance – began to have its effect. Along with other influences, it led to a sharp rally in the depressed stock market by the end of January.

The tougher policies with which the Lifeboat chiefs had been aiming, since the previous August, to reduce their commitments, now began to show up more plainly. The troubled story of Cannon Street Acceptances, chronicled in Chapter 7, had already culminated in the calling in of a receiver in September 1974. In November, the appointment of a receiver marked the collapse of the larger Triumph Investment Trust but this, the biggest crash of a fringe bank to date, did not seriously worsen the already nerve-ridden atmosphere, a fact which made it easier for the Lifeboat thenceforward to adopt a bolder line over refusing additional support. In January, a receiver was called in to First Maryland, a subsidiary of the crumbling Stern property group, whose Nation Life Insurance concern also failed. February 1975 saw the appointment of a receiver at Burston Finance, earlier the subject of considerable support from the Crown Agents, as well as from the Lifeboat. The parent Burston Group went into liquidation after its 65 per cent stake in its authorised bank subsidiary, Burston and Texas Commerce Group, was taken over by the US concern Texas Commerce Bank, which held the other 35 per cent. Not long afterwards Audley Holdings, a smaller concern controlled by the collapsed Cornwallis Estates, a subsidiary in turn of Kayrealm, which was in receivership, failed.

In March 1975, London and County Securities collapsed with ultimate losses put at over £50 m. Following the report in January 1976 of the Department of Trade Inspectors into L and C's affairs, and police enquiries, Mr Caplan, the former chairman, who was by then living in California, and Mr Trevor Pepperell, a former L and C director, were charged in 1978 with theft and other offences, and eight other businessmen faced a range of charges in connection with the company's affairs.

In November 1980, Mr Pepperell was jailed for twenty months after being convicted on charges in connection with the London and County Securities Group's affairs. Two other former directors in the group, one of them Mr Brian McMenemy, were fined. At a later trial, Mr Pepperell was sentenced, in 1981, to two years' imprisonment, after admitting other charges connected with the group's affairs. Mr McMenemy at the same time received an eighteen month suspended jail sentence after pleading guilty to certain charges. Two others formerly holding office with the group received suspended sentences of eighteen months' imprisonment. The British authorities sought the extradition from the United States of the London and County Securities Group's former chairman, Mr Caplan, to face charges against him.

A receiver was appointed in May to the once fast-growing David Samuel Trust, which later went into liquidation. One director, Mr Leslie

Lavy, became bankrupt in 1978, disclosing debts of more than £19 m,[6] personal guarantees of DST's liabilities accounting for the bulk of his debts. (An order of discharge from the bankruptcy, suspended for six months, was made in December 1980). Total debts of £23.2 m were disclosed by Mr Herbert Towning,[7] managing director of DST, in a public examination in the London Bankruptcy Court, in 1978; Mr Towning too had given personal guarantees of DST's liabilities.

From this stage in the support operation, the Bank of England gave important extra assistance by shouldering the responsibility for repaying the remaining outside depositors in a number of collapsed fringe banks – almost certainly including London and County Securities, Triumph Investment Trust and Cannon Street Acceptances.[8] This was a substantial burden to the Bank, which may well involve it in costs totalling many millions of pounds.

The acquisition of secondary banks by larger groups, which usually took over the outstanding support loans from the Lifeboat, gathered pace from the winter of 1974/75 onwards. In September 1974, British Bank of Commerce was acquired by National and Grindlays Bank (afterwards Grindlays Bank). Then in August 1975 there was a more dramatic development when the large Mercantile Credit finance house, which had had to make £19.5 m of provisions against property loans, and which had £167 m on loan from the Lifeboat, was purchased for £32 m by Barclays Bank, already the holder of a stake of some 18 per cent in it. Barclays took over Mercantile's support loans, which helped towards the reduction of total Lifeboat lending by some £200 m to £950 m in the third quarter of 1975.

In May, the name and northern business of Northern Commercial Trust was acquired by the major Dutch bank, Algemene Bank Nederland, for £2.5 m. A large stake in NCT had been held by Authority Investments, the quoted company with a considerable proportion of its shares held by Lord Lever's family. Authority owns the London banking concern Knowsley, which took over NCT's London loan book, much of it against property. Some £32 m of Lifeboat lending was at the same time transferred from NCT to Knowsley and a good deal of this was still outstanding at the end of 1980.

The Vavasseur group, reconstructed in 1974, continued to sell assets, its disposals including the sale of First Investors and Vavasseur unit trust management business to Henderson Administration, and the reduction to 25.5 per cent of the stake in Roeday Properties, which went into receivership. Losses continued and another reconstruction of the

Vavasseur capital became necessary in 1975. In his statement of January 1976 with the 1974/5 accounts, Sir Ian Morrow, the new chairman, aptly summed up the position by saying the company had operated 'with the support of the Bank of England "Lifeboat Committee" on the understanding that the company would carry out a policy of orderly realisation of assets until . . . it became a viable operation'. Ultimately, in 1977, the much scaled down Vavasseur was effectively absorbed into the related Mills and Allen International advertising concern. In 1979 the remaining Lifeboat support loans were paid off with the help of a bank loan.

At Cedar Holdings, the £72 m emergency rescue package from the four institutional shareholders and Barclays Bank was incorporated, with some further refinements, into a refinancing plan in October 1974. Voting control passed to the four institutions through the issue to each of them of one 'A' share carrying ten million votes, some of the most heavily weighted shares ever created. But it then emerged that the group, which had considerable properties, had been so hard hit by the tumble in property values that all its share capital and reserves had been lost and it had a capital deficiency of £6.3 m. There was a tense moment in late-1974 when there was questioning whether the rescue should go on. However, it was continued, and in April 1975, following further prolonged negotiations involving prominent loan stock holders among others, Cedar's capital was reconstructed in a way which lightened the burden of debt by changing part of it into preference share capital, thus enabling the business to continue with a positive quantity of shareholders' funds. However, existing ordinary shareholders ended up with a reduction of their previous holdings. Revised arrangements were also made under which the institutions bought the properties at prices recognising the general downturn in values. By mid-1977 Cedar's borrowings from the institutions had been reduced to only £10 m and by mid-1978 to £5 m; the Bank of England had nothing to pay under its offer to reimburse any losses to the institutions up to £2 m. The Morrisons and most other directors left Cedar in the spring of 1975, when Mr Simon Coorsh, an experienced businessman who had held prominent posts in Sir Issac Wolfson's Great Universal Stores group, moved in to preside over the company's resumption of new business, albeit on a limited scale.

The revised Cedar board noted that loans of £362,000, including accumulated interest, were outstanding in mid-1975 to certain former directors and an officer of the group, and to executives of a subsidiary; it reached a settlement with one former director and took legal action against two former directors and a former executive for recovery of the debts owed.[9]

Following a period of revival, Cedar was taken over in 1979 by the big Lloyds and Scottish finance house – controlled by Lloyds Bank and Royal Bank of Scotland Group – for £9.6 m, and the remaining support loans, then of under £4 m, were repaid.

The biggest headache for the Lifeboat committee arose from mounting problems at First National Finance Corporation (FNFC). This large and venturesome group typified many activities of the secondary banking era and had prospered strongly in the boom but was now hard hit through its exposure to the slump in the property and share markets. In 1974, the group had put aside £36 m of provisions, with the result that there was a £6 m pre-tax loss on the year's business, compared with an £18 m profit in 1973. But by 1975, when the scale of the disaster in the property industry had become more widely apparent, the position had deteriorated further. The group's borrowings from the Lifeboat were also very large, £350 m late-1975.

A number of the clearing bankers among the Lifeboat crew were certainly reluctant to allow the position to continue unaltered, in view of the huge sums involved. A report was commissioned from Kleinwort Benson, the company's merchant bank, as to whether FNFC's business might be split, so that its basically sound consumer credit side would continue, while the rest of the assets, largely associated with property, were separated off to be collected by the Lifeboat through a realisation operation. This arrangement, however, proved not generally acceptable to the clearing banks, which would have been left with the less attractive assets.

Meanwhile, the Lifeboat strengthened its own managerial grip on FNFC in view of its very large financial exposure there, and major board changes became inevitable in the circumstances. Lord De L'Isle resigned as chairman and from the board in the summer of 1975 and Mr John Glyn, who had become a director, and a deputy chairman, early in 1974, was appointed chairman, while Mr Richard Langdon, who was already on the board, became deputy chairman. In May 1975, Mr Maurice Denton, a senior official seconded from the National Westminster Bank, moved in as full-time joint managing director alongside Mr Pat Matthews. Two senior clearing bankers, Sir Richard Pease, a vice-chairman of Barclays Bank, and Sir Michael Wilson, a vice-chairman and former chief general manager of Lloyds Bank, also joined the FNFC board in mid-1975. Mr Alan Challis, the Crown Agents' former finance director, who had become a deputy chairman of the FNFC in 1973, had resigned in August 1974.

By the middle of 1975, FNFC's shares, which had reached 139 p in 1972, had collapsed to only 4.5 p. The full extent of the predicament which lay behind such a rating emerged when the half-year results were drawn up. 'The unaudited consolidated balance sheet on 30th June 1975 discloses that there are no assets available for Shareholders and that there is a further deficiency of £33 m', was how the position was later summed up for shareholders. Such had been the setback in the property market and the scale of FNFC's commitment to it that a further £91.5 m of provisions against loss became necessary for the half-year up to mid-1975, bringing the accumulated provisions, including sums set aside in 1972–4, to £144 m. This meant that by 30 June 1975, FNFC was providing, against the relevant assets of £464 m, for possible losses of no less than £137 m, reducing the net value of these assets to £327 m; a further £7 m put aside for 'guarantees and other contingencies' raised the provisions to £144 m. This is how the picture was presented to shareholders when reorganisation proposals were put forward in December 1975:

3. Analysis of Provisions
The analysis of the cumulative provisions that have been made by the Directors of the Company as at 30th June, 1975 is as follows:

	Gross £'000	*Provisions* £'000	*Net* £'000
Loans, advances and other customers' accounts			
Housing development	87,544	31,267	56,277
Housing re-development and investment	62,974	20,878	42,096
Commercial and industrial properties	88,451	30,096	58,355
Hotels	23,810	6,707	17,103
London and County Securities Limited	5,000	5,000	–
Other loans not secured by property	28,733	13,886	14,847
Consumer credit (net of deferred charges)	125,463	3,411	122,052
	421,975	111,245	310,730

3. Analysis of Provisions (*continued*)

	Gross £'000	Provisions £'000	Net £'000
Quoted investments	6,090	4,075	2,015
Unquoted investments	5,430	4,767	663
Properties held under contracts for sale	18,619	6,100	12,519
Associated companies	12,348	10,800	1,548
	464,462	136,987	327,475

Guarantees and other contingencies	7,000
	143,987

The movement in total provisions
is as follows: –

Cumulative total as at 31st December, 1972	6,351
Further amount charged in 1973	13,234
Further amount charged in 1974	35,780
Further amount charged in the 6 months to 30th June, 1975	91,429
Provisions utilised on disposal of assets	(2,807)
Cumulative total as at 30th June, 1975	143,987

The Group has continued its practice of charging interest to all accounts. The provisions shown therefore include both principal and interest.[10]

It is worth pausing over this table since it so clearly exhibits the way in which much secondary bank business was vulnerable to the storms of 1974/5, in particular to the tempest in the property and share markets. The clearly healthy state of the consumer credit side is one bright spot. But the heavy exposure to property is obvious. Widespread difficulties among house-builders, with whom the group had much lending business and some share links, doubtless accounted for the £31 m of provisions against £88 m of loans for 'housing development', while the similar amount put aside against much the same total lending in the 'commercial and industrial properties' field, reflects the problems prevailing there. The £19 m of 'properties held under contracts for sale' (£6 m of loss provisions) is clearly connected with the £72 m deal, which had originally looked so profitable, to sell many blocks of flats. The £63 m of 'housing re-development and investment' loans, with loss provisions of £21 m, reflects the extensive involvement in this then troubled area. The fact that nearly £9 m had to be provided against losses on quoted and unquoted investments previously worth £11.5 m shows what misfortune the group had had with some of its holdings of this kind, many of which were in the housebuilding and property field. Among its quoted share interests, FNFC had sizeable holdings in companies in these then hard-pressed industries, such as Regalian Properties and Royco Group, and Fairview Estates, while it also had unquoted interests in private building firms. The 'other loans not secured by property', totalling £29 m, against which there were loss provisions of nearly half, £14 m, were principally advances against the security of share investments. They presumably included substantial loans to individuals (and perhaps companies) who had used them to buy blocks of shares and were feared to be unable to repay when the shares had tumbled. It is not known whether the shares principally in question were in hard-hit property and secondary banking companies or who the borrowers were.

When the full extent of FNFC's provisions in the light of the property crisis, and the fact and size of its deficiency of assets, became apparent, the question of radical changes again arose. Some clearing banks were reluctant to continue support indefinitely. But the Bank of England was adamant that FNFC should continue as one entity with the Lifeboat support which had been firmly provided throughout. The Bank took the view that the atmosphere was still somewhat fragile at this stage, and that success to date in rebuilding confidence should not be jeopardised. The clearers favouring a more drastic solution bowed to the central bank's views. It has been widely thought that the Bank of England felt a sense of special obligation to FNFC because of the helpful way in which that group had responded to its request, at the outset of the whole upheaval in December 1973, to take over the management of London and County Security Group; however, there is no evidence that such an argument was put to the Lifeboat committee.

By now, a major construction of FNFC's capital had become inevitable, to deal with its large deficiency. A scheme was accordingly prepared, and approved at the end of 1975, by which the Lifeboat's support loans were to be funded into a variety of redesignated and redefined loans, to be repayable as and when conditions made this possible. Shareholders were told the directors had 'concluded it will be in the best interests of all concerned that the Group should continue to carry on its business with a view to eventual disengagement from the property sector in which it has suffered so severely. It is intended that the business should be carried on over a period sufficient to enable it to deal with the Group's loans and other assets to the best possible advantage. They have also concluded that, meanwhile, the original business, the Consumer Credit Division, which is still profitable, should continue to operate on established lines'. They added, significantly, in seeking shareholders' agreement to the new arrangements, that 'in the absence of a comprehensive reorganisation steps would have to be taken to place the company in liquidation'.

Mr Matthews stayed on until March 1976 and then resigned, eventually receiving a severance payment for loss of office. Still a fairly wealthy man from earlier business ventures, he now works as a financial consultant and art dealer. Six directors left during 1975/76 and two afterwards, a total of £120,000 being paid to three directors whose service contracts were terminated by the company. The new chairman said that 'after taking legal advice it was clear that compensation was payable upon the termination of service contracts of certain directors'. Mr Matthews sold his shareholding, which had been worth nearly £10 m in 1972 when the shares stood at 139 p, for a few pence a share, so that his link with the business he had created in happier times was severed.

FNFC has continued to conduct an extensive programme of completion of housing and other properties which had accrued to it as security for unrepaid loans and, as opportunity has offered, of the sale of its property assets. Its net deficiency rose to £79 m at the end of April 1977, but this had been more than halved to £29 m by the end of October 1980. At that time FNFC was still borrowing £225 m from the Lifeboat support group. The consumer credit side has meanwhile prospered.

In November 1974, United Dominions Trust, the largest borrower of Lifeboat support loans, with £500 m at the peak, received a new chairman, who was very much out of the top banks' own stable: Mr Leonard Mather, formerly chief general manager and afterwards vice-chairman of the Midland Bank, of which he remained a director. One of Mr Mather's first tasks was a new scrutiny of the group's loan portfolio, which was outside the main instalment credit business and included some £160 m of lending in the troubled house-building sector. As a consequence, provisions of £25.8 m were disclosed in the 1974/75 accounts, which also included £21.1 m of write-offs, mainly against investments in companies at home and abroad. UDT showed an overall loss of £54.8 m and its shareholders' funds were slashed from £95 m to £37 m in 1974/75. Mr Mather announced early in 1975 that dependence on the Lifeboat must be reduced and that this 'will entail a reduction in the scope of our activities'. Property lending was scaled right down and a lengthy programme of selling off overseas and other peripheral interests was embarked on.

UDT recovered gradually and by mid-1980 had reduced its Lifeboat borrowings from £500 m to some £100 m. But it was unable, after the shocks of the mid-1970s and in the difficult trading conditions of later years, to rebuild its capital to the extent necessary for a satisfactory long-term independent existence. In August 1980 it was announced that the Trustee Savings Banks (TSBs) would take over UDT's major instalment credit business. Then, in January 1981, a £106 m counter-bid for the whole of UDT was foreshadowed by Lloyds and Scottish, the large clearing-bank backed finance house which had earlier bought Cedar Holdings. But the TSBs successfully riposted with a larger full offer of £110 m for UDT.

As 1975 went on, some of the most resilient of the Lifeboat's passengers strengthened their position enough to be able to dispense with its assistance, though loans or borrowing facilities from the big banks were often made available for a time. Bowmaker, the finance house controlled by the C. T. Bowring insurance broking group, was the first to manage without Lifeboat finance; it was 'landed' in the late autumn of 1975, having already repaid a good part of its borrowings under the £89 m Lifeboat support made available to it, and having fixed up a medium-term loan from leading banks and the Bank of England with which to pay off the rest. As a company with a consumer credit business bringing a continuing flow of repayments, and little exposed to the property market, it was well placed to recover as soon as circumstances allowed. (In 1980, the whole Bowring group was bought by the large US company Marsh and McLennan.)

Rather similarly placed was the smaller Wagon Finance Corporation, which left the Lifeboat in 1976, having fixed up £30 m of borrowing facilities, much on a medium-term basis, from a consortium of banks. Keyser Ullmann had recovered sufficiently by 1976 to quit the Lifeboat, having repaid its support borrowings which had been £65 m in the early months of 1975. This banking group, where a leading clearing banker,

Mr Derek Wilde, succeeded Mr Edward du Cann MP as chairman in March 1975, will be the subject of a separate study in a later chapter.

One or two smaller finance houses turned to their clearing banks in the critical years of the mid-1970s for borrowing facilities which were given a measure of Lifeboat backing after the big banks and the Bank of England formed the support group in December 1973. Medens Trust, the Isle of Wight-based finance house, had, in the light of the disturbed money market conditions in late-1973, fixed up borrowing facilities with its clearing banks. As the general crisis in the financial world escalated, these were continued through the clearer principally concerned, with the backing of the support group. A larger borrowing facility provided by institutional shareholders was used only briefly and to a limited extent, while further bank standby facilities which would have been available were never required. The general cash scarcity of the time thus presented no troublesome problems. In the adverse climate, however, Medens cautiously kept new business almost entirely to motor contracts, and the impact of the prevailing situation was shown in the drop in its pre-tax profits, from £480,000 in 1972/73 to £160,000 in 1973/74 after substantial additional provision for doubtful debts. By 1978/79, the profit level had more than recovered to reach £638,000. In 1979, it was noted that the banking division's advances to the property sector had been reduced and were by then insignificant. In 1981, Medens Trust ceased to be independent when it was taken over by the merchant bank group Brown Shipley Holdings for £3.8 m.

The way in which the big banks could help smaller financial customers through the difficulties of several years is illustrated by Duboff Brothers, in the unquoted Consolidated Finance Holdings group. The £2.5 m secured loan facility previously mentioned which the National Westminster Bank had accorded Duboff in the first half of December 1973 – and which afterwards, for a time, came under the Lifeboat group's wing – was continued and grew over several years in which Duboff, in common with so many others, was obliged to make substantial loss provisions against its own lending. From 1976 the resultant accumulated losses pushed Duboff into a deficit position and by the end of 1978 it had a £2.66 m deficiency of shareholders' funds, despite gradual sales of an extensive range of the parent CFH's share stakes and other interests. In 1979, after drawings on the secured loan facility had reached £5.7 m (it grew further to 6.7 m when all outside deposits were repaid), a settlement was reached which is of interest in the general context of the Lifeboat operation. Duboff raised a new loan of £2.2 m from another bank. This paved the way for the settlement, under which some £2.2 m was repaid to the National Westminster Bank, which assigned the residual balance of £4.7 m owed to it to a consortium including a company in, and directors of, the CFH group for a consideration of only £50,000. Thus, effectively, the National Westminster accepted a loss of over £4 m. The result was to leave Duboff, which in 1979 was concentrating on financial management (it ceased taking deposits in 1978) with a positive quantity of shareholders' funds.

Looking back later, Mr Harvey Cohen, the chairman, recalled, in an interesting view of the crisis, how meetings were held every two or three months with the National Westminster Bank to discuss company policy during the years when the loan was continuing and sales of assets were gradually taking place. A feature was the clearing bank's insistence that all outside depositors should be fully repaid before the 1979 settlement – an arrangement in tune with the Lifeboat principle that all depositors with supported secondary banks should be completely protected.

As the process of take-overs, capital reconstructions, closures and recovery continued among the various secondary banking concerns helped by the Lifeboat, the reading on the City's confidence barometers moved from 'critical' to 'chronic' and then to 'convalescent', and the burden on the big banks slowly lightened. From a peak of £1285 m in March 1975, when the Bank of England was carrying more than its normal share of a tenth, the Lifeboat support loan total fell back to £914 m at the end of 1975 and to £783 m a year later.

But the amount was to remain large for some years and the crisis period of the mid-1970s was not to end without further major upheavals. These difficulties, in whose handling the Bank of England itself assumed the key role, are now to be considered, along with the varying experiences of some smaller banks outside the Lifeboat, before an appraisal of the whole major episode is presented.

11 Later Troubles and a Summing-up

> By our system, all extra pressure is thrown upon the Bank of England. In the worst part of the crisis of 1866 . . . there was no other lender to new borrowers.
>
> Walter Bagehot, *Lombard Street*, 1873

The Bank of England's acceptance of responsibility for support costs beyond the £1200 m limit set to the combined Lifeboat operation in August 1974 meant that it had itself to shoulder the full burden of dealing with new crises which broke out at individual banking houses later. This proved no light task, for the Bank subsequently mounted two potentially highly costly supporting actions, and took certain other protective measures, before the secondary banking troubles had run their course. The most important was the rescue of Slater Walker Securities (SWS), culminating in the Bank's take-over of the Slater Walker bank. It is ironic, but perhaps scarcely surprising, that SWS, the best-known of the new financial enterprises in the boom years, should also have figured so prominently in the later crisis period.

SWS weathered nearly two years of the mid-1970s' upheaval, despite the emphasis which it had placed in 1971–3 on the expansion of its interests in property and banking. It was helped by its rapid action to turn assets into cash after widespread problems had hit other parts of the secondary banking industry. Thus, although a net loss, after extraordinary items, of £25 m was reported for 1974, the crisis which eventually revealed a number of deep-seated problems did not break out until October 1975. It was touched off in an unexpected way, by developments in the East, notably the affair of the 'Spydar's web'.

During its earlier phase of expansion internationally, SWS had had major interests in Hong Kong and also in Singapore, where it had effectively controlled the 'Tiger Balm' conglomerate, Haw Par Brothers International. It had sold its stake in Haw Par in mid-1974, but Haw Par still owed $29 m to the Slater Walker bank. This amount mainly

138

represented finance which had been provided towards an earlier take-over by Haw Par of a substantial stake in Slater Walker Securities (Hong Kong) – formerly Kwan Loong – which SWS had sold off in late-1973. There was anger in Singapore about the terms of that deal under which, it was felt in some quarters there, Haw Par – in the days when it had been linked with SWS – had paid too much.

Still more important was the affair of the 'Spydar's web'. Spydar Securities, a private Hong Kong company, was the vehicle for an executive incentive scheme for SWS executives involved in operations in the Far East. This company made gross profits of $1.9 m (some £1.1 m) for its participants, including Mr Slater and Mr Richard Tarling, who was until mid-1974 chairman of Haw Par and a SWS director. Much of the gain was on holdings of fast-rising shares in two companies, Kwan Loong and another Hong Kong concern, King Fung (later Southern Pacific Properties), which had shot ahead when the then SWS-linked Haw Par group had applied its Midas touch by itself purchasing holdings in them in the early 1970s. Blocks of both shareholdings had gone to the private Spydar company, for the benefit of Mr Slater, Mr Tarling and four other executives, at the 'ground floor' price at which the SWS group had bought its much larger holdings. 'Knowing that the shares in Kwan Loong and King Fung would automatically go to a premium *solely* because of our involvement, we would obviously allocate shares to our executives at cost price concurrently with the purchase by the company, *as had always been our practice with incentive shares throughout the world*',[1] Mr Slater afterwards recalled (present author's italics in latter passage). However, controversy subsequently arose and dwelt particularly upon the secrecy of the deal and upon whether Spydar had acquired its share in Kwan Loong and King Fung at the same time as had the Haw Par group or whether the deal had been back-dated to give the Spydar holders the benefit of a cheap purchase cost after the shares had in fact climbed higher.

This was the matter which, with other aspects of Haw Par's affairs, led the Singapore Government afterwards to seek the extradition of Mr Slater and Mr Tarling, claiming that they had conspired, with others, to make £1 m of profits through Spydar; other charges, mostly relating to Haw Par's accounts, were also brought. Mr Slater was discharged at the first hearing. Mr Tarling was eventually extradited, and convicted and imprisoned in Singapore, on only a limited range of charges concerning the accounts, having been found in Britain to have no case to answer on the others. (However, on Singapore's appeal, the affair had reached the House of Lords where five Law Lords had split 3:2

in finding there was not a case for Mr Tarling to answer on certain of the Spydar charges). Mr Tarling also appealed against the verdict on the charges on which he was convicted in Singapore.

The Spydar affair was beginning to cast a long shadow before it by the autumn of 1975. Singapore's Finance Minister, Mr Hon Sui Sen, had spoken in Parliament in July of evidence of 'serious wrong-doing' and two inspectors had been appointed in Singapore to investigate the affairs of Haw Par, including Spydar.

On Friday, 24 October, having notified the Bank of England of his intention four days earlier, Mr Slater resigned as chairman and a director of SWS, stating that 'matters connected with the recent inquiry into the affairs of Haw Par in Singapore have received adverse publicity which is damaging to SWS'. During the four days it was arranged that the financier Sir (then Mr) James Goldsmith, who was a friend of Mr Slater's and whose interests had built up a considerable shareholding in SWS, should take over as the group's chairman. Four senior personalities from City of London merchant banks joined the board: they were Lord Rothschild, then the chairman, and Mr Ivor Kennington, a director, and later a deputy chairman, of N. M. Rothschild and Sons, and Mr Charles Hambro, chairman, and Mr Peter Hill-Wood, a director, of Hambros Bank. M. Dominique Leca, a director of Sir James Goldsmith's key company, Générale Occidentale (GO), and formerly chairman of Union des Assurances de Paris, also became a director of SWS.

Sir James was to devote a great deal of time and energy to the affairs of the troubled SWS in the succeeding two years. Previously mainly known in British financial circles as chairman of two British companies in his GO group, the large Cavenham food business and Anglo-Continental Investment and Finance – the latter was once described by Mr Slater as 'a very high flying vehicle'[2] – he became a much better known public figure as a result of his chairmanship of SWS. He was knighted in Sir Harold Wilson's resignation honours list in 1976.

The new board of directors could not be certain at the outset whether, without additional support, Slater Walker Securities was solvent or not. They soon concluded that substantial provisions against loss would have to be made, but could not quickly assess the required amount. Meanwhile, the Bank of England, concerned about the risks from troubles at such a large and well-known financial concern, had immediately provided the SWS bank with a very large secured standby borrowing facility. In November, 1975, the terms of this financing arrangement were refined and amended, with some reduction in the amount. The standby became a secured advance facility up to £70 m and the Bank also provided guarantees for £40 m of the Slater Walker bank's lending, and future interest on it. Stiff terms for the ultimate repayment of this aid were stipulated, though these were ultimately overtaken by later arrangements.

For months two leading firms of accountants called in by Sir James Goldsmith, Peat Marwick Mitchell and Price Waterhouse, worked on a detailed scrutiny of SWS's affairs. Then, in September 1976, the full extent of the group's problems was publicly revealed. The new board published particulars which disclosed that, without the Bank of England guarantee, the Slater Walker bank would have been insolvent because of its bad debts and losses.[3] Major provisions totalling £66.1 m against losses in various areas of the business were recommended, although the Bank of England's guarantees made that part of the suggested provision which related to the banking side unnecessary. Very large total provisions were included in SWS' 1974/75 accounts, which revealed a total net loss for the year, after heavy extraordinary items, of £42 m, compared with a revised one of £30 m for the previous year 1974.

SWS, under its new board, struggled on for nearly another year, selling off investments and properties as far as was possible, endeavouring to recover what it could of the loan portfolio, and reducing debt, while continuing the investment management and insurance businesses. But overall losses persisted and shrinkages in capital and reserves were such as to make possible future breaches of the loan stock trust deeds. By the summer of 1977 it had become clear that the next stage for the ailing group must be decided on. After prolonged debate, it was effectively dismantled, but in a way which very much muted the impact of the outcome. In a major deal, the Bank of England itself took over the tottering bank, Slater Walker Ltd (SWL), together with certain property and other assets, on terms which were generous enough to allow the rump of the SWS group to continue as a viable non-banking financial services business, strong enough to meet its obligations on its foreign currency borrowings, under the altered name of Britannia Arrow Holdings. The arrangement also gave the group enough funds to enable it to reach agreement with its sterling loan stock holders for the redemption of these stocks at a reduced price; Sir James Goldsmith made it clear in putting the relevant proposals to stockholders that the alternative to agreement could be the liquidation of the group.[4]

Mr Geoffrey Rippon, MP, the former Conservative Minister, became chairman of Britannia Arrow from December 1977 in place of Sir James

Goldsmith, who then resigned from the board, along with the four City of London personalities, Lord Rothschild, Mr Charles Hambro, Mr Hill-Wood and Mr Kennington, who had become directors of SWS with him after Mr Slater's departure. (M. Leca had retired from the board shortly before).

The settlement with the Bank staved off the danger of what would have been the biggest and noisiest crash of the secondary banking crisis; no financial group of the size of Slater Walker Securities had collapsed in the mid-1970s upheaval or for many years.

But the Bank of England's support operation for SWS may well turn out to have been very costly, if anything like the sum it put aside against losses on this account, believed to be some £35 m, proves to have been needed. The accountants' report noted that the Bank's £40 m guarantee of SWL's loan book was likely to be required in full. Since taking over SWL, the Bank has made a payment to that company under the guarantee which, it is reasonable to suppose, was as much as £40 m and which may have been more – allowing for the fact that unpaid interest due after 11 December 1975 was also guaranteed. That the payment was on this scale is also suggested by the fact that, during the accounting period in which it was made (1 January 1977–28 February 1978) the value of SWL's outstanding loans, net of provisions, was dramatically reduced, from £60 m to £15 m. The possible prospective large losses on the Slater Walker loan book doubtless account for the great bulk of the £35 m or so of provisions made by the Bank on account of SWS.

Meanwhile, the Bank has been following the course adopted by many bank creditors with hard-pressed debtors. It has been striving to get back what it can and has, in some instances, reached settlements in which it has accepted less than the sum due. In other cases – as further described in Chapter 13 – it has, however, taken bankruptcy proceedings against certain debtors.

To what extent the Bank may finally incur actual net losses on its support of SWS will depend largely on what offset it may have against losses on the loans through any capital gains on the property it took over as part of the deal, such as the office block at 100 Fetter Lane, London, which it sold off to an institutional buyer in 1979/80. The extent of recoveries against debts owing will also be a factor.

The Bank's decision to complete the SWS support operation on such potentially costly terms was reached after lengthy consideration with the revised SWS board and its advisers of the various alternative available possible courses. The idea of ending support, and allowing SWS and its bank to collapse, had been rejected partly to avoid a default on the group's Euro-currency borrowings and more generally to prevent a damaging blow being administered to financial confidence. Much attention must have been given to striking the final balance between the interests of the remaining business which was to continue as Britannia Arrow Holdings, the loan stockholders, and the public interest, as represented by the Bank of England. The decision to make the settlement was endorsed by the Court, the Bank's governing board, apparently by a large majority, but not without at least one dissenting voice being raised. Most directors seem to have felt that the Bank had become effectively committed to completing this support operation on the best terms available when it first provided major backing on Mr Slater's departure in October 1975.

The private banking concern Jacobs Kroll, a section 123 company run by Mr David Kroll, an accountant, and Mr Jack Jacobs, was another case where the Bank of England had to take protective action after the Lifeboat's doors were closed. In mid-1973 a half share in it had been bought by a Slater Walker associate, Equity Enterprises (EE), an investment, entertainment and betting shop business, of which SWS and the TV personality Mr David Frost together owned more than half. EE, which had millions of pounds of loans owing to Slater Walker – including $7 m borrowed to finance the purchase of the US concern Russeks – bought the rest of Jacobs Kroll in September 1975; the idea then was that JK would become part of the Slater Walker bank, but this did not happen. EE was itself in such deep waters, with investment losses and cash problems, by late-1975 that a fundamental reorganisation of its loan structure was needed to preserve it as a going concern. A number of schemes to this end were considered but not adopted.

In November 1975 Jacobs Kroll ceased trading as a prelude to liquidation and it was disclosed that arrangements were being made by the Slater Walker bank, in consultation with the Bank of England, to protect depositors with nearly £1 m in JK; in other words, the Bank shouldered responsibility for seeing that these people were repaid.

As to Equity Enterprises, which became Hemdale Film Group, a bid for it at 3p a share was made by two of its directors, Mr John Daly and Mr Derek Dawson, who acquired the stake of 29.6 per cent held by SWS – which had itself taken over Mr Frost's holding – and ended up with over 80 per cent of the shares. The Slater Walker bank released EE from repaying to it £3.2 m of loans, and arranged the cancellation of nearly £2 m more represented by loan stock; under other arrangements, it also received a repayment of £1.1 m out of the proceeds of the sale of the old Russeks (renamed Redlaw Enterprises).

The other large secondary bank which the Bank of England shielded from sudden collapse to the point of itself also acquiring much of the business was Edward Bates and Sons, which had become an authorised bank as the fringe banking crisis was breaking out in December 1973 and which was a subsidiary of the quoted Edward Bates and Sons (Holdings). Bates experienced recurrent pressure on its deposits and was hit additionally by prospective large losses on its Welfare Insurance subsidiary, which it ultimately sold at a loss of nearly £10 m in 1975 to the National Westminster Bank and London and Manchester Assurance, the latter eventually buying out the National Westminster's stake.

In September 1974, Bates appealed, as the last successful applicant, to the Lifeboat support group, which helped by buying out part of its shipping loan portfolio, an interesting example of the diversity of ways in which the Lifeboat could assist troubled fringe banks. In May 1975, Bates sought to improve its position by bringing in Arab interests; First Arabian Corporation (FAC), a Luxembourg-based holding company owned by a number of prominent Arab interests, took a 25 per cent shareholding. The Bank of England obtained a 'letter of comfort', in line with its new principle of parental responsibility where overseas share-holders had or acquired sizeable stakes in British banks; in this, FAC 'recognised that their shareholding (in Bates) carried an obligation to support [Bates] which went beyond the limited liability represented by their shares', as the Bank of England afterwards explained.[5]

But there was more trouble to come. In May 1976 the Bates directors realised that the scale of the provisions needed against loans Bates had made to the more speculative end of the property and Greek shipping markets[6] put the solvency of the group in doubt. Bates' shares were suspended from quotation and an investigation showed that the position was much worse than the board had recognised. By this stage, though, a large proportion of Bates' £67 m of deposits were from Arab sources and are thought to have included sizeable quantities of some of the Gulf States' sterling balances. In view of this, and as Bates was an authorised bank, the Bank of England decided itself to protect the concern's depositors. Eventually all the share capital was lost and the group proved to have a substantial deficiency.

Long negotiations followed and eventually the Bates bank was taken over by a mainly Arab consortium, including interests of the multi-millionaire Mr M. M. Al-Tajir, Ambassador of the United Arab

Emirates in Britain; Barclays Bank International took 20 per cent in the altered and recapitalised concern, Allied Arab bank. Before this transaction the Bank of England had itself acquired certain loans and other assets of the Bates bank, so eliminating its net deficiency. The assets were placed in a new subsidiary company, EBS Investments, through which the Bank is carrying out the task of turning the assets into what cash can be realised. There can be no doubt that this piece of protective action led the Bank to make loss provisions of many millions of pounds, probably up to £30 m or so. The Bates holding company went into liquidation. (The Bank of England noted, in announcing the reconstruction arrangements in August 1977, that a 'significant' contribution towards reducing the old group's deficiency had been made under the earlier 'comfort letter'.)

The Bank of England also monitored the fortunes of other banking concerns which found the going rough and provided some financial help in a few further cases. One was Wallace Brothers Bank, formerly Wallace Brothers Sassoon, the product of a merger between E. D. Sassoon and Wallace Brothers; the Crown Agents had a 27 per cent stake in the combined group as a consequence of their 40 per cent holding in E. D. Sassoon. Wallace, which had a long history as a well-known trading company with Eastern interests and whose managing director was Mr J. J. Grafftey-Smith, expanded even after 1973 – its gross assets were £128 m in 1975, against £96 m in 1973 – but its business proved highly vulnerable to the property crisis. The Bank of England closely followed the situation and is believed to have provided financial assistance through a line of credit of some £10–12 m at ordinary interest rates. However, problems continued. The Bank of England then called on the big Standard Chartered Bank, which, as a non-clearing bank had not been part of the Lifeboat support team, to help as its contribution to the handling of the secondary bank crisis; Standard Chartered was already interested since it had a loan of about £2 m outstanding to one Wallace Brothers company.

In December 1976, Standard Chartered took over Wallace Brothers (Holdings), the group holding company, with its subsidiaries, on terms which reflected the acknowledged problems on the property side. To sweeten the deal, the Bank of England made a large line of credit of some £20 m available on reasonable interest rate terms through Standard Chartered, but this was not long used to any great extent. Important changes in the top management of the acquired company, notably the resignation of Mr Grafftey-Smith, had occurred several months before take-over discussions began.

After a scrutiny of its assets by a team put in by Standard Chartered, the Wallace Brothers group turned out to have such problems on the property side that it was in a deficit position to the extent of some millions of pounds. Standard Chartered has since gradually disposed of the non-banking assets (mainly property); it did not sell the banking side of Wallace, but this is being steadily phased out. Standard Chartered's loss in connection with Wallace, for which provision has already been made, seems unlikely to be more than £1 m or so. There is clearly no prospect that any price for the take-over of Wallace will be payable, under the acquisition terms, to the original shareholders.

The Bank of England also kept in very close touch with Anglo-Portuguese Bank, which carried out a quick slimming-down operation in the crisis: its gross assets were reduced from £190 m to £104 m in the year to January 1975. In April 1975, Anglo-Portuguese, hitherto owned by the family trusts of Sir Isaac Wolfson, was taken over by Norwich Union Insurance for £12 m and renamed A. P. Bank. In this instance the Bank of England's activity was essentially that of watchfulness and moral support.

In January 1977 another authorised bank, the long-established Ionian Bank, which had in 1958 come newly under the control of Mr Michael Behrens and Mr John Trusted, both stockbrokers, decided to effect an orderly run-down of its banking business, its principal activity. The Bank of England provided a stand-by borrowing facility, probably of not more than £5 m, to cover any short-term liquidity problems during this process. It is not thought that any losses are likely to have fallen on the Bank of England in this case. Ionian had incurred losses after making substantial provisions on its lending, part of which was to British Bank for Foreign Trade, a company of which Mr Behrens and Mr Trusted were directors and in whose shares they had interests.

The Bank of England also kept a close watch over the resolution of problems at Bank of Cyprus (London), which in 1975 incurred a net loss of £3.6 m after making £2.3 m of exceptional provisions for bad and doubtful debts, mainly against property loans. A subvention of £3.6 m was injected by the bank's parent company and a major board shake-up took place. In wording which gives an interesting insight into how the protective arrangements, already referred to in Chapter 9, for foreign-controlled banks in Britain worked out in a case of serious losses, the Bank of Cyprus (London)' 1975 report and accounts recorded that 'The ultimate holding company [Bank of Cyprus (Holdings)] has given an undertaking of financial support for [the London bank] in line with the policy of the Bank of England regarding foreign banks operating in the

United Kingdom and has also made arrangements for financial support to be provided by the Central Bank of Cyprus.' Bank of Cyprus (London) weathered the troubled years satisfactorily with this aid and continues trading normally.

The widespread banking and property crisis created a more adverse environment for many financial businesses other than those with which the Lifeboat support group and the Bank of England were specially concerned. Consequently, it strengthened the case for smaller companies to pass under the wing of larger groups. Thus, the period from the start of 1974 brought frequent news of take-overs, as well as of capital reconstructions and, in some cases, failures reflected in the calling in of receivers.

In January 1974 Western Trust and Savings, a section 123 company, with its parent, Western Credit Holdings, passed under the control of the large American group Philadelphia National Bank, from which it had already received financial backing. Then in 1979 it was bought by Royal Bank of Canada for £10.5 m, and has enlarged its banking activities.

Hawtin, the former Dental Manufacturing, which in the early 1970s had strongly expanded its banking, second mortgage and consumer credit activities through its section 123 subsidiary, Hawtin & Partners, found itself with serious problems as a result of the fall in property values in 1974, while it had large Euro-currency and other long-term borrowings. A solution was found by an agreement in December 1974 for the sale of Hawtin & Partners for a nominal price to Gilwise, a member of the large US group Gulf + Western Associates, which had earlier provided substantial finance to the Hawtin group.

Cripps Warburg, a 123 company and, later a listed bank, was taken over in February 1975 for a nominal price by Williams and Glyn's Bank, (the English clearing bank in the Royal Bank of Scotland Group) from which it had received additional finance. A bank official concerned in the transaction remembers fishing in his pocket for the grubby £1 note which constituted the acquisition price.

In the autumn of 1974, the wide-ranging Jessel Securities group was confronted by acute problems at its London Indemnity and General Insurance (LIGI) subsidiary, which was hit by the effect of rising interest rates on the value of its securities and by its income bond holders' withdrawals. Jessel decided to inject £13 m more capital into LIGI; it put in £6.5 m but was unable to meet a call for the other £6.5 m in October 1974. This led to an application by the Jessel group for a provisional liquidator for LIGI and provoked a crisis for Jessel Securities itself by rendering unsecured loan stock immediately repayable; the quotation of its shares was then suspended. Values of others of the group's assets also fell heavily and, after lengthy attempts to negotiate a survival scheme, and a programme of sales of assets, Jessel Securities was eventually put into liquidation. Jessel's one banking interest was a holding of a fifth in the Midlands concern G. R. Dawes Holdings; this was bought by directors of that company, which later went voluntarily out of business, making a substantial distribution to shareholders.

At the Corinthian Securities banking concern, owned by Corinthian Holdings, there was a substantial reduction of deposits as a result of the general crisis. Established lines of credit were drawn on and additional sums were put up by a shareholder, Charles Wolfson Charitable Trust, which, in December 1976, raised its holding from 18 per cent to 29.9 per cent. Major management changes took place in July 1976, under which the chairmanship passed first to the late Col. H. S. J. Jelf and, following his death in November that year, to Mr Henry Prevezer; both had previously been non-executive directors. The group incurred a net loss of some £1 m in 1974, after provisions against banking advances and falls in the value of securities. A period of retrenchment, consolidation and rationalisation followed, bringing a return to profitable operation. In November 1980, Corinthian Holdings made an agreement to sell its Corinthian Securities banking subsidiary to the large US steel group Armco for £1.29 m.

A loan which would have been financed through the Lifeboat support group was approved in 1974 for Henry Ansbacher, the merchant banking subsidiary of the Fraser Ansbacher financial and property concern, but it was never drawn upon. The Fraser Ansbacher group experienced considerable problems in the mid-1970s and incurred losses of £6.5 m, largely on property and investments, during the years 1975–8. It recovered well in the late-1970s under revised management headed by Sir Samuel Goldman, a former Second Secretary in the Treasury. Now renamed Henry Ansbacher Holdings, the group carried out a capital reconstruction in 1979, following a decision to concentrate on the merchant banking business of Henry Ansbacher; its R. Fraser Securities property subsidiary had earlier been disposed of and its last remaining interest in the Robert Fraser & Partners investment banking subsidiary was sold early in 1980. Some 49.6 per cent of the shares of Henry Ansbacher Holdings is owned by the US-based Lissauer metals group, which first took a share stake against £1.7 m of new capital in

1976 and later channelled in £3 m of new capital; another 18.9 per cent is owned by the Grand Metropolitan hotels and brewery group.

Few banking and financial concerns weathered the crisis years without their share of worries. But a number of smaller groups, as well as the great majority of larger banks, came through satisfactorily without serious problems or loss of independence. There were, however, often setbacks in profits because of bad debt provisions; precautionary cutbacks in business were frequently made. A number of companies had well-timed injections of capital from existing or new large shareholders in the years 1973–5. It is worth recalling some names in this category, along with one or two comments on their successful survival.

Leopold Joseph Holdings received £2.3 m of new capital when, in July 1974, two West German State banks, Bayerische Landesbank and Bremer Landesbank, became shareholders with a combined stake of 25 per cent in its equity. Leopold Joseph made a precautionary reduction in loans and advances in 1973/74 and saw only a standstill in its profits in 1973/75; it was fortunate in having little property lending. (It is interesting to recall that, soon after Leopold Joseph's shares were floated on the Stock Exchange in 1971, Mr Gerald Caplan's London and County Securities revealed that it had bought a holding of about a quarter of them. This was one of the first occasions on which the ill-fated London and County Securities had come to the public's notice. There was talk of a full-scale bid by London and County, but any such idea was frozen out by the board of Joseph, which said it wanted no link with London and County. The London and County shares in Joseph were sold off by a placing through the stock market in 1972).

Wintrust, too, weathered the storms well. As the chairman, Mr George Szpiro, said in mid-1974, the board had seen the economic and financial climate deteriorating from the previous summer and had reduced the level of its advances, particularly to the property and financial sectors. However, the company's profits declined between 1974/75 and 1976/77, partly because of the need to make provisions against property and other lending.

Gresham Investment Trust, and its banking subsidiary Gresham Trust, a section 123 company, came satisfactorily through the crisis, though the group suffered a sharp drop in profits in 1974/75. The chairman, Mr Peter Wreford, has recalled that, although a substantial part of Gresham Trust's loans were in the property development field, 'our exposure was less than that of many other concerns, which were often lending up to 90 per cent or 100 per cent of the security, and taking a share in the borrowing company's development property'. Gresham was lending not more than 70 per cent of the value of security and was not taking a stake in developers' profits; 'we were also much more careful in looking at the properties'.[7]

Among financial companies and finance houses which emerged satisfactorily from the testing years was London Scottish Finance Corporation, a Manchester-based company engaged in making small personal loans and not involved in financing commercial or property borrowers or purchases of Stock Exchange securities. A shortening of repayment periods for lending after the onset of the crisis made possible a substantial cutback in borrowings, and lending was also reduced; profits were sharply lower in 1973/74. In 1976, a stake of just under 20 per cent in London Scottish was bought by FIMS, a subsidiary of the US group ISC Financial Corporation, against £230,000 of additional capital. This holding passed later to Edward Lumley (Finance), Lloyd's brokers, being held through Goseford Financial Management and was, in 1979, increased to 25 per cent.

Manson Finance Trust, where Cedar Holdings had had a 10 per cent interest which was sold in 1974, was another which came well through the crisis years and remained independently in business; in 1974 the Danish group F. L. Smidth took a 20 per cent stake, later raised to 29.6 per cent, in Manson. In 1980 Hong Leong took a 51 per cent stake.

It is now possible to gather together a list of the many banking concerns assisted to a greater or lesser degree through the Lifeboat support operation, to survey the experience of other concerns, some of which required much help in other ways, and to note the major changes the crisis years wrought in the structure of the secondary banking industry. A more general assessment of the whole rescue strategy, including its benefits and costs, will be given in the final chapter.

Schedule I on pages 152–61 shows the companies with which the Lifeboat support group was concerned in one way or another. It lists 25 groups, counting the previously related Northern Commercial Trust and Knowsley as one. As already noted, one company, Henry Ansbacher, was accorded a right to draw on the Lifeboat, but never did so. Including it, although it is shown in the later Schedule II from page 162, the number would be 26, the figure publicly given by the Bank of England as the total of those for whom the Lifeboat support group's 'control' committee 'approved support of varying degrees'.[8]

Schedule I briefly sums up the experience of the 25 companies in the crisis years and also shows how radically the ownership structure of this part of the secondary banking industry changed after the onset of the crisis. Of the 25, eight collapsed and another, Sterling Industrial Securities, was radically scaled down under the Crown Agents' supervision and later sold. Of the rest, no fewer than eleven had by the early months of 1981 passed, in whole or substantial part, under the control of larger groups, a process which generated much repayment of Lifeboat loans by the new owners. Several, including some later taken over, had recovered under their own power and dispensed with Lifeboat backing, which in one or two cases had been brief and indirect. But by late in 1980, only a handful of the 25 remained as independent entities in the banking business. Lifeboat lending had been cut to some £500 m by the end of 1979 when only United Dominions Trust, First National Finance Corporation and Knowsley were borrowers; this figure had been further reduced a year later, mainly through large repayments by UDT.

In other parts of the British banking industry outside the ranks of the primary sector, the hurricane which blew in 1973–5 also left a much altered scene. Schedule II notes the varied fortunes during the crisis years of a number of other banking and financial concerns which were not helped through the Lifeboat but some of which, including Slater Walker Securities and certain other concerns, received financial assistance from the Bank of England. Of 24 companies listed, which represent – though by no means exhaustively – a further large part of the secondary banking sector of the mid-1970s, a number are, for one reason or another, no longer in the banking business, while several others have in whole, or in substantial part, been taken over by larger organisations, including the Bank of England.

It is worth noting that there have been considerable variations in the ways in which acquired secondary banking companies shown in Schedules I and II were subsequently dealt with by their new owners; many, in the finance house sector and elsewhere, have been further developed, while a few in less promising areas of secondary banking have been scaled down. Further reference to the supervision of the banking sector since the crisis will be made in the final chapter.

Meanwhile, in the next two chapters a closer look will be taken at two secondary banking groups – Keyser Ullmann and Slater Walker – which, because of their size and the scale and nature of their problems, are notably illustrative of the crisis.

APPENDIX

This appendix surveys a wide range of secondary banking and financial companies (those outside the ranks of the High Street clearing banks, the principal merchant banks, the discount houses, and others regarded as making up the primary banking system). It shows how they fared in the 1973–75 crisis and notes the extensive changes which resulted from that experience in the secondary banking sector. Those companies helped by the 'Lifeboat' operation are considered in Schedule I; the others are reviewed in Schedule II.

SCHEDULE I BANKING CONCERNS ASSISTED IN THE SECONDARY BANK CRISIS WITH SUPPORT LOANS THROUGH THE JOINT OPERATION (THE LIFEBOAT) RUN BY THE BANK OF ENGLAND AND THE LONDON AND SCOTTISH CLEARING BANKS

Company	Board included	Total assets ($£m$)	Experience in crisis
(Banking status, and whether shares quoted on the Stock Exchange: in each case as at end of 1973)	(30 Nov. 1973 unless otherwise stated. Those still directors end of 1979 marked with an asterisk*)	(Last balance sheet up to end of 1973, unless otherwise stated)	including maximum amount of support loans, if known, and sequel
Audley Holdings			
section 123 co. (subsid. of Cornwallis Estates, afterwards in liquidation; ultimate holding co. Kayrealm, afterwards in receivership). Not quoted	Woolf Abrahams, Anthony Adair, James P. Holding, directors	2	Provided with support loans. Receiver appointed May 1975

Beverley Bentinck Listed bank (finance house). Not quoted. (Now British Credit Trust, owned by Bank of Ireland. Until May 1978, subsid. of Northern Foods). Shares of successive parents quoted	Nicholas Horsley, chairman, David Smith,* managing director	38	Had some loans, backed by support group; these later repaid. Taken over in May 1978 by Bank of Ireland from Northern Foods for £11 m
Bowmaker Listed bank (finance house) and section 123 co. (Subsid. of C. T. Bowring, whose shares were quoted; Bowring group, including Bowmaker, taken over in 1980 by Marsh and McLennan of the US)	Edgar Bowring, chairman, Gilbert Cooke,* deputy chairman and chief executive (afterwards deputy chairman), T. G. Stevenson,* deputy chief executive (later managing director)	243	Received support loans within £89 m maximum. Left Lifeboat in autumn of 1975, when remaining support loans were repaid and co. received a new medium-term loan from major banks and the Bank of England
British Bank of Commerce section 123 co., whose shares were quoted. (Now Grindlays Bank (Scotland), owned by Grindlays Bank)	Alexander Stone, chairman, Earl of Harewood, Sir Jack Lyons, directors	59	Received support loans of £13.9 m at the peak. Taken over in September 1974 for £3.3 m by National and Grindlays Bank (now Grindlays Bank)

SCHEDULE I (*continued*)

Company (Banking status, and whether shares quoted on the Stock Exchange: in each case as at end of 1973)	*Board included* (30 Nov. 1973 unless otherwise stated. Those still directors end of 1979 marked with an asterisk*)	*Total assets (£m)* (Last balance sheet up to end of 1973, unless otherwise stated)	*Experience in crisis* including maximum amount of support loans, if known, and sequel
Burston Group Burston Finance subsid., a section 123 co. Group's shares were quoted.	Neville Burston, chairman, Sir Bernard Waley-Cohen, Bt, deputy chairman, W. T. Robinson, managing director and chief executive	100	Burston Finance provided with support loans. Receiver appointed to it in Feb. 1975. 65 per cent holding of Group in Burston & Texas Commerce Bank taken over in 1975 by Texas Commerce Bank of the US, which already held 35 per cent. Parent co. afterwards in liquidation
Cannon Street Investments (Cannon Street Acceptances subsid., a section 123 co.). Parent co.'s shares were quoted. Quotation still suspended end of 1980	Herbert Despard, chairman, W. T. Hislop,* managing director (chairman from 1974)	122	Cannon Street Acceptances received support loans up to £20m; receiver appointed to it in Sept. 1974. CSI reconstructed as subsid. of National Westminster Bank
Cedar Holdings section 123 co. Was quoted	Jack Morrison, chairman, Michael Morrison, deputy chairman and managing director, David Fischer (USA), managing director. William Broadfield and	128	Loans of up to £22m made available by Barclays Bank and financed through Lifeboat. These loans part of package by which institutions also put up £50m. Capital reconstruction 1975. Loans repaid within fol-

	Brian Oram, non-executive directors, representing institutions		lowing few years. Taken over by Lloyds and Scottish in 1979 for £9.6m
David Samuel Trust section 123 co. Not quoted	Leslie Lavy, chairman, Herbert Towning, managing director	38	Provided with support loans. Receiver appointed May 1975. Went into liquidation Nov. 1976
Duboff Brothers section 123 co. (Consolidated Finance Holdings ult. hlg co.). Not quoted	Harvey Cohen,* chairman and joint managing director, J. J. Fine, joint managing director, Bernard Duboff,* Samuel Duboff,* G. D. Berger,* G. H. Chamberlain, directors	9.5	Loan facility, initially of £2.5m, and ultimately of £6.7m, provided by National Westminster Bank, for a time under wing of Support group. Co. sustained losses leading to £2.66m deficiency by end of 1978. Settlement in 1979 under which £2.2m repaid and Natwest claim to over £4.5m assigned, against £50,000 payment (see text), leaving co. with positive shareholders' funds
Edward Bates and Sons (Holdings) Edward Bates and Sons subsid., a section 123 co. (Listed bank from Dec. 1973). Holding co. was quoted	James Gammell, chairman, Dennis Barkway, John Robertshaw, Peter Brandt, Tom Wyner, directors	74	Received some support loans in autumn of 1974, Lifeboat buying out part of shipping loan portfolio. Sizeable Arab shareholding, and Middle East deposits, from May 1975. Later, reconstruction under which part of business, recapitalised, emerged as Allied Arab Bank, with predominantly Arab shareholders and Barclays Bank International stake. Bank of England took over remaining assets of Bates bank for realisation through EBS Investments, now a Bank of England subsidiary. Holding co. in liquidation

SCHEDULE 1 *(continued)*

Company	Board included	Total assets (£m)	Experience in crisis
(Banking status, and whether shares quoted on the Stock Exchange: in each case as at end of 1973)	(30 Nov. 1973 unless otherwise stated. Those still directors end of 1979 marked with an asterisk*)	(Last balance sheet up to end of 1973, unless otherwise stated)	including maximum amount of support loans, if known, and sequel
First Maryland section 123 co. (Ultimate holding co. owned by Mr W G Stern and his family trusts). Not quoted	William Stern, chairman	18	Provided with support loans. Receiver appointed in Jan. 1975
First National Finance Corporation† Listed bank (afterwards section 123 co.) Quoted	Viscount De L'Isle, VC, chairman, Percy (Pat) Matthews, deputy chairman and managing director, Alan Challis, deputy chairman, John Black, Leslie Maxted,* Richard Langdon,* (deputy chairman, June 1975), Leonard Sainer,* Jocelyn Hambro, directors. (John Glyn,* chairman from June 1975; director 1974)	543	Received support loans totalling £350 m at peak. Capital reconstruction end of 1975, under which support loans divided into direct, deferred and income loans, with defined terms. Support loans reduced to £225 m at 31 Oct. 1980. Net deficiency of £79 m (30 Apr. 1977) more than halved to £29 m (31 Oct. 1980). Extensive programme of realisation of property and certain other assets undertaken

(Holdings) Was quoted	48	Harry Soning, chairman, Harvey Soning, deputy chairman	Provided with support loans. Receiver appointed June 1974
Keyser Ullmann Holdings (Keyser Ullmann subsid., a listed bank). Holding co.'s shares were quoted	433‡ (31 Mar. 1974)	Rt. Hon. Edward du Cann, MP, chairman, Jack Dellal, deputy chairman and managing director, Roland Franklin, Ian Stoutzker, Stanley Van Gelder, managing directors. Sir David Nicolson, L. L. Paisner, Barnett Shine, directors (Derek Wilde,* chairman and a director from March 1975).	Received support loans, of £65 m at peak. Loans repaid by 1976. Stand-by facilities from clearing banks provided for a time thereafter; dispensed with from Jan. 1977. Taken over for some £43 m in 1980 by Charterhouse Group, into whose Charterhouse Japhet bank KU banking company being absorbed. (See also Dawnay Day Group – Schedule II)
London and County Securities Group Banking subsidiary a section 123 co. Was quoted	129	Gerald Caplan, chairman and managing director, Robert Potel, deputy chairman, Lord Bradbury, F. A. Davies, N. G. A. Evans, Woolf Perry, Rt. Hon. Jeremy Thorpe MP, directors	Received support from a special consortium (see text) and afterwards received Lifeboat support loans. Joint co. planned by Bank of England and FNFC in Feb. 1974 to run the banking co. Announced in Mar. 1975 that banking company to be placed in liquidation; its total deficiency estimated at over £50 m. Group was the subject of a Dept. of Trade investigation (report published Jan. 1976). Holding co in liquidation

SCHEDULE 1 (*continued*)

Company	*Board included*	*Total assets (£m)*	*Experience in crisis*
(Banking status, and whether shares quoted on the Stock Exchange: in each case as at end of 1973)	(30 Nov. 1973 unless otherwise stated. Those still directors end of 1979 marked with an asterisk*)	(Last balance sheet up to end of 1973, unless otherwise stated)	including maximum amount of support loans, if known, and sequel
Medens Trust section 123 co. Not quoted	J. A. K. Collins,* chairman, G. F. Corber, managing director. L. Brett,* director (later managing director)	11 (30 June 1974)	Clearing bank borrowing facilities fixed up in late-1973 were continued with backing of support group. Borrowing facility provided by institutional shareholders used briefly and further available bank standby facility never required. Co. taken over by merchant bank group Brown Shipley Holdings in 1981 for £3.8 m
Mercantile Credit Subsid. a section 123 co. Was quoted	Daniel Meinertzhagen, chairman, Victor Adey,* deputy chairman and managing director (chairman from 1976)	377	Received support loans, of £167 m at peak. Loans repaid when co. taken over by Barclays Bank for £32 m in 1975
Morris Wigram section 123 co. (afterwards Schlesinger). Not quoted	H. L. Denton, chairman, Alan Morris, deputy chairman. T. C. G. T. Elwes, managing director. D. Heimann, M. J. Wigram, directors	30	Received support loans of about £10 m. Taken over for a nominal price in 1974 by Schlesinger Organisation, which repaid the loans. Schlesinger bank bought in 1980 by Slavenburg's Bank, of Holland

Northern Commercial Trust section 123 co. Not quoted. (Authority Investments, quoted, held 27%)	Sir John Foster, QC, chairman, Sidney Friedland, managing director. Brian Sandelson, director	90	NCT (apart from London loan business) taken over in 1975 by Algemene Bank Nederland, of Holland. Support loans of some £32 m, previously provided to NCT, transferred to Knowsley, by which London business of NCT taken over. Support loans on reduced scale still outstanding at end of 1980 to Knowsley
Knowsley section 123 co. (wholly owned by Authority Investments)	Sir John Foster,* QC, chairman, Sir John Langford-Holt,* MP, Dennis I. Lever,* Brian Sandelson,* directors		
Sterling Industrial Securities section 123 co. Not quoted	Lord Mais, chairman, Sidney Davidson, managing director, Sidney Finley, the late Bernard Wheatley (Crown Agents), directors	33	Received Lifeboat loans and larger support loans from Crown Agents, a substantial shareholder. Co. became the subject of a controlled running down of its business under the *aegis* of the Agents. Later sold
Triumph Investment Trust G. T. Whyte banking subsid. a listed bank. Group shares were quoted	Tom Whyte, executive chairman, becoming chief executive August 1974, when Lord Chelmer became chairman; Leonard Richenberg, deputy chairman and managing director	203	Provided with support loans (from Lifeboat) of up to some £30 m and some £5 m, in addition to an existing deposit of £5 m, from Crown Agents. Receiver appointed Nov. 1974. Now in liquidation

SCHEDULE 1 (*continued*)

Company (Banking status, and whether shares quoted on the Stock Exchange: in each case as at end of 1973)	Board included (30 Nov. 1973 unless otherwise stated. Those still directors end of 1979 marked with an asterisk*)	Total assets (£m) (Last balance sheet up to end of 1973, unless otherwise stated)	Experience in crisis including maximum amount of support loans, if known, and sequel
Twentieth Century Banking section 123 co. Not quoted. (Owned from 1972 by Bovis, now subsid. of P&O). Both successive ultimate parents quoted	Peter Gordon,* managing director	62	Received support loans. Acquired, as part of Bovis group, by P&O in Mar. 1974
United Dominions Trust[†] Listed bank. (Old Broad Street Securities subsid. a section 123 co.). Quoted	Sir Alexander Ross (retired Mar. 1974), chairman, Gilbert Standing, (chairman, Mar.–Oct. 1974), (Leonard Mather,* chairman and director from Nov. 1974)	896	Received support loans of some £500 m at peak. Prudential Assurance and Eagle Star Insurance put up bulk of £30 m against convertible stock in 1974. Property lending cut right back and a range of overseas interests disposed of from 1974. In 1980, agreement for instalment credit business to be bought by Trustee Savings Banks. Remaining support loans almost fully repaid in 1980. Full take-over bid of £110 m by TSBs successful in early 1981

J. H. Vavasseur Vavasseur Trust subsid. a section 123 co. (Group now part of Mills and Allen international†). Quoted	Sir Gordon Newton, chairman, David Stark, deputy chairman and chief executive, Jeremy Pinckney, Gervase Thomas, Timothy Renton MP,§ directors	52	Received support loans. Two capital reconstructions. Remaining support loans repaid, with the help of a clearing bank loan, in 1979. Co. effectively absorbed into Mills and Allen International in 1978
Wagon Finance Corporation† Listed bank (finance house). Quoted	The late Edward Bonser, chairman, Stephen de Bartolomé,* (later chairman) Joseph Chopping,* managing director. George Warburg, Arthur Winspear*	43	Received support loans, of some £8 m at peak; these were repaid in 1976. Co. then ac- corded loan facilities, including some medium-term, from a number of banks and accepting houses

NOTES

'Banking status' refers to the position at 30 Nov. 1973. The term 'Listed bank' means those in the Bank of England's lists for statistical purposes (*BEQB*, Dec. 1973, pp. 538–41), referring to the position at 31 Oct. 1973, as subsequently amended for developments up to 30 Nov. 1973). 'Listed banks' generally comprise those treated as banks under 8th Schedule of Companies Act 1948 and section 127 of Companies Act 1967, and those authorised under Exchange Control Act 1947. 'section 123 co.' denotes a concern holding a certificate under section 123 of the Companies Act 1967.

'Quoted' means that the shares were listed by the Stock Exchange at the end of 1973.

* See table heading, 2nd col.

† indicates co's shares quoted end of 1980.

‡ Group figure, including banking (shown as comparable fig. in 1975 accounts).

§ MP from March 1974.

SCHEDULE II   EXPERIENCE OF SOME OTHER BANKING AND FINANCIAL CONCERNS IN THE CRISIS YEARS AND AFTERWARDS

Company	*Board included*	*Total assets (£m)*	*Experience in crisis and, if relevant, afterwards*
(Banking status and whether shares quoted on the Stock Exchange: in each case as at end of 1973	(30 Nov. 1973 unless otherwise stated. Those still directors end of 1979 marked with an asterisk*).	(Last balance sheet up to end of 1973, unless otherwise stated)	
Anglo-Portuguese Bank (now A. P. Bank) Listed bank. Not quoted	Sir Isaac Wolfson, chairman, Sir Charles Hardie, Viscount Monckton, Peter Bunce* (general manager), directors	190 (Jan. 1974)	Total assets rapidly reduced to £104 m by Jan. 1975. Co. taken over in Apr. 1975 by Norwich Union Insurance for £12 m
Chancery Trust section 123 co. (subsid. of Chancery Consolidated, afterwards acquired by Arbuthnot Latham Holdings). Parent co.'s shares were quoted	Michael Renton,* chairman, afterwards deputy chairman of Arbuthnot Latham Holdings; David Holmes, director (until 1975)	22 (Chancery Cons., £28 m)	Group very liquid at onset of secondary banking crisis, after lately virtually disengaging from property. Chancery Consolidated (and Chancery Trust) taken over by Arbuthnot Latham Holdings in Dec. 1975 for £4.9 m
Corinthian Holdings† Corinthian Securities banking subsid., a section 123 co. Quoted	Frank Collis, chairman, Mrs Gloria Eban, the late Col. H. S. J. Jelf, Henry Prevezer,* (chairman from 1976), directors	16	Reduction of deposits as result of secondary banking crisis. Drew on established lines of credit and Charles Wolfson Charitable Trust, a shareholder, provided additional sums, later raising its interest to 29.9%. In Nov. 1980, agreement made to sell Corinthian Se~~curities to Armco of the US for £1.29 m~~

Cornhill Consolidated Group‡ Included Cornhill Consolidated co. Not quoted	John Morris, A. J. Allright, J. L. Beetwell, directors	21 (31 May 72 – Dept. of Trade Inspectors' estimate)	Liquidation of Cornhill Consolidated co. decided on in Jan. 1974, co. accorded no Lifeboat loans. Group afterwards in liquidation
Cripps Warburg Listed bank. Not quoted	Milo Cripps, George Warburg, John Morgan, directors	31	Taken over by William and Glyn's Bank in Feb. 1975 for a nominal price
G. R. Dawes Holdings† G. R. Dawes subsid., a section 123 co. Holding co.'s shares quoted	Howard Dawes, chairman	21	Holding group put into voluntary liquidation in 1977 so that shareholders could obtain full cash value of assets, including industrial interests. Substantial distribution to shareholders
Dawnay Day Group Banking subsid. section 123 co. Was quoted	David Finnie, chairman until Nov. 1974; Sir Peter Parker, chairman 1974–7; Edward Hatchett,* chairman from 1977	65	Prudential Ass. provided unsecured borrowing facility of £10 m in 1974. Banking activities reduced. Taken over for £16.6 m in 1980 by Hume Holdings, a subsidiary of Rothschild Investment Trust (now RIT). In April 1981 it was arranged that the Dawnay Day banking company should be taken over by a new company, Holding Financier, being formed by Mr Guy Naggar, until then deputy chief executive of Keyser Ullmann (KU), to run KU's European banking operations in France and Switzerland which he was 'buying out'

SCHEDULE II (*continued*)

Company	Board included	Total assets (£m)	Experience in crisis and, if relevant, afterwards
(Banking status and whether shares quoted on the Stock Exchange: in each case as at end of 1973	(30 Nov. 1973 unless otherwise stated. Those still directors end of 1979 marked with an asterisk*).	(Last balance sheet up to end of 1973, unless otherwise stated)	
F. C. Finance† Listed finance house (Subsidiary of Co-operative Bank)	Lord Wilson of Radcliffe, chairman, John Donaldson,* managing director. (Sir Arthur Sugden,* chairman and director from 1974–80)	71	Holding co. provided increased backing and advances in 1974; profits in 1974 and 1975 affected by provisions against loans and land held for development. In 1980, Co-operative Bank bid to buy out remaining 18% publicly held shares for £1.4m
Fraser Ansbacher (now Henry Ansbacher Holdings†). Henry Ansbacher, listed bank, a subsid. Quoted	Sir Maxwell Joseph,* chairman until 1976, M. N. Richardson, deputy chairman, J. R. Cowen, managing director, J. M. Button,* director. (Sir Samuel Goldman,* KCB, chairman and director from 1976)	42	Support loan for Henry Ansbacher banking subsid. approved in 1974, but never drawn. Group incurred losses of some £6.5m, mainly on property and investments, in 1975–8. Capital reconstruction, and change of name, in 1979, following concentration on merchant banking business of Henry Ansbacher; subsidiaries R. Fraser Securities (property) and Robert Fraser and Partners (investment banking) disposed of. After reconstruction, 49.6% of shares held by Lissauer Group, of the US, which had channelled in some £3m capital after initial investment of £1.7m, and 18.9% by Grand Metropolitan

Gresham Investment Trust† Gresham Trust subsid. section 123 co. Parent co.'s shares quoted	Peter Wreford,* joint chairman and joint managing director, Maurice B. Baring,* joint chairman, Norman Baldock,* joint managing director	18	Weathered crisis years satisfactorily; profits fall 1974/75 Continues trading normally
Hawtin and Partners section 123 co. (subsid. of Hawtin†) Parent co.'s shares quoted.	Frank Hawtin,‖ chairman	41 (Group total)	In 1974/75 Gilwise, a member of the US group Gulf + Western Associates, took over Hawtin and Partners for a nominal consideration
Hodge Group Julian S. Hodge, a listed bank, among the group's subsids. Was quoted	Sir Julian Hodge, chairman, W. G. Pullen, deputy chairman, Sir Andrew Maitland-Makgill-Crichton, S. E. Taylor,* directors	278	Taken over in Nov. 1973 by Standard and Chartered (later Standard Chartered) Bank for over £42 m
Ionian Bank Listed bank. Not quoted	Sir Robin Brook, chairman, B. W. S. Irwin, deputy-chairman, Michael Behrens, John Trusted, directors	54	Decided in Jan. 1977 to effect an orderly run-down of its banking business, its principal activity. Bank of England made available stand-by facility of some £5 m to cover any short-term liquidity problems
Israel-British Bank (London) Listed bank. (Subsid. of Israel-British Bank, of Israel). Group shares were quoted	Harry Landy, chairman, Joshua Bension, director	62	Co. and Israeli parent ceased business in 1974 and both were placed in liquidation. Contributions made to liquidation fund by Bank of England and Bank of Israel

SCHEDULE II *(continued)*

Company	*Board included*	*Total assets (£m)*	*Experience in crisis and, if relevant, afterwards*
(Banking status and whether shares quoted on the Stock Exchange: in each case as at end of 1973	(30 Nov. 1973 unless otherwise stated. Those still directors end of 1979 marked with an asterisk*).	(Last balance sheet up to end of 1973, unless otherwise stated)	
Jacobs Kroll section 123 co. A half share in the co. bought in mid-1973 by Equity Enterprises, controlled by Slater Walker Securities and David Frost. EE bought rest of JK in Sept. 1975. Not quoted	David Kroll, Jacob Jacobs, directors	12.75	Receiver appointed Nov. 1975. 'Unconnected' depositors repaid through arrangements made by Slater Walker and Bank of England
Jessel Securities Investment company with insurance, unit trust management, and industrial interests. No direct banking interests, though 20% stake in G. R. Dawes Holdings. Quoted	Oliver Jessel, chairman, M. V. St Giles, T. F. H. Jessel MP, directors	202	Difficulties from autumn 1974, when receiver called into the London Indemnity and General Insurance subsid. Later in liquidation

Leopold Joseph Holdings† (Subsid. Leopold Joseph & Sons a listed bank). Quoted	Sir Hugh Weeks, chairman, Baron Alexis de Redé,* deputy chairman, Louis Heymann,* executive director, Viscount Kemsley,* Prince Rupert Loewenstein,* directors	74	Weathered crisis years satisfactorily in independence; profits level in 1973–5. Stake totalling 25% in holding co. acquired against capital injection of £2.3 m in July 1974 by two West German State banks, Bayerische Landesbank and Bremer Landesbank
London Scottish Finance Corporation† Quoted	Harry Livingstone, Roland Landman,* joint chairmen, Jack Livingstone,* managing director	9	Weathered crisis years satisfactorily in independence. In 1976, stake of 20% bought by FIMS, subsid. of US group ISC Financial Corporation, which put additional capital into LSFC. This stake later passed to subsid. of Edward Lumley (Finance), Lloyd's brokers
Manson Finance Trust† Quoted	A. Lawson,* E. E. Goldie,* joint chairmen	6	Weathered crisis years satisfactorily in independence. In 1974, F. L. Smidth group, of Denmark, took stake of 20% (raised in 1975 to 29.6%) and lent £1 m. 51% stake taken by Hong Leong, 1980

SCHEDULE II (*continued*)

Company	Board included	Total assets (£m)	Experience in crisis and, if relevant, afterwards
(Banking status and whether shares quoted on the Stock Exchange: in each case as at end of 1973	(30 Nov. 1973 unless otherwise stated. Those still directors end of 1979 marked with an asterisk*).	(Last balance sheet up to end of 1973, unless otherwise stated)	
Moorgate Mercantile Holdings† Quoted	Julius Silman,* chairman, Julius Levinkind,* managing director	20	Co. was refused rescue operation in Dec. 1973. Special manager and receiver, Rupert Nicholson, appointed. Capital reconstructed and co. later recovered, shares being re-quoted 1978
Slater Walker Securities (Was parent of Slater Walker, listed bank). Now Britannia Arrow Holdings.† Quoted	Jim Slater, chairman, A. J. H. Buckley, managing director, B. Banks, M. J. Booth, J. K. O'Donnell, R. Rowe, Richard Tarling, Ian Wasserman, directors	588	In Oct. 1975 received from Bank of England line of credit; this fixed in Dec. 1975 at £70 m. Bank also guaranteed principal of loans up to £40 m and future interest. In Sept. 1977, Slater Walker banking company taken over, with some SWS property, by Bank of England. Loan stock changes at SWS, involving repayment, on altered terms, of sterling loan stocks. Remaining (chiefly investment management) business of SWS, renamed Britannia Arrow Holdings

Wallace Brothers Bank Previously Wallace Brothers Sassoon Bank. A section 123 co. (Subsid. of Wallace Brothers (Holdings)). Not quoted	D. R. S. FitzGerald, chairman, J. J. Grafftey-Smith, managing director	96	Taken over by Standard Chartered Bank in Dec. 1976 on terms likely to involve nil consideration. Loss of up to £1m or more on the acquisition subsequently provided for by purchaser. Business of Wallace (not consolidated in Standard Chartered accounts) is being gradually phased out
Western Trust and Savings section 123 co. (Subsid. of Western Credit Holdings). Holding co. was quoted	H. N. Sporborg, chairman, R. C. Priestland,§ managing director, Russell Taylor,§ director	32 (Group total)	Control of Western Credit acquired in Feb. 1974 by a subsidiary of Philadelphia National Bank of US, Arbuthnot Latham Holdings retaining minority interest. Group completely acquired by Royal Bank of Canada in Feb. 1979 for £10.5 m
Wintrust† Listed bank. Quoted	George Szpiro,* chairman and joint managing director, Richard Szpiro,* joint managing director	37	Weathered crisis years satisfactorily in independence; profits declined 1975–7

NOTES

'Banking status' refers to the position at 30 Nov. 1973. The term 'Listed bank' means those in the Bank of England's lists for statistical purposes (*BEQB*, Dec. 1973, pp. 536–41), referring to the position at 31 Oct. 1973, as subsequently amended for developments up to 30 Nov. 1973). 'Listed banks' generally comprise those treated as banks under 8th Schedule of Companies Act 1948 and section 127 of Companies Act 1967, and those authorised under Exchange Control Act 1947. 'section 123 co.' denotes a concern holding a certificate under section 123 of the Companies Act 1967.

'Quoted' means that the shares were listed on the Stock Exchange at the end of 1973.

* See table heading, 2nd col.

† indicates co's shares quoted end of 1980.

‡ For detailed reference to Dept. of Trade Inspectors' report, see note 5 to Chapter 7.

§ Still respectively managing director and director of Western Trust and Savings end 1979 (as at 30 Nov. 1973).

‖ Still chairman of Hawtin, end 1979.

12 Case Study One: Keyser Ullmann

At that time [1973] we had a lot of money and the City were telling me "lend it out, lend it out".

Mr Jack Dellal, former deputy chairman of
Keyser Ullmann Holdings[1]

Among the banking companies caught up in the upheaval, Keyser Ullmann attracted a large share of public attention, and not without reason. It embarked on a remarkable lending spree just before the crisis and was later forced to draw substantially on the Lifeboat's support loans. It had also to make such large provisions for losses on its loans that it incurred very heavy losses and saw its shareholders' funds reduced at one stage to less than a third of their previous level. How did it all happen?

The business had a relatively quiet history before the 1970s. It traced its origins back to the formation in the last century of the investment banking business of A. Keyser; in 1962 it acquired the Ullmann banking business and in 1965 became Keyser Ullmann (KU). The earnings record was staid in the next few years, net disclosed profits being £0.6 m in both 1968/69 and 1970/71. But in the early 1970s the bank, particularly through its managing directors, Mr Roland Franklin and Mr Ian Stoutzker, became very active in the corporate finance field; one very substantial and profitable part of this business was its role as financial adviser to some of the companies associated with Sir James Goldsmith.

The next years brought several important changes and developments. in 1970, on the retirement of Mr Charles Keyser, Mr Edward du Cann MP became chairman. Mr du Cann had a City background as a pioneer in the post-war revival of the unit trust industry; he was also chairman of Central and District Properties.

In March 1972, a significant new stimulus to the KU group's growth occurred, when Prudential Assurance put up £7.5 m for a shareholding of over a fifth in the quoted Keyser Ullmann Holdings (KUH) parent company. This connection reinforced the standing of KU and a month later the group successfully made a share exchange offer at £69 m, for Central and District Properties. Also in 1972 KU joined in the vogue for forming consortium banks – British banks set up by several inter-national partner banks to operate in the Euro-markets and otherwise – and became one of a number of banks which established London Interstate Bank.

The next major event in a period of busy activity was KUH's £58 m take-over, in the winter of 1972/73, of the fast-growing Dalton Barton Securities (DBS), which owned a section 123 bank and which was run by Mr Jack Dellal and Mr Stanley Van Gelder. KU and DBS already had some link before their merger. In particular, KU held a 24.4 per cent stake in Swordheath Properties, a property dealing subsidiary of Matlodge, which had much flat property in West London, and which DBS owned on a 50:50 basis with interests of the brothers Mr David Kirch and Mr Peter Kirch.

After the merger, the Dalton Barton side remained based at Hyde Park House, Knightsbridge, in London's West End, through which much lending continued to be done, whereas the old KU operated from Throgmorton Street, and later from Milk Street, in the City of London. Mr Dellal assumed the office of deputy chairman of KUH and he and Mr Van Gelder both became additional managing directors, alongside the existing two, Mr Roland Franklin, whose family had been connected with Keysers for four generations, and Mr Stoutzker, who is his brother-in-law.

In the financial year to 31 March 1973, the group made increased net profits of £9.0 m, compared with £4.4 m in 1971/72; in his annual statement Mr du Cann noted the acquisitions of Central and District Properties and Dalton Barton as the major features of the year 1972/73, and recorded that KU was by then retained as corporate finance adviser by more companies than at any previous time.

KUH's cash and shareholders' funds received a major boost when, in September 1973, Central and District Properties (C and D), bought against an issue of KUH shares only a year and a half earlier, was sold for cash to the large Town and City Properties, realising a net profit of some £28 m. Framed copies of the cheques for the £97 m cash price afterwards stood in the office of Mr Dellal, who had been largely responsible for arranging the sale. This deal, not long before the eve of the secondary banking crisis, was much better timed for KUH than for the buyer, Town and City, which, as noted above, was to face major difficulties in the crisis years after its period of expansion.

With the large profits of the C and D sale having increased KU's capital and its capacity to lend, the stage was now set for the fresh upsurge in advances which Mr Dellal afterwards recalled that he was urged by 'the City' to make at this time. As will be seen, lending did indeed proceed briskly, and the group's total advances, which had been £161 m at 31 March 1973, climbed rapidly; a year later, they were put at £254 m after their value had been reduced by substantial loss provisions following the start of the general crisis.

What sort of advances structure had the company built up – and swiftly built up – by the time the crisis struck the City of London at the end of 1973? So much has become known that it is possible to attempt to sketch the broad shape of the loan book which constituted much the most important asset of the group and on which very heavy losses were to be faced.

Out of a total loan book approaching £300 m before the deduction of loss provisions, over £100 m had been lent to only four main borrowers, none of whom could pay the money back when it became due.

One large slice of the lending was to Mr Ronald Lyon's wide-ranging Ronald Lyon Holdings property group, which was to crumble in May 1974. It appears that loans to this group (much personally guaranteed by Mr Lyon), together with other advances to him personally (including finance for the building of a new yacht) amounted to around £20 m, against which substantial provisions must later have been needed. Various of the Lyon interests were charged to KU and were taken over by it as security.

Another major debt owing to KU on the outbreak of the crisis was from a further big private property group, that of Mr William Stern. By 1978, this debt, with accumulated interest, amounted to £20.5 m. This is how Mr Stern, who became bankrupt in 1978, following a petition by KU, with debts of more than £104 m, almost entirely arising from his guarantees of his companies' borrowings, described to the author how his debt to KU had arisen: 'They didn't lend £20 m. They lent only about £10 m. Of the £10 m, £7 m was a loan made in relation to the sale to my companies of a residual portfolio of Central and District's properties for £9 m: they lent £7 m and I paid £2 m for these. They (KU) lent the £7 m in Swiss francs at the then rate of SwF 7.90–8.00 to the £; after the pound fell against the Swiss franc, there were exchange losses of £7–8 m, making a debt of £14–15 m; the rest was interest.' Mr Stern was not the only player in the secondary bank and property drama who incurred big losses through borrowing in foreign currency; a number of others who raised foreign currency loans at lower interest rates than prevailed in Britain found that their sterling debt was sharply magnified by the pound's major drop in the mid-1970s.

Much the most dramatic and widely-discussed feature of KU's lending was the sum of £17.25 m, later raised to £21.75 m, which was advanced to C.S.T. Investments, the £100 private company effectively controlled by the young Mr Christopher Selmes, to finance the controversial take-over, in the autumn of 1973, of Grendon Trust, whose then chairman was the Duke of St Albans. Grendon's assets included property; in the still euphoric atmosphere of the autumn of 1973, MEPC, the large property group, was also a keenly-interested would-be bidder for Grendon.

In the event, the KU loan which, with unpaid interest, eventually mounted up to some £27 m, proved irrecoverable; by June 1975 CST Investments had a deficiency of £27.49 m.[2] The circumstances of the bid and its financing have been vividly related, with their findings, by the two Department of Trade Inspectors, Mr Joseph Jackson, QC, and Mr Kirkpatrick Young, TD, who investigated CST Investments and also Dowgate and General Investments, a quoted investment trust in which there were considerable Selmes holdings and which lent £5.2 m, unsecured and not repaid, towards financing the bid for Grendon.

The initial loan facility from KU to CST Investments – then apparently not exceeding £16.5 m – was against the security of the Grendon shares to be acquired. It was also the subject of a personal guarantee from Mr Selmes, for whose operations KU, through its Dalton Barton side, had previously lent on two occasions. A personal guarantee was also obtained from a 22-year-old colleague of Mr Selmes' whom the Inspectors later recorded as having said to them that he had about two minutes' notice that he was to sign a personal guarantee for £16.5 m.[3]

The take-over of Grendon went through in the late-autumn of 1973: its sequel was simple and catastrophic. The Inspectors quote Mr Dellal as saying that it 'was a loan which was supposed to have unravelled itself very quickly. The idea was that they were going to sell this off, that off, and the other off – everything'.[4] In the expression of the Inspectors, the takeover of Grendon 'was to be an asset-stripping operation'.[5] As such, and indeed from any viewpoint, it went disastrously wrong. The Selmes team moved into Grendon in November 1973, and they found more problems than they had anticipated. For instance, the Monotype Corporation, earlier acquired by Grendon through transactions involving the Edward Bates secondary bank, which the Inspectors also discussed, was running unprofitably. Then, within a few months, the crisis of the property industry, where many Grendon assets were, broke out. The £17.25 m loan, later raised to £21.75 m, was not repaid; the Inspectors say in their report that the amount KU had to write off this loan was £21.75 m, not counting loss of interest and other expenditures.[6] Mr Selmes eventually went to live abroad (he gave no oral evidence to the Inspectors) and in August 1974 KU took over the management of Grendon. The Inspectors also chronicle how Mr Selmes was released from his personal liability, through his guarantee on this huge debt, in return for a Henry Moore sculpture valued at £20,000, £16,000 of shares and a debt of £114,000 'binding in honour only'. The agreement, under which the young financier was let off his vast liability, was afterwards described by Mr Derek Wilde, KUH's new chairman, who had formerly been a vice-chairman of the big Barclays Bank, as 'the most astonishing piece of paper I have ever seen'.[7]

The Inspectors refer to the release of Mr Selmes from his guarantee as 'an extraordinary, almost incredible, story'.[8] They remark, of the approval for the ill-fated £17.25 m advance: 'no-one at the merchant bank (KU) took an overall look at the transaction from what one might term a banking point of view. This was a commercial transaction in which the idea was to buy a company and sell it off in one way or another, as yet not worked out, as quickly as possible at a huge profit'. Of the outcome, which resulted in the full eventual debt, with accumulated interest, proving irrecoverable, they record that Mr Wilde said the episode was 'an enormous disaster'; they also quote the comment of Mr Edward du Cann, the KU chairman that the loan 'was a very great mistake, it should never have occurred'.[9] It must be rare indeed in banking history for the amount lost on a loan transaction to be, as in this case – because of interest and other costs – more than the total amount originally lent.

KU's largest loan exposure of all was through its financing of the mainly flat-owning interests of Peureula Investments, in which Mr David Kirch and his brother Peter had substantial holdings. Mr David Kirch, after working for a time in the Lloyd's insurance market and afterwards owning a meat company, went into the property business with his brother Peter in 1962, when he was 24. An early enterprise was the purchase, for more than a quarter of a million pounds, of twenty-three houses in Earls Court, West London, which were then producing an income of only £1000 a year. According to Mr David Kirch's recollection, quoted in an article in the *Evening Standard* in 1970,[10] this was the brothers' 'first big gamble'. 'Someone showed us . . . we had paid £100,000 more than his top valuation. Which wasn't very cheerful. We issued a cheque for the 10 per cent deposit which wasn't covered at the time. We had to borrow to cover the 10 per cent on the cheque and then we had the serious trouble of raising the other 90 per cent'. However, the venturesome pair succeeded in obtaining the necessary finance and then proceeded to build their residential empire of flats and other property further. In Mr Kirch's words in the same interview, 'once you had dealt with figures of a quarter of a million things do become much easier'. In his case, they did indeed.

In the early 1970s, the Kirch brothers bought into a quoted company, the former Peureula (Sumatra) Rubber Estates, which was renamed Peureula Investments. KU was banker to Peureula, as was Barclays Bank. There was the further, significant, association which KU had with the Kirch ventures through the joint shareholdings, already noted, in Matlodge and Swordheath Properties. KU made large loans, which eventually amounted to over £30 m, to Peureula, whose pre-tax profits more than doubled to some £1.8 m in 1972.

However, soaring interest rates from late-1973 and the property crisis created unhappy conditions for the heavily-borrowed Peureula, whose previously high flying shares dropped away; the company was then taken over by the private Kirch company, Chesterbeech, so coming out of the quoted sector. Conditions worsened and the huge loans, eventually amounting, with interest, to some £35 m, could not be repaid by the Chesterbeech group of companies. As a result of this, it must be assumed that KU, directly or indirectly, controls a group of companies owning thousands of flats and other property. Considerable sales of these assets had already taken place by the end of 1979. Meanwhile KU had provided several million pounds against losses on this part of its lending. Mr David Kirch was quoted in *The Sunday Times* of 17 December 1976 as saying: 'They (KU) can only ever *hope* to get their money back, which they won't.' (Author's italics) Mr Kirch, who now lives in Jersey, afterwards remarked to the author: 'The bank (KU) had a partnership with us in Matlodge and Swordheath Properties. If I ever again went into a venture involving large-scale borrowings, I would certainly always want the bank or financial institutions lending for it to participate as a shareholder.'

Within KU's loss book, which spanned a much wider range than these major four big loans, and some 80 per cent of which related to property, there were a number of other substantial advances running into several

million pounds. The bank was a creditor for more than £5 m to
Guardian Properties, which failed in 1974 after receiving some Lifeboat
support. It was also among the banks which financed the large private
property interests, of some £90 m at their peak, of Mr David Lewis;
these ran into difficulties in 1974 and, being unable to repay in full,
eventually reached accommodations and ultimately settlements with the
various bank creditors. K U was a creditor to this borrower for around
£6–£7 m, a considerable part of which must have been irrecoverable.
Another loan was one of several million pounds, not all recovered, to
a company associated with the late Prince Stanislas Radziwill, husband
of the late President John Kennedy's sister-in-law Lee. Prince Radziwill
had also been a participant in certain Australian property ventures
which the Crown Agents were involved in. A considerable number of
further loans to companies, mostly concerned with property, and
individuals, many of sizeable amount, were also made. Loans to hotel
interests amounted to between £5 m and £10 m.

In November 1973, the cash-rich K U, which had previously occasionally made credit facilities available to London and County Securities,
extended £12.5 m of further secured borrowing facilities to that, by then,
ailing, concern. In November drawings under it were repaid, but K U
took over £10 m of L and C's loan book, and with it, in effect, a number
of sizeable loans to individuals. A £2.6 m loan from L and C's bank to
Mr Rolf Schild – who was in the headlines in 1979/80 when he and his
wife and daughter were held by kidnappers in Sardinia – was also taken
over by K U,[11] which subsequently started legal proceedings for the
recovery of the money; Mr Schild denied liability.

The first impact of K U's adverse lending experience was publicly shown
when the K UH group's accounts for the year to 31 March 1974 referred
to provisions and losses of an exceptional nature, charged to the
banking company's reserves; the following year's accounts, presented
on an altered basis of full disclosure, showed that the provisions had
been £30.6 m, resulting in a 1973/74 pre-tax loss of £12.8 m. Disclosed
shareholders' funds at the end of March 1974 were £100.3 m. Cushioned
as it was by the highly profitable sale of Central and District Properties,
K U had weathered the early stages of the secondary banking upheaval
without serious liquidity problems. But by the late summer of 1974, it
was receiving support loans from the Lifeboat.

In July Mr Dellal, a deputy chairman, and Mr Van Gelder, formerly
the chiefs of the Dalton Barton side, resigned from the K UH group,
where they had been managing directors, and from the board, after-

wards receiving compensation for loss of office totalling £27,000. In the following March Mr du Cann resigned as chairman and as a director of KUH, though he remained chairman, at a £25,000 a year salary, of the Cannon Assurance subsidiary. Mr Derek Wilde, a vice-chairman and former senior general manager of Barclays Bank, moved in with the blessing of the Bank of England and the Lifeboat support group, to be full-time chairman of the KU group. The other two of the four previous managing directors, Mr Roland Franklin and Mr Ian Stoutzker, resigned in July 1975. Mr Roy Fenton, who had been a senior Bank of England official, became KU's chief executive, a post he held until his death in 1979.

By the spring of 1975, KU was drawing some £65 m of support loans. As Mr Wilde told shareholders in his first annual statement: 'Without that help, it is difficult to see what answer might have been found to our problem'.[12] The group's results for 1974/75 further revealed the major scale of the setback which the group had suffered. There was a pre-tax loss for the year of £59 m after additional provisions of £64 m for bad and doubtful debts and other purposes, including £13 m to cover the future interest cost of sums borrowed to finance loans on which full interest was not being received, had been made relating to the year itself; a further sum of £18.5 m for unpaid interest due was also earmarked. As Mr Wilde stated: 'In all we have provided against doubtful debts this year a sum of £82.5 m and together with the outstanding provisions of earlier years we have a total of £119 m out of which we have written down our advances to the figure of £176 m.'[13] Shareholders' funds (capital and reserves) had been slashed to £42.6 m; they were to be further reduced by additional provisions and losses to £30.4 m by the end of September 1976. Thereafter, the figure showed some increase, reaching £44 m by 1980.

The revised management team set about tackling the process of recovering what could be obtained in connection with loans in default, the great majority of which were against property. It was to be a lengthy task. The realisation operation was conducted by a department headed by Mr Karol Ashken, the Polish-born director who had come over to KUH and its board with Dalton Barton. The job was not easy as the property market remained fragile for some time. KU had to channel in some £15 m more cash to complete partly finished buildings they had taken over as security for unrepaid loans. It had also to set about seeking to sell, not merely thousands of flats, but various other properties. These included new office blocks, such as the Conoco building in Blackfriars Road, London, begun by Prince Radziwill's interests, which was completed, and eventually sold, and the Sean Lemass building in Dublin, started by the Lyon group. Mr Lyon's new yacht was completed and sold by KU for several million dollars in 1979. Other assets taken over as security for loans not repaid had also to be sold off: these ranged from shares in quoted companies to oil paintings.

Confidence flowed back to KUH under its new management and by 1976 the Lifeboat support loans, which had reached £65 m at their peak but had been gradually declining, were repaid. KU received stand-by borrowing facilities, which were used on occasion, from the big banks; these were dispensed with in 1977. From 1977/78 the more compact group began to earn profits again. With a considerable eventual reflow of money from realisations of its written-down assets and only modest new lending business, the group became an interesting potential 'cash box' with the additional appeal of large tax losses. Then, in 1980, KUH was taken over for £43 m by Charterhouse Group, the investment and financial concern with industrial interests which owns the Charterhouse Japhet merchant bank, an accepting house. The two banks are being combined, the Keyser Ullmann name being dropped. Mr Wilde, who became non-executive chairman of the combined bank and deputy chairman of the Charterhouse Group, remarked at the time the merger details were announced that, had KUH continued on its own 'It would undoubtedly have taken a long time to re-establish our reputation.'

One further matter which should be referred to is that of lending to directors. The accounts for 1974/75 disclosed that 'secured loans made by the [KU] banking subsidiary in the ordinary course of business to companies in which directors had an interest of not less than 10 per cent in the equity share capital and loans to directors personally' reached a maximum of £7,446,559 in 1974/75.[14]

A substantial part of this was accounted for by secured lending to companies in which Mr Dellal and Mr Van Gelder had minority shareholdings up to early in 1974, Court Hotels (London) and its Comfort Flats and other subsidiaries. KU, originally through Dalton Barton, made loans to these companies which, by 1973, are thought to have been in the £2.5–3 m range; however, within the following year this debt mounted up, with interest, to £4.5 m or more. Mr Dellal has commented to the author that the loans to Court Hotels and its subsidiaries were made in line with the principle of providing finance to customers one was well acquainted with. It is to be remembered that in the boom days when these loans were first made, the Dalton Barton lending operation had had virtually no bad debt experience.

In 1973, a 25 per cent stake in Court Hotels was bought by Tollman Hotels and the Dellal-Van Gelder holding, previously some 20 per cent, was cut to about 10 per cent. This reduced stake was in turn disposed of when Tollman bought a further holding giving it control of Court Hotels. However, this remaining holding had evidently not changed hands before the beginning of KU's financial year 1974/75 and is believed to have been included, to the extent of at least £4.5 m, in the total of lending to companies in which directors had interests of at least 10 per cent. In the event, the KU loans to Court Hotels turned out most unfortunately. Court Hotels went into receivership, owing large debts, and KU had to make big loss provisions, probably of some £3 m, against this lending.

In addition, KU had made sizeable loans, believed to have amounted to some £600,000 in March 1975, to Mr Dellal's private company, Allied Commercial Exporters. These were all repaid in due course with interest without loss to the bank. Mr Dellal had no personal loans from the KU bank. Mr Van Gelder had reduced an overdraft which had at one time exceeded £400,000 to under £100,000 at the time of his resignation, and it is understood that settlement arrangements were later made in connection with this balance.

Substantial loans were made to Mr du Cann, who owed the KU bank an amount which reached considerably more than half a million pounds before it was repaid in 1979, some four years after he had ceased to be chairman and a director of the group.

Much of the lending by KU to Mr du Cann arose in this way. In 1972, an interest in International Life Insurance (UK), which had started as the British arm of Mr Bernie Cornfeld's Investors Overseas Services (IOS) empire, and which was ailing following the troubles and adverse publicity surrounding IOS, became available. Arrangements were made around June 1972 for a minority holding in ILI (UK) to be bought from Value Capital, a Bahamas company associated with the controversial Mr Robert Vesco, a former associate of Mr Cornfeld. The idea was that under the wing of KU and Mr du Cann, and with the prestige of the latter as a prominent politician, ILI would be rescued from threatened decline and set on a more prosperous path. However, after considerable discussion, a larger, controlling, interest of 57 per cent in ILI (later renamed Cannon Assurance) was acquired by the KUH group, and a holding of some 15 per cent, (131,250 shares) was bought by Mr du Cann, finance for his purchase being provided by KU.

The average cost per share of the shareholding acquired by Mr du Cann was considerably lower than that of the stake bought by KUH itself. The reason for this difference was that the KUH group was acquiring a majority holding. A legal wrangle with overseas interests over the title to the holdings was eventually settled – further payments being made – in 1978, in a way which firmly established the title of the buyers.

Mr du Cann had left the KU chairmanship and board more than three years before this settlement was reached in May 1978 but he had remained as chairman of the KUH-controlled Cannon, which duly recovered and prospered. In 1979, Cannon was bought by a Canadian concern, Cascade Group for £9.6 m and, for his holding, Mr du Cann received some £1.4 m, yielding him a profit reported to be of about £1 m, subject to capital gains tax, on the cost of his investment. He clearly felt that, in shouldering the debt to finance his shareholding in Cannon – in whose recovery he played a notable part – he had incurred a significant personal risk for the sake of undertaking the much-needed revival of that then ailing concern. He was quoted as saying, after the Cascade take-over, giving rise to his £1 m pre-tax profit, was announced, that everyone was willing to criticise people who took risks and were successful but that in 1972 he had taken a real business risk in trying to keep ILI viable.[15]

Mr du Cann also had some further loans from KU, partly secured otherwise than on the Cannon shares. It is believed that the total he owed to KU at the time of his resignation in March 1975 was around £500,000. Allowing for interest due, this sum had risen considerably further by early 1979. After the sale of Cannon to Cascade, Mr du Cann repaid all his outstanding borrowing from KU, with interest. He remained chairman of Cannon Assurance for some time after the Cascade take-over until he left in February 1980.[16]

The remaining two former managing directors of KUH, Mr Roland Franklin and Mr Ian Stoutzker, also had certain borrowings from KU. But perhaps the most significant personal transaction in which Mr Franklin was concerned did not involve a loan but a deal, later put into reverse, for the sale of his flat.

At the end of 1974, the London flat of Mr Franklin and his wife in the smart Regents Park area of London was sold to Keyser Ullmann for £275,000. When, a few weeks later, in January 1975, the matter came up before the board for the normally routine approval of the use of the company's seal to complete the purchase deal, certain others of the directors – not all of whom had previously known of it – voiced criticism of the transaction. The timing of the sale had certainly been unhappy. At this stage, several weeks into 1975, KU was fully in the eye of the secondary banking and property storm. It was drawing heavily from the Bank of England's Lifeboat, and was just ending a financial year's trading which was to result in a £59 m loss after provisions of £64 m, the great bulk of which were against possible losses on property lending.

Buying a luxury flat from one of its managing directors for £275,000 at such a time was, as one other director pungently put it, 'the sort of business KU needed like a hole in the head'. Moreover, so uncertain and near-paralysed was the property market that, although Mr Franklin had obtained a professional valuation of the flat at £275,000, it was possible for others to feel doubts whether the flat was really worth this sum in the prevailing conditions.

At any rate, the flat episode brought to a head a certain accumulated discontent among some other directors at decisions, as they saw it, being made, so that they became *faits accomplis*, by a small inner group of top directors, some at least of whom also happened to be debtors of the company. An approach was made to Prudential Assurance – which held 17 per cent of KUH and whose investment manager, Mr Ronald Artus, was on the board – and subsequently the matter was discussed with Sir Jasper Hollom and the Governor of the Bank of England, Mr Richardson. The Bank asked for a report on various matters. This report was prepared by Mr Richard Langdon, senior partner of Spicer and Pegler, KUH's auditors; it is believed to have covered lending to directors. Eventually, early in March 1975, Mr Franklin agreed, in response, as it was recorded, to the request of certain directors, to buy back the flat and this was done, apparently with the help of a loan.

As it happened, it was shortly after this episode, towards the end of March 1975, that Mr du Cann resigned as chairman and a director of KUH, saying that his public duties and other commitments had increased very much during the recent months and that it seemed essential to him to reduce them; Mr Wilde then became chairman.

Mr Franklin's loans from KU remained considerable for a time after he had left the group in July 1975, but no losses were incurred on them. On occasion KU provided some finance to private companies in which Mr Stoutzker had interests. There was never any possibility of losses being incurred by KU on these loans.

Particulars of loans to individual KUH directors and related companies have not been published by the group, but its accounts have given figures which, though they may to some degree reflect borrowing by other directors, are consistent with the narrative above. While the maximum of such loans in 1974/75 was £7,446,559, the highest figure during March 1975 (by when Mr Dellal and Mr Van Gelder had left the board) was £5,309,213 less at £2,137,346.[17] The maximum March 1975 figure had fallen another £572,885, to £1,564,461,[18] by 3 April 1975. Mr du Cann ceased to be a director of the KUH board a week earlier, on 27 March 1975. By the end of March 1976, when Mr Franklin and Mr Stoutzker were no longer directors, the total had fallen £1,319,390 further to only £245,071.

13 Case Study Two: Slater Walker

> Mr Moxon said he would be glad to know what was the amount of bad debts made by the Bank [of England] during the past half year . . . He understood that a portion of the property was locked up as advances made on account of the Thames Embankment, and in other ways which did not leave the money available for general banking and commercial purposes; and if that were so, he should express his disapproval of such a policy.
>
> Extract from debate in the Bank of England Court, 13 September 1866, about the Overend and Gurney crisis; quoted in Walter Bagehot, *Lombard Street*, 1873

This work has already noted the rise of Slater Walker Securities (SWS) and its later crisis which led to the large-scale and potentially very costly Bank of England rescue operation, culminating in the Bank's take-over of the Slater Walker bank which, without the central bank's backing, would have been insolvent. But SWS was so prominent in the growth, and the fading, of the secondary banking industry that some aspects of it merit a further glance. Incidentally, it is ironic to recall that the Slater Walker bank had earlier been through several changes of control and name, under one of which, as Anglo-French banking Corporation, it had had problems which had previously, in 1931, brought it to the Bank of England's notice, although on that occasion the Old Lady of Threadneedle Street had herself done nothing for it.[1]

The full report of the review of SWS's financial position by Peat Marwick Mitchell and Price Waterhouse, which was commissioned by the new board after Mr Slater's departure and the start of the Bank of England's support in October 1975, has never been made public. But a summary of it by the accountants themselves was released in September 1976, along with SWS's accounts for 1975, prepared by the new board, and a statement by Sir James Goldsmith, the new chairman. (These papers will be referred to as the September 1976 documents[2]). The

183

summary gives a rare insight into the workings of a secondary banking and financial business of the period. Its portrayal of the position, with some significant criticisms, is essential to the study of the crisis and of lessons to be learned from it.

In dealing with the Slater Walker Ltd bank (SWL), the accountants noted that it was 'regarded in the SWS Group as an "in-house" bank whose prime function had been to service the needs of the Group and the Group's clients. Thus some £68 m of SWL's advances, out of a total of £91 m at 31 October 1975, were to companies in which SWS had or previously had an interest, or to individuals to finance shareholdings in such companies'. The accountants ascribed what they called the 'inherent weaknesses' of SWL's lending to three factors. One was the small number of very large loans within the £91 m total: four loans, ranging from £5 m to almost £18 m, accounted for more than half, 51 per cent, of the total portfolio. A further sixteen loans of over £1 m accounted for another 31 per cent of the lending. The result was that, out of the total loans – 150 – only 13 per cent by number made up 82 per cent of the money on loan. A clear example of too many eggs in too few baskets.

A second 'inherent weakness' was the fact that no current interest payments were being required on about two-fifths of the loan book: 'the terms on which some £36 m of the loans were granted included provision for the rolling up of interest'. A third weakness, in the accountants' view, arose from the 'mismatching of the maturity dates of assets and liabilities; liabilities due within 3 months amounted to £57 m, whereas assets realisable within 3 months were £22 m. The loan portfolio included some £62 m of loans (before provisions) with an expected repayment date of over two years'.

The accountants considered that loss provisions of £29.2 m, on top of existing provisions of £9.6 m, would have been needed against the SWL loan book as at 31 October 1975, but for the Bank of England's £40 m guarantee, which was seemingly eventually required in full. The greater part of these provisions would have related to a small number of accounts within the £68 m lent to companies in which SWS had an existing or former interest, or advanced to individuals to finance the purchase of shareholdings in such companies. The largest provision recommended was one of £15.5 m in respect of a single situation. This was the lending to Charles Spreckley Industries,[3] a collapsed public company, and its private parent company, Cambourne Securities. At the end of 1975, SWS's holdings included £1.8 m of 9 per cent partly convertible unsecured loan stock 1983 in Charles Spreckley Industries.

Another major loan on which a loss, of around £5 m, was incurred was the US $29 m (£16.8 m) owed by Haw Par Brothers International, of Singapore. After lengthy negotiations, SWL had agreed to take $20.5 m (£11.8 m) in settlement of this controversial debt. The $8.5 m (£5 m) discount included some $1.9 m (£1.1 m) 'representing the estimated gross profit earned by the six executives from the disputed [Spydar] executive incentive arrangements', as was explained in an appendix about the agreement with Haw Par in the September 1976 documents. Mr Slater, Mr Tarling and the four other participants in Spydar undertook to repay the money to SWL by mid-1981: they 'agreed to join in the settlement arrangements and to reimburse £659,772 and US $742,902 to SWL on 30th June 1981, being together (at the time of their agreement) the equivalent of US $1.9 million'.[4] The £5 m loss involved in the Haw Par settlement contributed to SWL's doubtful debts exceeding the £29.2 m originally mentioned and apparently requiring the full £40 m Bank of England guarantee of principal to be brought into force.[5]

The September 1976 documents also noted that, in two areas of activity, investments and property, SWS had assets that were bringing in much less income than the cost of the money borrowed to finance them. The accountants mentioned that borrowings in the property division were £60.8 m, of which £47.8 m represented 'intra-group indebtedness' – money lent from other parts of the SWS group – 'with the rolling up of interest' Gross income from all the properties, a major part of which were being developed or awaiting development, was only £1.5 m in a full year. Provisions of £14.8 m, net of surpluses, were recommended against property.

A provision totalling £13.3 m was recommended in respect of SWS's general investments and those in associated companies; this was more than a quarter of the book value of these holdings. The largest provision recommended was one of £5.6 m against loss on the holding in Equity Enterprises, the company in which SWS participated jointly with Mr David Frost. It was also noted that the Slater Walker bank has had to make substantial provisions in respect of loans to some of the associated companies and others in which the group held investments, as well as in respect of loans to finance purchases of shares in them by directors of such companies. One example was a £5 m provision against loans in connection with Equity Enterprises.[6]

A further point made was that SWS had 'substantial shareholdings' in four companies caught up to a major extent in the secondary bank

crisis – Cannon Street Investments, Grimshawe Holdings, Charles
Spreckley Industries and Triumph Investment Trust. The total book
value of these 'substantial' holdings was down, at the end of September
1975, to less than £0.3 m.

The September 1976 documents brought out the unusual nature of
some of the SWS group assets. These included sugar options, costing
£0.4 m, of which £0.3 m was lost, and paintings with a 'carrying value'
of £0.7 m, which the new board wrote down by half. Another asset was a
sporting estate on the River Spey in Scotland, the Tulchan Estate,
valued at £2 m at the end of September 1975.

The reporting accountants remarked of SWS's investment management division that it appeared to them to be well run and managed in an
orthodox manner.

Of Slater Walker Insurance (SWI), which had actuarial liabilities of
£42.5 m on its life insurance activities and which operated insured
pension schemes on behalf of over 29,000 people, the accountants'
summary identified several problem areas. One was that the investments
on this side contained 'too many holdings of portfolio investments of
questionable value'. (Mr Slater afterwards commented that during the
relevant period the market as a whole dropped substantially and that the
policy of maintaining a high degree of liquidity meant that any
opportunity of taking advantage of the subsequent revival of the market
by reinvestment was lost). Property holdings were also considered to be
too high a proportion – at 16 per cent – of the market value of the
insurance portfolio.

Further, the accountants, considering the management and investment policy of the insurance side, remarked that 'in the crucially
important area of investment policy Mr Slater . . . exercised a dominant role . . . SWI management in no way influenced the selection of
investments within [the broad parameters specified by the SWI actuary],
nor were the dealings formally approved or ratified by either the board
or the executive committee'. The accountants noted that in 1976, to
avoid a likely difficulty over its solvency margin, SWI transferred certain
investments in companies which had lost their stock market quotation
to SWS at their pre-suspension prices. These investments included
partly convertible loan stock of the collapsed Charles Spreckley
Industries.

The accountants believed that the need for many of the provisions
recommended for the Slater Walker bank (SWL) should have been
apparent earlier in 1975. They considered that a review at the interim
stage of the need for provisions against doubtful debts would have

resulted in a loss being disclosed by the SWS group for the first half of 1975, in place of the £2.2 m pre-tax profit actually announced on 19 August 1975. Shareholders were also told that, as a result of the provisions made, the group's borrowing powers had been exceeded and they were asked to approve an increase, which they did.

The September 1976 documents included a list of large loans outstanding from SWL to directors or recent directors of SWS at the end of 1975. There were personal loans totalling £772,840 outstanding to Mr Tony Buckley, who had resigned as managing director of SWS in September 1975, and one of £225,757, as well as a house mortgage loan of £88,537 (£314,294 in all) owing from Mr John O'Donnell. Another director, Mr Ian Wasserman, had a personal loan of £94,642 and a house mortgage loan of £58,637, a total of £153,279. (Later documents showed that Mr O'Donnell and Mr Wasserman owed £276,808 and £153,040 respectively at the end of 1976, a year in part of which both were still SWS directors). Shareholders were also told that loans totalling £352,000 to companies controlled by Mr Jim Slater were outstanding during the year but had been repaid in full. A house mortgage loan of £118,149 was outstanding to the wife of Mr Slater, and guaranteed by him.

Did SWL (now owned by the Bank of England) lose or expect to lose any money on these loans or other loans to its directors or staff? The accountants pointed out that at the end of October 1975, just after Mr Slater's resignation and two months after that of Mr Buckley, there were outstanding from SWL loans of £1.2 m in which two directors who had resigned during 1975 were interested. Of the £1.2 m, £1 m had been advanced during 1975. No provision was recommended against the house mortgage loan to Mrs Slater or the £352,000, afterwards repaid, to Mr Slater. The accountants said that loans outstanding at the end of October of £751,000 to the other ex-director, clearly Mr Buckley, had included £500,000 which had been advanced after it had been decided he would leave the SWS group. 'The accountants were informed that the reasoning behind this loan (£500,000) was to enable the borrower to buy shares in a company which he planned to develop with the intention of improving the inadequate security for the earlier advance. The accountants were of the opinion that at the time of their review, there was a shortfall of some £325,000 in the security held by SWL for these loans, and a provision was recommended.' Mr Slater, in his book, recalls that it had been agreed between himself and Mr Buckley in the autumn of 1975 that, in view of the reduced size of SWS, it made no sense for Mr

Buckley to remain with the company. Mr Buckley had institutional friends in the City who were prepared to back him in a 'shell' operation and he had chosen Floreat Investment Trust as his vehicle for the purpose. Mr Slater adds that as a result of past loans to cover investment in companies such as Equity Enterprises, Mr Buckley had lost money on balance and owed Slater Walker the shortfall. He received no compensation when he left SWS but Mr Slater arranged for him to borrow approximately £500,000 against his Floreat shares, which were fully asset backed. 'As I saw it, the gain in the Floreat share price would help provide cover for the existing loan, and as a result he would be able to repay both loans', Mr Slater says, adding: 'In the event Tony did not make a success of Floreat and it worked out very badly for the company as a result'.[7]

The reporting accountants mention that there was a shortfall of some £200,000 in the security held for loans and a house mortgage totalling £303,000 to one director and that a provision was recommended. Mr O'Donnell, with a debt of £314,294 to Slater Walker at the end of 1975, is the only director whose known borrowings can be consistent with a figure of £303,000 owed at the end of October that year. (Mr O'Donnell resigned as a director and left the SWS group in 1976, afterwards becoming a director of a private company, H & L Vintners, which was put into liquidation in 1978; he was later committed for trial on a charge in connection with H & L's affairs.

In the early months of 1981, the Slater Walker banking company – a subsidiary of the Bank of England – filed bankruptcy petitions against Mr Buckley and Mr O'Donnell.

Mr Slater, who had at one time been worth millions of pounds, became known in the late-1970s as a 'minus millionaire'. Although his loans from SWL were repaid, he had extensive borrowings from elsewhere, taken to finance personal investments including farmland, paintings and some SWS shares, as he has explained in his book. After his resignation from SWS, his personal liabilities substantially exceeded his assets; he owed money to a joint stock bank, two insurance companies and a merchant bank, and his 'shortfall' was over £800,000.

Mr Slater's creditors proved understanding, however, in line with the general reluctance of financial institutions to force debtors into personal bankruptcy in the secondary banking crisis. They took a friendly and pragmatic line and agreed to give time for the build-up of Mr Slater's new private venture, the Strongmead property company in which he received backing from Lonrho, the conglomerate group with African interests headed by Mr Tiny Rowland. Later Mr Slater wrote some children's books and his financial position evidently improved. He was reported in October 1979 as saying that he was no longer a 'minus millionaire', that he had repaid the Lonrho loan, but that his net indebtedness was still more than £200,000, and that he had two major outstanding loans amounting to £750,000, which were due in 1981 and 1982.[8]

Mr Slater was, of course, due to reimburse his share of the amounts due in respect of the Spydar Securities arrangements to the Bank of England's SWL subsidiary on 30 June 1981.

One further matter to which the reporting accountants drew attention was that purchases of SWS shares by four companies (one of them was Bion Securities) related to, but not subsidiaries of, SWS, with finance from the Slater Walker bank, might have contravened section 54 of the Companies Act 1948. This provision prohibits companies from financing purchases of their own shares, though there is a proviso exempting what is done in the ordinary course of business. The accountants noted that in the opinion of leading Counsel, there had been breaches of section 54. They also stated that Mr Slater had said he was responsible for the decision to make the loans and for the investment policy of the companies which included the purchase and sale of SWS shares. There was no suggestion that Mr Slater or any other SWS director had profited personally.

Mr Slater was subsequently prosecuted under section 54 in respect of £4 m of loans; he was acquitted in 1977 by the Guildhall magistrates in London. The Department of Trade, which had brought the case, then appealed and in March 1979 three Judges of the Queen's Bench Divisional Court, including the Lord Chief Justice, Lord Widgery, unanimously overturned the earlier decision of the magistrates to dismiss the charges. Mr Justice Davies, giving the main judgment, said the magistrates appeared to have been unduly influenced by arguments advanced over the proviso in section 54 (about the ordinary course of business). Mr Slater was afterwards convicted on the fifteen charges and fined £15 on each (the maximum fine being £100 on any count).

14 Appraisal and Conclusions

> The only thing men learn from history is that men learn nothing from history.
>
> Hegel

The Bank of England put aside a remarkable total of about £100 m for the possible cost to itself of the whole rescue strategy, while the clearing banks may still face a bill of up to perhaps £50 m, also already provided for in their accounts, for their own participation in the Lifeboat operation. These possible losses – as distinct from the much larger support *lending*, which was mostly ultimately repaid – show the magnitude of the burden the support operations may involve for those who conducted them. The fact that the central bank, a state-owned body, accepted responsibility for potential losses of such a scale, with a resultant drop in its payments to the nation's Exchequer, alone makes the measures taken to deal with the secondary bank crisis a matter of major public interest.

The estimate of some £100 m as the possible cost to the Bank of England has not been publicly given, but there are strong pointers to substantiate a figure of this order. It is believed that the Bank provided some £35 m against its support of the Slater Walker Securities (SWS) group, culminating in its purchase of the Slater Walker bank – for an orderly realisation of what could be recovered of the latter's assets – and of certain SWS property assets. A not greatly dissimilar sum is thought to have been provided for the support of the Edward Bates group, leading to the acquistion of the interests now included in the Bank's EBS Investments subsidiary. The combined prospective cost of the Bank's help with the handling of certain other troubled financial companies and its shouldering of responsibility as noted above for paying off outside depositors in several collapsed fringe banks, together with its one-tenth share in the risks of the combined Lifeboat operation, probably required further provisions of at least £30 m. It is, of course, too soon to know whether all the provisions made will eventually be required.

Evidence which has been published clearly points to provisions made by the Bank for its support operations on a scale consistent with the estimate of some £100 m. From 1974 to 1975, the Bank included annually in its accounts a single figure which comprised the year's provision for the support operation, either together with any new provision for the fall in the value of its holdings of gilt-edged securities or after the subtraction of earlier provisions no longer needed for falls in the value of gilt holdings.

In the four years 1974/75 to 1977/78, the Bank's[1] accounts disclosed total net provisions of £50.5 m in connection with the support operations, after the total had been cut back by unspecified reductions in provisions against gilt portfolios. The figure for support operations alone was thus higher, and, it is reasonable to assume in view of the large size of the gilt holdings, substantially higher than £50.5 m. In 1978/79, a further £8 m was provided, but since, in this year, there was a new provision against the gilt holdings, the further support provision was less than £8 m. All this is quite consistent with the assertion that the total loss provisions for the Bank's support operations were of the order of £100 m. (It is also notable that Sir Jasper Hollom told the House of Commons Select Committee 'the heavier losses are outside the Lifeboat'.)[2]

In the same five years, the Bank, as a State body, paid to the Treasury, in lieu of dividend, a total of £28 m out of its total operating profits (before tax) of £90.6 m, the net amount remaining going to reserve. This figure would clearly have been higher by a large amount, had the Bank's profits not been held down to the tune of £100 m or so by support provisions. The payment from the Bank to the Exchequer was thus substantially reduced by the loss provisions for the support measures. In this indirect sense, the resources of the nation's purse have been deployed in the support operation, as they have been more directly through the Government grant of £175 m to the Crown Agents.

The total provisions of the English and Scottish clearing banks for the Lifeboat operation conducted jointly with the Bank of England have not been separately identified but may well have exceeded £50 m. Near the end of 1980, the approximate maximum figure of possible loss to them is generally taken as some £50 m. Some loss in certain cases has received an offset from a margin of profit on the terms of support lending and it seems clear that much will depend on the eventual future of First National Finance Corporation, whose debts to the Lifeboat are still over £200 m, including £50 m of deferred loans.

The total provision of finance – as distinct from possible losses – involved in controlling the banking and related property crises was very large indeed. In addition to some £1300 m advanced through the Lifeboat, large loan resources were used by the Bank of England and by various investing institutions and banks to sustain further banking concerns hard hit by the upheaval. Many hundreds of millions of pounds more were supplied by the large banks to keep property groups afloat through this time of trial and to enable them to complete developments optimistically begun in the boom years. Much had later to be written off against interest and repayment not received; the big banks' provisions against their property lending in this period certainly exceeded £100 m. The total finance exceptionally provided must have run into billions of pounds: some estimates suggest it was £3000 m.

However, no exact account can be drawn up of the gains and losses from the support operation for Britain's secondary banks, undoubtedly the largest and most complex bank rescue campaign in history to date, nor of the related moves in the property field. Not only is it too early to assess the losses: the gains are not precisely quantifiable since they consist largely in the avoidance of dangers to the whole banking system which, because the worst did not happen, can never be the subject of more than judgment and estimate.

What is clear is that confidence in British banking was preserved and the rot was stopped from spreading beyond the fringe and secondary sector. Depositors were fully protected: no money was lost by ordinary depositors in banks helped by the Lifeboat support group or in those over which the Bank of England kept a close watch, except that it was not the general policy to protect persons connected with the ownership and management who had deposits in the supported bank. (It is worth noting that the Crown Agents organisation was one large-scale depositor which did face the loss of millions of pounds of deposits in fringe banks, presumably because its dealings with these banks had been on such a scale that it was regarded as part of the rescue team).

Another gain from the whole strategy was that problems were solved in such a way that no borrowing British bank defaulted on its obligations on Euromarket loans, something which would have had damaging repercussions on confidence in Britain and indeed generally in international financial markets.

In certain cases where a surviving secondary bank's assets had shrunk because of losses, loan stock holders accepted compromise settlements involving a reduction in their claims as a preferable alternative to greater loss in a liquidation. Likewise, ordinary shareholders agreed in a number of cases to substantial dilution of their equity shareholding as part of arrangements to stave off collapse. When fringe banks did eventually go into liquidation, they generally lost their whole investment.

The handling of the crisis by the Bank of England and the large banks gave a new impetus, of a kind which may be reckoned a benefit to banking stability, to the concept of joint-action rescues. Central banks had for centuries provided credit to ease panics caused by a bank's collapse, as the Bank of England did after Overend and Gurney's failure in 1866. Even the different idea of combined moves by the Bank of England and the big banks actually to fend off a bank's failure had been seen before – in 1891, when a range of banks guaranteed rescue loans made by the Bank of England to Baring Brothers.[3] But the crisis of the mid-1970s marked a new departure in introducing the principle of joint action by the central bank and leading commercial banks to deal with, not one, but a number of threatened banking disasters. The same combined approach, at least to the extent of co-operation in monitoring, was soon to be observed to some degree on the international scene, as noted in Chapter 9, reflecting a growing feeling that large banks could have more to gain than to lose by preventing pending collapses elsewhere in the banking community. But even at the end of 1980, there was still plentiful international debate about how far it is appropriate for commercial banks to adopt Lifeboat or safety net arrangements to protect their weaker brethren in times of crisis.

Retrospective appraisal must recognise that the keynote of the response by the Bank of England to the initial acute stage and subsequent long chronic phase of Britain's 1973–5 secondary bank crisis was the speed and efficiency of the rescue moves, with an emphasis on taking no chances where the financial community's strength and good name were at stake. The heads of the large banks responded most promptly, as has been seen, to the Bank of England's call to combined action in late December 1973 and the Bank provided continuing active leadership, not only in arranging and supervising the support lending but often in promoting, along with senior clearing bankers, eventual solutions through take-overs and in other ways, of the individual secondary banks' problems.

The main burden rested on Sir Jasper Hollom, with major back-up from Mr Blunden, an executive director; the Governor, Mr Richardson, who had played a crucial role in originally launching the Lifeboat operation, took a close interest throughout. Working relationships within the Lifeboat committee were generally harmonious, thanks not a little to Sir Jasper's unflappability – 'with him, a raised eyebrow is bad temper', a Lifeboat colleague remembers. But this did not preclude energetic debates on occasion, sometimes at even higher level than the committee itself, since the clearing bank members were sometimes rather less protectively-minded than the Bank. The Bank was generally (though perhaps not invariably), responsive to the views of the clearers, particularly on such major matters as its own financial participation in the combined support operation, the halting of the joint commitment at £1200 m, and the stiffer approach adopted from late-1974 onwards. In the later, potentially very costly, support operations for SWS and Bates, the Bank naturally made its own decisions, since it alone was providing the finance and carrying the responsibility for any losses. In 1975 Sir Jasper Hollom received a knighthood, an honour whose timing clearly recognised the prolonged and successful operation with which his name has been so much associated.

Was the support operation too comprehensive, expensive – and quiet? Could it have been effectively conducted at less potential cost on a more restricted basis? Some senior bankers privately expressed the view at the time that, while personal depositors with troubled fringe and secondary banks should be safeguarded, companies and other institutions which had lent to these banks should have known better and ought to be left to bear the consequences. This hard view, however, does not allow for the danger that default would have damaged the general reputation of the banking community and that, in view of the chains of lending through the new money markets, banks near the heart of the system could have been hit by such a policy.

Another critical opinion was that it was not necessary in the interests of confidence to rescue all affected banks. This approach envisaged, as one clearing banker summed it up privately, that 'if we had from the outset allowed two or three of the least respected names to collapse in a flurry of publicity with losses to their depositors, it would have served them right and would have acted like a quick piece of surgery on the City, cutting out the canker and enabling the rest of us to continue the more easily with our normal business'. This possibility was however ruled out, even in principle, as tension and the risk of spreading panic escalated through December 1973.

Another way in which the scale of the rescue strategy might have been limited would have been by arranging that, once general confidence had been strengthened by the knowledge of the Lifeboat's launching, the conditions for help should have been stiffened and support refused, or made more short-lived, in a greater number of cases. This kind of alternative is suggested by queries whether, for instance, it was entirely appropriate for Bank of England funds to be committed to support of the SWS group on such a scale that provisions of some £35 m were required. The persuasive answer usually heard to this is that once assistance had initially been provided, either through the Lifeboat or solely by the Bank of England, the ultimate cost to the rescuers would have been greater if a banking business had been left to fall into early liquidation than if it were nursed through to at least partial recovery. As has been seen, however, some stiffening in the Lifeboat's policy was seen from late-1974.

The general view in senior banking quarters was that the effort, even at a potential cost of £50 m or more to the clearers, was worthwhile. Here is how one senior official of a large clearing bank, Mr John Quinton, now a general manager of Barclays Bank, referred to the matter in a private talk about the secondary bank crisis, entitled 'The Fringe and Beyond', to the 300-strong London Branch Managers' Club of his bank in April 1975: 'Have we been right, in effect, to pay a premium of perhaps as much as £10 m as an insurance against loss of confidence in the banking system on the part of our own depositors, and internationally [against] a loss of confidence in the City of London? The answer is one we have brooded over long and often. On balance we feel that we were right to do what we did.'

If the uncomfortable conclusion has to be accepted that the comprehensive nature of the support operation was perhaps rather tender to certain banks which had taken high risks for high rewards in good times and now enjoyed ready protection in bad times, but that rescues had to proceed nonetheless, one clear policy lesson could be drawn from the crisis. This was that the system for supervision of the banking system had to be enlarged and strengthened to guard against a recurrence of the problems which had left the Bank of England and the large banks with so little choice of action when the crisis broke.

One of the first long-term institutional responses to the upheaval was that the Bank of England's Discount Office, which had hitherto been headed by Mr James Keogh, a long-time Bank man with a Military Cross from wartime service, was abolished in mid-1974 and its staff absorbed into the Chief Cashier's Office as the nucleus of an expanding supervisory organisation. A new more senior post, carrying responsibilities at policy level for banking supervision, was created at the same time; its first holder was Mr Blunden, who was succeeded, on his becoming a director in 1977, by Mr Peter Cooke. Following the mid-1974 reorganisation, Mr Keogh, who was the last holder of the traditional office of Principal of the Discount Office and who had, from 1972, held the rank of Adviser to the Governors, moved temporarily to other work until his retirement several months later at the end of 1974.

By 1978, the new organisation, known as BAMMS (Banking and Money Market Supervision Division) consisted of seventy people, nearly five times the strength of the former Discount Office.[4] It is significant that money markets too came under BAMMS' purview, considering the extensive use by secondary, and indeed the wider group of wholesale, banks generally, of funds from these markets; the long-delayed formation in 1979 of a Sterling Money Brokers Association placed yet another piece into the improved surveillance structure.

As the broader and more formal supervisory arrangements came into force, the Bank of England showed its awareness of such uncomfortable facts as that balance sheets could be designed to obscure rather than to reveal[5] and that high earnings might be an indicator of potential trouble from imprudent lending. Supervisory attention focused further on the importance of proper prudential ratios and balance sheet relationships as yardsticks for the safe conduct of a banking business. In 1975 the Bank published an outline of standards of capital adequacy and liquidity,[6] agreed with the clearing banks, which it was regarding as relevant to its supervisory process. One key prudential principle of this kind was that capital resources (including subordinated loan capital) should be enough to cover the 'infrastructure' (premises and equipment) of a bank plus some provision against loss on business risks, so that depositors' money should not be tied up for these purposes. Stress was also laid on the need to develop the right principles of matching – not too familiar a concept to all fringe bankers, as has been seen above – and the importance of sufficient liquid assests.

To make its surveillance a reality, the Bank also began to call for regular quarterly returns. Moreover, banking concerns were expected to supply new information on capital and reserves, and provisions, as well as details of large deposits and advances. The bank also wanted to know about standby borrowing facilities and contingent liabilities, as well as deals with associated companies and with directors.

In 1979, the European Economic Community's requirement that all banks should be authorised, coupled with the experience of the secondary banking crisis, led to the passing of the Banking Act, which placed supervision on a newly legal footing. The old categories of section 123, section 127 and other types of bank ranking were superseded and a system was introduced under which companies taking public deposits were required to obtain from the Bank of England either recognition as a bank or a licence as a deposit-taking institution. Recognition is for those which offer at least a considerable range of banking services and are of 'a high reputation and standing in the community'. By January 1981, 278 banks had been recognised and 280 further concerns had received licences.

Lessons of the banking crisis were plainly reflected in papers the Bank of England discussed with the banking community from 1980, spelling out the principles on which it planned to conduct its continuing supervision under the Banking Act. The first paper on liquidity, which aimed, among other things, at ensuring that wholesale banks engaged in 'maturity transformation' – borrowing short and lending longer – should be fully provided with liquid assets to meet any dangers from non-renewal of deposits, stirred a good deal of controversy. But its objectives showed that the Bank, at least, had absorbed the message from the crisis years.

The Bank of England is indeed justified in insisting that the banking community should not again risk running into crisis through excessive mismatching and scarcity of liquidity. It is also vital that the Bank should be firm in its decisions under the Banking Act about the status of individual banking concerns. Moreover, it is important that it should be supported in making right, if unpopular, decisions in awkward cases by a climate of opinion familiar with the dangers of the 1973–5 crisis.

How would any future banking crisis be handled? Clearly the main line of defence is that the tightened supervisory arrangements should fend off the risk as far as possible, just as, in the wider world context, surveillance, monitoring and international consultation are looked to as the means of providing against the risk of troubles in the vast international Euro-currency markets.

The Banking Act 1979 also provides for a new Deposit Protection Fund, created from levies on the banks, to safeguard 75 per cent of deposits up to £10,000 in any concerns that might collapse. This would protect small personal depositors but would provide no defence against any new crisis involving a flight of major money market deposits of the kind which took place from the secondary and fringe banks in 1973–5. Any more extensive protection would have been too costly; the banking system was also unwilling to encourage high risk-taking in any financial businesses which might think they were in a 'heads I win, tails I don't lose' situation, at the expense of the potential rescuers. The inference must be that, should another crisis of comparable dimensions to that in the mid-1970s arise in future, a new form of Lifeboat might be required.

A further eventual sequel to the banking crisis was the Companies Act 1980 bringing in, among other provisions, new curbs on directors' transactions which give rise to a conflict of interest and requiring greater disclosure in a number of respects.

In particular, the Act more closely restricts the exemptions from a continued general ban on loans by companies to their directors. Loans in the ordinary course of business, on commercial, arm's length terms, are permitted, but are subject to a limit of £50,000 and to disclosure of particulars in the lending company's accounts, except in the case of the top flight recognised banks. The latter, though not subject to any limit of size on their advances to directors, have to publish the aggregate of such lending in their accounts and to make particulars available for inspection by shareholders for a period before the annual meeting. Other deals which would have the effect of giving credit to directors are also controlled. Mr Reginald Eyre, the Parliamentary Under Secretary for Trade, put the matter in its context by referring to the milder provisions of the then existing company law when he told the House of Commons Standing Committee A, on the Companies Bill, on 29 November 1979: 'These provisions have been ineffective in preventing serious abuses, particularly by directors of "secondary" banks. Such abuses have, unhappily, been reported in recent years. Inspectors' reports have frequently recommended a tightening up of the law relating to loans to directors.'

It remains to be seen whether the new provisions will leave any significant scope in practice for very large loans to directors of recognised banks and licensed deposit-taking institutions. The matter could appropriately be kept under review. Indeed, there is much to be said for the recommendation of the Wilson Committee on financial institutions for some apparatus continuously to monitor the need for amendment of the law affecting financial institutions as business practices evolve.[7]

Another subject which has received much thought in the wake of the crisis is that of accounting practices and compliance with the series of accounting standards which the accountancy profession has issued in recent years. Public disquiet at the end of the 1960s about certain episodes showing the very varied value which different accounts could put on the same assets led to the formation of the Accounting Standards Committee and the secondary banking crisis provided further background for its work.

But, by 1980, there was a growing feeling that, although many accounting standards had been produced, companies might well become increasingly willing to breach them unless more was done to enforce compliance. Accordingly, a plan for a joint panel to review non-compliance with accounting standards emerged from discussions between the Consultative Committee of Accountancy Bodies, the Stock Exchange and the recently-formed Council for the Securities Industry, the City of London's top self-regulatory body.

This project envisages the establishment of a panel to review cases of alleged significant departures from accounting standards by companies whose securities are listed on the Stock Exchange or traded through an organised market. The arrangement would apply generally and not only to companies in the banking field. The idea is that instances of apparent breach of accounting standards could be raised with the panel by the Stock Exchange, by the professional standards committees of the accountancy bodies or by members of the public. If the panel concluded that the company's accounts had unjustifiably failed to comply with the standard in question, the matter would be referred to the Stock Exchange to consider such action as might be appropriate, presumably including a possible suspension of listing, unless and until the matter was put right.

The plan, which obviously owes a good deal to the City of London's generally successful exercise in enforcing a non-legal code of practice for bid activity through the Take-over Panel, had not been fully agreed by late-1980. If it is adopted, it will mark a significant step towards ensuring that common accounting standards are observed and so towards greater harmony with the position in other countries with active regulatory systems in the European Economic Community and elsewhere. But if the new scheme is not brought into effect, Britain could appear to be reverting to the more *laissez-faire* ways which existed in the past and could look increasingly out of step with West Germany, France, Holland, Belgium and other nations, including the United States, where the trend has been towards stricter surveillance.

Meanwhile, it is relevant to recall that in some cases where the accounting practices of fringe banks came under fire, auditors were also criticised, as, for example, by the Department of Trade Inspectors who investigated the affairs of London and County Securities Group. Consequent upon the report on L and C by the Inspectors, who were very critical of the role of the L and C auditors, Harmood Banner, Mr Richard Langdon, the liquidator of L and C, brought a multi-million pound action, alleging negligence, against the former partners of

Harmood Banner, then merged into the large accounting firm of Deloitte Haskins & Sells. The £8.5 m damages claim was settled in February 1980 with an agreed sum of £900,000 after the hearing on the case had been running in the High Court for some days, Deloittes continuing to deny all allegations of negligence. Mr Langdon said after the settlement that his claim had been for £5.75 m, plus interest from the date of the L and C collapse to March 1977. Of that, £4.3 m was 'a claim arising out of imprudent trading by the group' after the date of the auditors' report. 'The liquidator was advised by leading counsel that the claim was a proper one for the plaintiffs to bring. It was also consistent with the report of the Inspectors appointed by the Department of Trade. This part of the claim would have involved breaking new ground in relation to the legal liability of auditors',[8] Mr Langdon stated.

The last few pages show that much has been done to reduce the risk of another crisis but that a number of important points need to be watched if there is not still to be some danger of a recurrence of the upheaval or of undesirable aspects of banking in the mid-1970s. Perhaps the greatest hazard is that growing ignorance of the whole secondary banking affair may diminish the public awareness which should provide protection against any repetition of the story. For, ironically, so strenuously did the Bank of England struggle, in the interests of confidence, to prevent any resounding collapse during the whole crisis, that the very occurrence, or at least the immense scale, of this major episode in financial history has escaped the attention of many.

It would indeed be tragic if the events of the crisis were to remain so muffled, and knowledge of them so restricted, that the whole upheaval had to happen again one day because the dangers had not been widely enough appreciated and the necessary apparatus to prevent a fresh crisis brought fully in force.

It is grievous enough if a death in a traffic accident is required before road markings are changed for greater safety; where action has to wait upon two successive deaths, that must be black comedy. If the effectiveness of defences against a new major banking crisis were to be diminished through ignorance of what occurred in 1973–5 so that the whole thing could occur again before all the necessary lessons had been completely learned, then Marx's dictum that history repeats itself, first as tragedy and then as farce, would be all too abundantly borne out.

Abbreviations Used in Notes

BEQB	*Bank of England Quarterly Bulletin.*
BESB	'The Secondary Banking Crisis and the Bank of England's Support Operations' (May 1978). Paper by the Bank of England to the Committee to Review the Functioning of Financial Institutions, chaired by Sir Harold Wilson, K. G., M.P. (Hereinafter called the Wilson Cttee). Refs to paragraph nos, unless otherwise stated. (Reproduced in *BEQB*, June 1978, pp. 230–9).
BE Sup.	'Supervision of Financial Institutions'. July 1978. Evidence by the Bank of England to the Wilson Cttee. Refs to paper and para nos.
Blunden	'Recent Developments in British Banking'. Transcript of speech by Mr George Blunden, Director, Bank of England, Cardiff Business Club, 25 October 1976. Refs to page nos.
CAT	Minutes of Proceedings of Tribunal of Inquiry into the Crown Agents. (Mr Justice Croom-Johnson (Chairman), Lord Allen of Abbeydale and Sir William Slimmings). (From the Shorthand Notes of W. B. Gurney and Sons, 34 The Broadway, Westminster, SW1H OBH). Refs to day of hearing and page in cyclostyled minutes.
CLCB to Wilson	Evidence by the Committee of London Clearing Bankers to the Wilson Cttee, November 1977.
Evid. to Sel. Cttee	The Select Committee on Nationalised Industries (Sub-Committee C). Minutes of Evidence. Session 1977/78. Wednesday 18 January 1978 and Wednesday 25 January 1978. Bank of England. Report and Accounts for the year ended 28 February 1977. The Rt Hon Gordon Richardson, M. B. E., Sir Jasper Hollom, K. B. E., Mr George Blunden, and Mr P. A. S. Taylor. (Refs to page nos).
Fay	Report by the Committee of Inquiry appointed by the Minister of Overseas Development into the circumstances which led to the Crown Agents requesting financial assistance from the Government in 1974. Chairman: His Honour Judge E. S. Fay, Q. C.; other members: Sir Edmund Compton, G. C. B., K. B. E., and Mr P. Godfrey, F. C. A. 1 December 1977.

Ferguson/CST D. of T. Inspectors' Rpt	Ferguson and General Investments Ltd (formerly known as Dowgate & General Investments) and C. S. T. Investments Ltd. Investigations under section 165(b) of the Companies Act 1948. Report by Joseph Jackson, Q. C., and Kirkpatrick L. Young, TD, FCA (Inspectors appointed by the Department of Trade). 1979.
FT	*Financial Times.*
Hansard	Parliamentary Debates (Hansard), House of Commons Official Report.
Lombard Street	*Lombard Street: A Description of the Money Market.* Walter Bagehot, 10th edn (Kegan Paul, Trench Trubner, 1892).
L and CD of T. Inspectors' Rpt	London and County Securities Group Limited Investigations under sections 165(b) and 172 of the Companies Act 1948. (Also) Capebourne Limited, Standfield Properties Limited, Hibernian Property Co. Limited, Avon Land Securities Limited. Investigations under section 165(b) of the Companies Act 1948. Report by A. P. Leggatt, Q. C., and D. C. Hobson, M. A., F. C. A. (Inspectors appointed by the Department of Trade). 1976.
Return to Go	*Return to Go* by Jim Slater. (Weidenfeld & Nicolson, 1977; refers to paperback edn Futura, 1978).
RICS to Wilson	'The Property Boom 1968–1973 and its collapse'. A supplementary memorandum of evidence to the Wilson Cttee from The Royal Institution of Chartered Surveyors, July 1978.
SWS, EC and R & A 1975	Slater Walker Securities. Explanatory Circular and Directors' Report and Accounts 1975, published 15 September 1976.

Notes

CHAPTER 1   ACTION STATIONS AT THE BANK OF ENGLAND

1. *BEQB*, June 1971, p. 227.
2. Interview with Mr Hugh Jenkins, 1978.
3. Interview with Sir Kenneth Cork, 1979.
4. Interview with Mr Hugh Jenkins, 1978.

CHAPTER 2   THE LIFEBOAT LAUNCHED

1. Evid. to Sel. Cttee., p. 3.
2. The term 'Lifeboat' originated from an article by the author in the *FT* on 29 January 1974 headlined 'How the "Bankers Lifeboat" came to the rescue'. It quoted a top clearing banker as jocularly referring to the new combined operation as 'The National Joint Stock Bankers' Lifeboat Institution'. The banker who made the remark was Mr Leonard Mather, then a vice-chairman of the Midland Bank and afterwards chairman of United Dominions Trust.
3. Evid. to Sel. Cttee., p. 3.
4. Interview with Sir Eric Faulkner, 1979.
5. Collins, 1979.

CHAPTER 3   DEVELOPMENTS IN THE FINANCIAL SYSTEM, 1958–73

1. 'That controversial Euro-dollar market', *National Westminster Bank Quarterly Review*, August 1969.
2. BE Sup., 3, 10.
3. CLCB to Wilson, 10, 13.
4. Hill Samuel occasional paper, no. 3, May 1968.
5. Cmnd. 3293.
6. Barclays Bank, Report and Accounts for 1969, p. 27.
7. *BEQB*, Dec. 1969, p. 450.
8. Ibid., June 1971, p. 196.
9. The reference alludes to words in the later 1971 Budget speech.

CHAPTER 4   DEBUT OF THE SECONDARY BANKS

1. Charles Raw, *Slater Walker* (André Deutsch, 1977, pp. 353–4 and Coronet Books, 1978).

2. Jim Slater, *Return to Go*, p. 161.
3. L and CD of T. Inspectors' Rpt, 12.01–09 and 16.14.
4. *Return to Go*, p. 191.
5. Fay, para. 49.
6. Ibid., appendix XVII, table 1.
7. Ibid., paras 68–72 and 141.
8. Ibid., para. 30.
9. Ibid., paras 138 and 226.
10. Ibid., para. 329.
11. Ibid., para. 353.
12. Ibid., para. 266.
13. Ibid., para. 349.
14. Ibid., para. 332.
15. Ibid., para. 351.
16. Ibid., para. 359.
17. Ibid., paras 75–6, 142ff, 224ff, 329, 375, p. 157, and appendix XIV.
18. Ibid., paras 152ff and p. 157.
19. Ibid., paras 333ff and p. 157.
20. CAT, Day 83, p. 4.
21. *Return to Go*, p. 181.
22. L and CD of T. Inspectors' report, 3.09.
23. SWS EC and R & A 1975, p. 23.
24. *Management Today*, Aug. 1971.
25. First National Finance Corporation, Report and Accounts 1973, p. 9.
26. *FT*, 24 July 1974.
27. J. H. Vavasseur, Report and Accounts, 1973, p. 10.
28. 220 Law Reports, Queen's Bench, 1966, vol. 2, pp. 431ff.
29. BESB, paras 12–13.
30. *BEQB*, Dec. 1973, pp. 538–41.

CHAPTER 5 THE BOOM WHICH GOT OUT OF HAND

1. Ferguson/CST D. of T. Inspectors' Rpt, 1.22.
2. CAT, Day 52, pp. 10 and 35.
3. *Chartered Surveyor*, Dec. 1978 (Article 'Lessons to be learned from the past').
4. *Evening Standard*, 27 Mar. 1972.
5. *The Economist*, 25 Mar. 1972, p. 96.
6. CLCB to Wilson, table 54.
7. BESB, paras 20 and 22.
8. *BEQB*, Mar. 1974, table 12/1, col. 2.
9. Ibid., Mar. 1972 and Mar. 1974, table 8.
10. CLCB to Wilson, appendix D 8.
11. RICS to Wilson, 3.10.3.
12. *BEQB*, Mar. 1972 and Mar. 1974, table 10.
13. Ibid., Sept. 1973, pp. 308–14.
14. Ibid., Mar. 1974, table 8/1.

15. *The Economist*, 27 Jan. 1973, p. 56.
16. CLCB to Wilson, appendix D 4.
17. *The Economist*, 18 Mar. 1972.
18. Fay, para. 228.
19. Ibid., p. 157 and appendix XIV.
20. CAT, Day 25, p. 50.
21. CAT, Day 60, p. 43.
22. Judgment in High Court, Queen's Bench Div, 3 June 1977 (1975 S. No. 9823).
23. *FT*, 28 Nov. 1978.
24. CLCB to Wilson, appendix D 7.
25. RICS to Wilson, 3.11.5.
26. CLCB to Wilson, appendix D 10.
27. BESB, para. 19.
28. CLCB to Wilson, appendix D 7.
29. Interview with Sir Kenneth Cork, 1979.
30. *The Economist*, 15 Dec. 1973, p. 23.
31. Interview with Mr Richard Langdon, 1979.

CHAPTER 6   THE DASH FOR GROWTH – AND ITS CONSEQUENCES

1. *Return to Go*, p. 155.
2. Nigel Broackes, *A Growing Concern* (Weidenfeld & Nicolson, 1979) p. 221.
3. *Return to Go*, p. 155.
4. Interview with the late Lord Armstrong of Sanderstead, 1979.
5. *BEQB*, June 1972, p. 163.
6. *Hansard*, vol. 833, 21 Mar. 1972, col. 1347.
7. Hobart Paperback, no. 7. (The Institute of Economic Affairs, 1975).
8. *FT*, 8 Dec. 1977.
9. Douglas Hurd, *An End to Promises* (Collins, 1979) pp. 92 and 117.
10. *Hansard*, vol. 839, 29 June 1972, cols 1709–98.
11. *BEQB*, Mar. 1973, p. 16.
12. *The Economist*, 9 Dec. 1972, p. 15.
13. *FT*, 8 Dec. 1977.
14. Interview with Lord O'Brien of Lothbury, 1978.
15. E.g. *BEQB*, Dec. 1972, pp. 514–18.
16. *BEQB*, Sept. 1972, p. 327.
17. Cmnd. 5205, para. 23.
18. *The Economist*, 10 Mar. 1973, p. 80.
19. *The Times*, 31 July 1973, p. 2.
20. *BEQB*, Dec. 1973, p. 445.
21. Interview with Sir Julian Hodge, 1979.
22. L and CD of T. Inspectors' Rept, 9.83.
23. Ibid., 12.24.
24. Ibid., 5.44ff.
25. Ibid., 5.51.
26. Ibid., 16.15.
27. *Hansard*, vol. 866, cols 952ff.

CHAPTER 7 THE LIFEBOAT EMBARKS ON ITS MISSION

1. Blunden, p. 6.
2. Evid. to Sel. Cttee, pp. 9 and 4.
3. BESB, para. 28.
4. Ibid., para. 30.
5. Cornhill Consolidated Group Ltd (In liquidation). Investigation under section 165 (b) of Companies Act 1948. Report by David Calcutt QC and John Whinney FCA. (Dated 13 July 1977; published December 1980).
6. On 25 Jan. 1974.
7. J. H. Vavasseur, Report and Accounts for 1973.
8. Triumph Investment Trust, Report and Accounts for 1973.
9. *FT*, 16 Apr. 1975.
10. *FT*, 30 Aug. 1975.
11. Fay, para. 332.
12. Fay, para. 344.
13. CAT, Day 22, p. 49.
14. Fay, para. 355.
15. *FT*, 1 Aug. 1980.
16. CAT, Day 82, p. 11.
17. Fay, p. 157.
18. BESB, appendix A.

CHAPTER 8 THE PROPERTY CRISIS

1. BESB, para. 22
2. *Financial Statistics*, Dec. 1979. Table 81 and corr. tables in earlier issues.
3. *Investors Chronicle*, 31 Jan. 1975.
4. From Mr William Stern's Statement of Affairs.
5. Interview with Mr William Stern, 1979.
6. Fay, para. 342.
7. The Stern Group of Companies. Explanatory statement and proposals for moratorium and scheme of arrangement, 23 May 1975.
8. Interview with Sir Kenneth Cork, 1979.
9. Statement by Official Receiver, 14 Jan. 1977.
10. Interview with Mr David Lewis. 1980.
11. Ibid.
12. *FT*, 14 Dec. 1974.

CHAPTER 9 THE LIFEBOAT IDEA INTERNATIONALLY

1. Blunden, p. 6.
2. Robert Heller and Norris Willatt, *Can You Trust Your Bank?* (Weidenfeld & Nicolson, 1977) pp. 256–8.
3. *BEQB*, Sept. 1977, p. 326 (pp. 325–9 contain an interesting talk by Mr George Blunden on 'International Co-operation in Banking Supervision').
4. *BEQB*, Sept. 1979, pp. 298–301.

5. Evid. to Sel. Cttee, p. 13.
6. BESB, para. 44.
7. *BEQB*, Sept. 1979, p. 300.

CHAPTER 10   CRISIS CLIMAX AND TURN OF THE TIDE

1. BESB, para. 42.
2. Interview with Sir John Prideaux, 1979.
3. CAT, Day 87, p. 44. Also CAT, Day 240, pp. 16 and 21ff.
4. Fay, para. 346.
5. *FT*, 20 July 1978.
6. Ibid., 13 June 1978.
7. Ibid., 29 Apr. 1978.
8. BESB, para. 37, and *FT* (Lombard) 11 May 1978.
9. Cedar Holdings Ltd, Report and Accounts, 1975 and 1978.
10. First National Finance Corporation: letter to Shareholders headed 'Proposed Reorganisation', 8 December 1975.

CHAPTER 11   LATER TROUBLES AND A SUMMING-UP

1. *Return to Go*, p. 216.
2. Ibid., p. 166.
3. SWS, EL and R & A, 1975, p. 11.
4. Documents sent to SWS shareholders 3 Aug. 1977.
5. BESB, appendix C.
6. Ibid.
7. Interview with Mr Peter Wreford, 1980.
8. BESB, appendix A.

CHAPTER 12   CASE STUDY ONE: KEYSER ULLMANN

1. Ferguson/CST D of T. Inspectors' Report, 20.8.
2. Ibid., 29.14.
3. Ibid., 20.26.
4. Ibid., 20.41.
5. Ibid., 20.47.
6. Ibid., 1.16.
7. Ibid., 24.26–24.28.
8. Ibid., 31.22.
9. Ibid., 20.42, 20.47 and 20.71.
10. *Evening Standard*, 23 June 1970.
11. L and CD of T. Inspectors' Report, 9.114.
12. Keyser Ullmann Holdings Report and Accounts (hereafter KUH-RA) 1975, p. 4.
13. KUH-RA 1975, p. 3.
14. Ibid., p. 6.

15. *FT* 9 Mar. 1979.
16. Ibid., 2 Feb. 1980.
17. KUH-RA 1975, p. 6.
18. Ibid., 1976, p. 6.

CHAPTER 13 CASE STUDY TWO: SLATER WALKER

1. R. S. Sayers, *The Bank of England 1891–1944* (CUP, 1976, 2 vols) p. 533.
2. SWS, EC and R & A, 1975.
3. *FT*, 15 Sept. 1976.
4. SWS, EC and R & A, 1975, appendix E.
5. SWS, EC and R & A, 1975, p. 11.
6. *FT*, 15 Sept. 1976.
7. *Return to Go*, p. 217–18.
8. Ibid., pp. 226 and 268, and *FT*, 26 Oct. 1979.

CHAPTER 14 APPRAISAL AND CONCLUSIONS

1. Bank of England, Reports and Accounts, 1974/5–1978/9.
2. Evid. to Sel. Cttee, p. 11.
3. Sir John Clapham, *The Bank of England: A History, vol.* II, *1797–1914*, (CUP, 1944) p. 334.
4. BE Sup, 2, 7.
5. *BEQB*, June 1975, pp. 190–3.
6. *BEQB*, Sept. 1975, pp. 240–3.
7. Cmnd. 7937, 1111–19.
8. *FT*, 8 Feb. 1980.

Index

Ltd, & Co. etc have been omitted from company names.